"The fight to save City College is one of the most remarkable in the long history of progressive politics in San Francisco. It offers hope and practical lessons in opposing the neoliberal agenda of austerity, exclusion, and privatization. For decades, California bled dry the greatest public education system in the world. Turning that around will take years of struggle by the people demanding their lost rights and public investment in their children. As City College showed, victory is possible, and the battle will be led by the new working majority of color, who have already turned California blue and may yet save us from the depredations of the billionaires and madmen who rule America today."
—Richard A. Walker, professor emeritus, University of California, Berkeley, author of *Pictures of a Gone City: Tech and the Dark Side of Prosperity in the San Francisco Bay Area* (PM Press, 2018)

"The struggle and success of Free City proves that when people organize, persist, and resist injustice, they win!"
—Diane Ravitch, founder and president, Network for Public Education, author of *The Reign of Error: The Hoax of the Privatization Movement and the Danger to America's Public Schools* (Penguin Random House, 2014)

Free City!

The Fight for San Francisco's City College and Education for All

Marcy Rein, Mickey Ellinger, and Vicki Legion

Free City! The Fight for San Francisco's City College and Education for All
© Marcy Rein, Mickey Ellinger, and Vicki Legion
This edition © 2021 PM Press

ISBN: 978–1–62963–829–4 (print)
ISBN: 978–1–62963–845–4 (ebook)

Library of Congress Control Number: 2020934727

Cover by John Yates / www.stealworks.com
Cover art by MJ Creative / mollyjanecreative@gmail.com
Interior design by briandesign

10 9 8 7 6 5 4 3 2 1

PM Press
PO Box 23912
Oakland, CA 94623
www.pmpress.org

Printed in the USA.

Contents

APPENDICES

Foreword

Pauline Lipman

F*ree City! The Fight for San Francisco's City College and Education for All* is an anatomy of the five-year campaign that, as the authors explain, "turned a hopeless-looking defensive struggle against the announced closure of [City College of San Francisco] into a victory for the most progressive and expansive 'free college' measure in the US" and "unseated the entire leadership of the corporate-captured accreditation agency, removing one cudgel being used by the ed deformers." How did they do that? And what can we learn from it? Marcy Rein, Mickey Ellinger, and Vicki Legion, three of the participants/organizers, give us a point-by-point account from their vantage point of the twists and turns of forging student, faculty, and union community coalitions, how they "mobilize[d] San Francisco's love for the school to counter the media narrative" of failure, and how they reconceived the campaign to defend City College as an opportunity to fight for free community college for all, funded by a tax on the rich.

The fight for City College is magnified when we connect it with the broader neoliberal assault on public education. I live and work in Chicago, a laboratory for the corporate restructuring of education. Chicago has also been an incubator of resistance by parents, students, community organizations, educators, and their unions. Our battles in Chicago against school closings and privatization and the disciplining of teachers have played out across the country in teacher strikes, citywide campaigns led by communities of color to defend their schools, and parent and teacher organizing against high-stakes testing and austerity. As Karen Lewis, past president of the Chicago Teachers Union (CTU), reminds us, we are in a battle for the soul of public education.

Free City! connects the dots between the neoliberal assault on K–12 schools and the downsizing and corporate makeover of community colleges. The story of the move to take over and restructure City College is a replay of the attack on public schools in Chicago, Detroit, Philadelphia, Newark, and other US cities. The same shock doctrine, structural adjustment tactics that set up K–12 schools for restructuring, closing, and privatization were deployed against City College. As *Free City!* puts it, "This was a familiar script for students of austerity in education: cut funding, ask a nominally neutral body to analyze a district's finances, get a report calling for state takeover." The same cabal of billionaire venture philanthropists and corporate foundations and public private agencies in cahoots with the state that is engineering the remake of K–12 public education was behind the attack on City College. (In San Francisco, it was the Gates and Lumina Foundations and the Accrediting Commission for Community and Junior Colleges.) These neoliberal corporate policy drivers are determined to restructure schools, from kindergarten to university, as profit-making, business-oriented, workforce-training institutions. As in public K–12 schools, imposing high-stakes assessments, disciplining teachers and their unions, and narrowing the curriculum in schools serving working-class students of color are all part of their toolbox.

Community colleges have historically extended public education to people of all ages. They have opened up an opportunity for millions of working-class people, especially immigrants and people of color, for lifelong learning, to pursue new careers, to learn English or another language, or just to follow their intellectual and creative passions. The restructuring of City College—eliminating part-time students and "frills" like music, ethnic studies, and athletics, closing down community-based ESL programs, cutting back faculty, charging full tuition up front—was an attack on the heart of its community mission. It is not surprising that students, teachers, and community members organized to fight back. Their organizing resonates with resistance of parents and students of color and teachers against mass school closings in Chicago, Detroit, Philadelphia, and Oakland and the social movement teacher unionism of the CTU and the United Teachers of Los Angeles.

The five-year battle to save City College, like struggles parents and teachers have mounted against school closings and privatization in cities across the US, is part of a bigger battle for the city itself. In the neoliberal city, education, like other urban policies, is driven by corporate growth, real estate development, and the logics of the market. Whatever attracts investors and high-paid workers to the city is "good" urban policy. From

Chicago to New Orleans to San Francisco, "development" means pushing out working-class communities of color to make way for corporate real estate projects and gentrification. Closing public schools in low-income communities of color is integral to forcing out the people who live there, profiting off the land, and rebranding neighborhoods for a new, (generally) white middle- and upper-middle-class clientele. What is at stake is the future of the city itself—who can live there and who the city is for. This is what was at the heart of the battle to defend City College in San Francisco against a power bloc composed of the tech sector and real estate developers and their allies in City Hall who wanted to close the college as part of a land grab for inflated market rate housing.

I don't read the takeover of City College as only motivated by profit. Driven by intertwined logics of capitalism and white supremacy, the takeover is part of redefining the city as a space of whiteness and affluence. A space stripped of its working-class and immigrant history. A corporate city of race and class exclusions. City College is a community institution. It's a school with radical political history, with an identity connected to ethnic studies, community programs, and revolutionary movements. The college's history, its students, its intellectual and cultural richness, and its publicness are materially and symbolically counter to the corporate branding, privatized lifestyle, whiteness, and rampant gentrification that are remaking San Francisco for hedge fund investors and high-paid tech workers. It is this contest over race and capital and the meaning of the city that defines the battle for City College. A city council person quoted in *Free City!* makes this clear: "There is a pervasive sense that we are losing the city we once loved, along with the community, one person at a time. . . . [N]o one is immune to the wave of displacement that is sweeping our Bay Area." This could be said for nearly every city in the US.

Demands like "Free College for All" are a critical component of maintaining the cities we love and making them more inclusive, more public and collective, and more just. But, as *Free City!* shows, this is a battle against powerful forces of racial capitalism, and political clarity is critical. Clarity about who the enemy is and strategies to not only resist but to unite across our multiple experiences and structural differences (of race, class, gender, sexuality, immigrant status) to transform defensive demands into proactive campaigns. A key piece is systematic reflection on actual struggles for justice by those who are deeply involved and opening them up to scrutiny in ways that help us all develop more political clarity.

This is a challenge in many respects. *Free City!* exposes the collaboration of the state and predatory capital to siphon the lifeblood out of an institution that has been a working-class education anchor and center of public intellectual activity. It clarifies that the neoliberal agenda to destroy public community colleges and turn them into mills to train a labor force for the unequal, globalized economy is also a prong in the spatial remake of the city. But this is fundamentally a book about organizing, about the complexities and challenges of bringing many sectors of community together into an evolving campaign to make the fight for one school a fight for the city.

Free City! takes us through the assault on City College, the alliance of corporate and public forces that led it, and their strategies and tactics. It dissects the challenges and learning of the organizers who came together to defeat it, their steps and their missteps. The authors break down how the campaign countered the outsized megaphones and unlimited resources of the corporate policy makers and think tanks and their racialized discourses of failure and markets, how they exploited contradictions in the alliance of neoliberal corporate/state actors, how the campaign built organization and consciousness over time, the need for flexible tactics, the pivotal role of research to uncover the motivations and political and economic alliances behind the attack on City, and the evolving and sometimes conflicting positions and roles of students and faculty, unions, and community organizations. The book invites us to engage, debate, be in a conversation about strategy and tactics, about ends and means, about the politics of race and class, about education and urban space, and about turning defensive battles into organizing for "non-reformist reforms"—reforms like "free college"—that undermine existing social arrangements and prefigure the economically and socially democratic and just society we so desperately need. By inviting us inside the struggle, the book encourages us to systematically analyze the dialectics of power that shape our contexts and to reflect deeply on strategies and goals. *Free City!* is a gift to all of us.

They Love It Enough to Fight for It

O n the first day of every semester, Edgar Torres leaves the door to his City College office open for students who get lost in the sprawling Ocean Campus. If they pop their heads in, they get friendly directions from Torres, longtime chair of the college's Latin American and Latino/a Studies Department. Maybe the visitors glimpse the children's art and the vivid weaving of an Aztec calendar that brighten the walls of the narrow room in the seventy-year-old building.

Depending on the year, perhaps Shanell Williams stopped by. She grew up in San Francisco's Fillmore District and landed at City College at eighteen years old, right out of the juvenile justice and foster care systems. No one in her family had graduated from college. Like so many students, she had to work while she was taking classes, but after several years she graduated with plans to transfer to the University of California, Berkeley.

Maybe the student was Martín Madrigal, from Turlock, in California's Central Valley. Martín came to City after four tours in the United States Army in Iraq, seeking to explore his identity and realize his dream to teach math.

Or maybe the student was Win-Mon Kyi who stepped up for the college where her Burmese immigrant parents learned English. "My mom was taking ESL at Downtown Campus when she was pregnant with me," Kyi said. Working at her parents' Mission District pizza shop after high school, Kyi saw displacement changing the neighborhood day by day. She had just started taking classes at City when the school faced the threat of closure. "CCSF was being sanctioned around the same time that I was focusing on the pushout. I wasn't able to articulate so much as to the solution and the root causes of this crisis that impacted my community; that investigation, that transformation, found me while I was going to City College still trying to figure out my path," Kyi said.

Everyone in San Francisco has a City College story. Since its founding in 1935, the school has sunk deep roots in the city, becoming part of family life across generations and educating nearly one out of seven San Franciscans in its peak years. It began as San Francisco Junior College, serving a working-class city that depended on its bustling port and industries ranging from shipbuilding to printing. It opened just a year after the militant general strike that led to the deaths of two strikers and the unionization of all the major West Coast ports in the United States. It has trained San Francisco's firefighters and chefs, nurses and X-ray techs and drug counselors, taught English to waves of new immigrants, and offered steps up the career ladder and paths to new lives and lifelong learning.

"We're the school of second and third and fourth chances," said Alisa Messer, English teacher and strategic leader in American Federation of Teachers (AFT) Local 2121, the union for City College faculty. A lifelong San Franciscan raised in the city's Richmond District, she's seen "the way the city has come through, when asked. . . . San Franciscans love the college."

They love it enough to fight for it.

CHAPTER ONE

San Francisco's Community College
Before 2012

C ity College of San Francisco's (CCSF) main campus, high on a hill in
the city's Ingleside district, affords a sweeping view of the city the
school has served since the 1930s. Closest to Ocean Campus, as it's called,
you see the southeastern neighborhoods of the city, its last remaining
working-class strongholds. Beyond them, more of the city's forty-seven
hills ripple down to the San Francisco Bay, and you can see ships if the
fog's not in.

Walk around Ocean Campus, and you'll see a jumble of buildings that
show the school's history. "Temporary" modular units, some dating from
1969, house CCSF's award-winning student newspaper the *Guardsman*
and various classes—music and math, drama and business. The Multi-Use
Building, the newest structure, has geothermal heat and smart classrooms,
some of them extra large to accommodate play spaces for child development classes and multilingual practice for health care interpreters.

The *Pan-American Unity* mural painted by Diego Rivera in 1940 enliv-
ens the lobby of the campus's pocket-size theater, and sculptures dot the
grounds, including "St. Francis of the Guns," a statue cast from the metal
of guns surrendered in a 1969 buyback program. "One of the instructors in
our very low-level ESL class showed us the art pieces around campus and
told us the stories and the values behind them," said Khin Thiri Nandar
Soe, a student activist who landed at City after fleeing the military regime
of Burma [Myanmar]. "That made me feel at home. Before, I felt very
foreign, like an alien, but the values I treasure are not so different from
the school's."

By 2012, City College was one of the largest schools in the largest
community college system in the US, serving more than ninety thousand students.[1] It offered college credit and noncredit (adult education)

courses at eleven campuses and almost two hundred neighborhood sites.[2] Different sites had their specialties. The aircraft mechanics certificate program operated at San Francisco International Airport, automotive and motorcycle mechanics and other technical programs were head-quartered at Evans, in the industrial area between Highway 280 and the Bay. Downtown Campus, on the edge of the financial district, hosted the hospitality and culinary arts programs and the Educated Palate restaurant. Many visual arts programs were held at Fort Mason Campus, not far from Fisherman's Wharf. Allied health classes mostly took place at John Adams Campus, on the edge of the Haight-Ashbury neighborhood. The highly rated programs in registered nursing and radiology had offices at Ocean, as did many of the classes offered by the departments in the Diversity Collaborative.[3] Music and Fine Arts Departments offered both theory and practice classes.

About half of CCSF's offerings were free, noncredit, community-serving adult school classes, which in most other places statewide were run by K–12 districts. By far the biggest program was English as a Second Language (ESL), an indispensable resource in a city where two out of five people were born outside of the United States.[4] Classes in neighbor-hood community centers extended the school's reach and allowed access for more vulnerable students—like the theater and painting classes for people on the autism spectrum and nutrition classes where seniors gathered for low-cost hot lunches.

Over the years, the school wove a strong net of student support ser-vices, including: childcare centers and parenting classes; programs for older students returning to college; Second Chance, for formerly incar-cerated students; Project SURVIVE, a peer education program geared to preventing sexual violence; a women's center, a veterans' center, and a cluster of retention centers serving students of color.

The statewide community college network is home to about three-quarters of California's Black and Latinx college students; in 2012, nearly three-quarters of CCSF students were students of color, most of them low-income or working-class. Like those at other schools around the state, most of CCSF's workers have union representation: the faculty through the American Federation of Teachers (AFT) Local 2121, the staff through a chapter of Service Employees International Union (SEIU) Local 1021, the department chairs through their own Department Chairperson Council (DCC), others with the Building Trades Council and Stationary Engineers.

Through more than four decades of contract negotiations, AFT 2121 built one of the strongest contracts for part-time faculty in the US. Faculty who worked more than half-time got health insurance. Part-timers had preference for full-time positions, and while they still earned less per hour than full-timers, the pay gap was smaller than at most other schools.

City College grew rapidly in the post–World War II years, flowered with the social justice movements of the 1960s, and sustained the inspiration of that era even in the decades of backlash and austerity that followed.

World War II to the 1970s: Laying Foundations, Opening the Door

Returning veterans flooded San Francisco after World War II, joining the thousands of people who had come to California for home front jobs. Veterans had GI Bill dollars to spend on education and flocked to City College. The school ballooned to 5,000 students in 1946 and more than doubled in the 1960s, from 8,400 in fall 1962 to 17,763 in 1971.[5]

Employers needed a technically trained workforce to run California's powerhouse industrial economy, and Californians clamored for more public postsecondary education. In response, the state legislature approved the Master Plan for Higher Education in 1960. The plan established three tiers of colleges: the University of California, open to the top 12 percent of high school graduates; the state colleges, open to the top 33 percent; and the community colleges (no longer called junior colleges), open to anyone eighteen or older who could "benefit from instruction."[6]

The Master Plan achieved world renown for its ringing promise of tuition-free college for all—though its new requirements pushed more students of color out of the state colleges and universities and into the community colleges, including in San Francisco.[7]

Although their top-billed mission was transfer preparation, transfer was always a small part of what went on at most urban community colleges, with associate degrees, workforce education, English language instruction, and lifelong learning playing far bigger roles. Community colleges always had to work with far less public funding than the upper tiers of the public higher education system. They received two-thirds as much funding per student as the state colleges and only about one-third as much as the schools in the University of California system. This contradiction between broad mission, the deep needs of many students, and the scant resources available would break open in 2012.

Still, the swelling wave of community college students fought to make the promise of open access real and to have community college education promote justice and equality. At the community college on Grove Street in Oakland's flatlands, the Black Panthers ran study groups, fostered debate on the Vietnam War and other issues of the day, and launched a successful multiyear campaign for a Black Studies Department with credits transferring to University of California. Activists started a free health clinic and a work-study program for people who had recently been released from prison. Black Panther Party minister of culture Emory Douglas got his art training at City College of San Francisco.

Not far from City's main campus, the Black Student Union (BSU) and the Third World Liberation Front at San Francisco State spearheaded what became the longest student strike in US history. The strike, which ran from November 1968 to March 1969, quadrupled the number of Black students in the two years after the strike, won the nation's first College of Ethnic Studies, and inspired the opening of college doors and Ethnic Studies Departments on hundreds of campuses nationwide. AFT Local 1352 struck alongside the students in unity with their demands for radical changes in the university. A significant layer of City College faculty came of age during these movements and brought their values with them. They tried to make a ladder with many rungs, so that the least privileged students would have support to climb as far as they were willing to try.

California's community college system became the biggest, the most affordable, and, many said, the best in the country. With programs and services for everyone from grandma to preschoolers to traditional college-age students, people thought of these as "Democracy's Colleges."

Backlash, Austerity, and Education "Reform"

Open admissions policies affirmed access to public higher education as a right for all—and opposition to open-access became a part of the backlash against the civil rights movement that propelled Ronald Reagan into the California governor's office in 1966. Reagan campaigned on "law and order," promising to "put welfare bums back to work" and "clean up the mess" of student protest at University of California, Berkeley.[8] Richard Nixon rode the same law-and-order message into the White House in 1968 and 1972. Postwar US prosperity crashed in the global recession of 1973. A politics of austerity took hold that moved from social spending to social control—a tidy fit with law-and-order priorities.

Economic anxiety married backlash in the "tax revolt" kicked off by California voters' passage of Proposition 13 in 1978. The measure was spearheaded by commercial real estate interests. The proposition virtually froze residential and commercial property taxes that had supported public schools and services; properties could only be reassessed when they were sold. Since corporate properties turned over rarely compared to private homes, most corporate property taxes were locked at their 1970s assessment.

State revenue tanked. White flight to the suburbs—aided and abetted by federal housing policy—intensified the racial impact of the tax freeze on cities. Schools were starved of resources.[9] San Francisco was hard hit; some five thousand jobs in schools, libraries, parks, and public works were lost and transit fares were doubled. One author summarizes: "The axe fell most heavily on human services."[10]

To cope with the impact of Proposition 13, voters passed Proposition 98 in 1988, guaranteeing a percentage of state spending to public education from kindergarten through community college.[11] State and local jurisdictions raised regressive sales taxes and user fees. From 1980 to 2004, the California State University system raised fees a stunning 1,188 percent.[12] After nearly a half-century of being free, California community colleges began charging modest tuition in 1984. A mantra of scarcity entered the lexicon: "Education will need to do more with less." State revenues became a larger part of community college budgets, making them more vulnerable to the ups and downs of the business cycle and Sacramento politics. As scarcity bit the schools, California began its huge prison expansion. The state Department of Corrections first projected the need for expansion in 1982, and voters passed a prison construction bond the same year. During the 1990s, the state would build nineteen new prisons and just one university.

The seventeen members of the California Community Colleges Board of Governors (BOG) appointed by the state governor make policies that apply to all 116 colleges and appoint the statewide chancellor. In 1991, the BOG convened the Commission on Innovation and charged it with figuring out "how the community colleges in California could *serve an increasingly larger population of students without requiring any additional state expense*," wrote Marty Hittelman, then president of California Federation of Teachers' (CFT) Community College Council.[13] The commission included several corporate executives, with a sprinkling of college administrators and elected officials. It recommended more televised courses, application of the total quality management model to improve results, and central-ized state-level contract bargaining for all the community college districts, including the California State University and University of California. "These corporate ideas never die," Hittelman observed nearly forty years later. Nowhere did the commission suggest the obvious: allocate more funds to support a focus on quality education in the segment of postsec-ondary education serving the students with the greatest needs.

By 2003, California's community colleges were facing draconian state budget cuts and demands to cut classes to cope with shortfalls. CCSF took a leading role in organizing against the cuts, even creating a "missing stu-dents" art project that traveled all over the state.[14] Statewide mobilizations blunted the severity of the cuts and held down tuition increases. The March 17, 2003, protest at the state capitol in Sacramento drew more than ten thousand people, surpassing organizers' expectations. It marked "the moment when community colleges discovered their mojo and ceased being roadkill," wrote Jonathan Lightman, longtime executive director of the Faculty Association of California Community Colleges (FACCC), an independent lobbying group.[15] The March in March became an annual event.

City College swam against the tide of austerity for twenty years. It continued to expand into the 2000s, opening new campuses in the largely Latinx Mission District and in Chinatown, responding to community organizing and demands; the Chinatown Campus had been thirty years in the making. In 2001 and 2005, San Francisco voters passed bond issues to complete those campuses and help finance new buildings for the aging Ocean Campus, including a state-of-the-art Performing Arts Education Center (PAEC). In 2007, City College was profiled by the *New York Times Magazine* as one of the top eleven community colleges in the country.[16]

The Great Recession landed hard on California in 2008. State reve-nues, already shrunken from thirty years of austerity policies, tanked by a third.[17] The 2009 state budget cut spending on K–12 education by more than $9 billion. City College saw its state funding plummet by $25 million from 2008 to 2012, a huge hit, given that the school's revenues ran a bit over $220 million. During the 2009–2012 budget crisis, California slashed $1.5 billion from the budget for community colleges, and colleges statewide cut out 21 percent of their academic year classes and over 60 percent of summer classes.[18]

Budget cutbacks compounded stress for people at the college. Plumbers, painters, and other crafts positions were critically understaffed; hundreds of repair tickets accumulated across the campuses, and fixes happened with the speed of molasses. Faculty tore their hair out over ten-year-old computers that would not allow them to open attachments. As she sat in a lecture hall in the Science Building, Vicki Legion counted eight large holes in the walls, left behind by hurried electricians. Bathroom stalls in need of repair were often taped off for weeks. Support staff were overworked and underpaid, and getting an invoice approved could take months and more than one trip to the accounting office downtown. Some students were not getting their financial aid in a timely manner. It was a slow grind that seemed to go on and on.

Gnarlier problems rooted in austerity and structural racism also came to a head in 2009–2012. As a community college, CCSF was open to all comers, so many students arrived unprepared for college-level work. Placement tests in English and math determined whether they could take college level courses for credit or would have to take noncredit remedial courses first. No surprise that students hoping to transfer to university from the under-resourced high schools in low-income communities of color were often placed in remedial classes. They could get stuck at that level for as many as five semesters before even starting to get college credit. "It feels like high school all over again," one student observed. Since the average real cost of a year of community college ran as high as $20,000—mainly for living expenses—remediation as practiced became both discouraging and expensive.[19]

Differences over changes to placement criteria and the remediation sequence opened a bitter rift that would widen in the following few years.

Instead of Cutting Classes, a Strategy for Belt-Tightening

City College chancellor Don Griffin supported the need to change placement policies, even as he labored late into the evening over the school's budgets, straining to find ways to keep cutbacks away from the classroom. A former Black Panther, Griffin had taught psychology and statistics and worked as an administrator at CCSF since 1969, when his support for the Third World Student Strike at San Francisco State cost him his job there.

Rather than simply cutting classes, Griffin's strategy for dealing with budget cuts was to protect student enrollment numbers and to "keep the family together," minimizing teacher layoffs. Ensuring that students had access to classes maintained the best possible baseline for state appropriations, which were based on enrollment.

Under Griffin's belt-tightening program, the faculty took a negotiated 2.9 percent pay cut, and administrators, including Griffin himself, took a 5 percent cut. The college also left some administrative vacancies unfilled, and longtime administrators simply took on more work.

Other community college presidents thought that Griffin's strategy for resisting the downsizing underway across the state was brave, ranging toward "nervy." And, indeed, as the Great Recession dragged on for five long years, the belt-tightening that had worked to get the college through typical recessions failed to balance the budget. The college dipped into its financial reserves—although only at their lowest point in 2011 did the reserves dip below the state-recommended minimum of 5 percent of annual expenditures.[20] The state cut money for special services—book vouchers, childcare, disabled student services—and the college could only partially fill the gaps. Although Griffin was committed to minimizing class cuts, he had to cancel summer classes in 2010 for the first time ever.

Renaming Austerity: California Turns from Open Access to "Student Success"

Public schools serving students in kindergarten through high school (K–12) had been targeted by foes of the public sector for decades. *A Nation at Risk*,[21] issued in 1983 by a Reagan administration commission, sounded themes that would gradually enter daily parlance to become common sense: US education was "drowning in a sea of mediocrity," and the purpose of education was to boost US global economic competitiveness. The Business Roundtable, composed of the CEOs of the top two hundred US-based multinationals, charged to the rescue. By 1990, it had launched a national drive for adoption of state content standards, state-mandated tests, and rewards and sanctions tied to test results.[22] Reformers from the private sector and both political parties blamed teachers and their unions for most education problems and legitimized the transfer of public funds to privately run charter schools. Changes codified in 2001 federal legislation dubbed No Child Left Behind pushed standardized testing and punished and ultimately closed many poorer schools. Nationwide, districts closed schools attended by two hundred thousand students per year, mostly in Black and Latinx communities.[23]

Around the turn of the millennium, corporate-linked foundations took on a prominent role in funding policy research and pilot projects in K–12 education reform. One of the top three was the foundation started by Microsoft founder Bill Gates. Along with Lumina—a foundation seeded with funds and personnel from the student loan industry—Gates would help the "reform" project jump the fence from K–12 to community colleges.

Community college reformers contended that the colleges had succeeded in providing "access" but had failed miserably at "success," with success defined as "obtaining a credential of economic value" by completing a degree or certificate. Broader definitions of success were simply off the table. The reformers began talking about a "completion gap," the difference between the number of students who enter community college and those who complete a certificate or degree. They stressed the importance of full-time attendance and a fast track to graduation in closing the gap. They also lauded performance funding (or outcomes funding) as a way to encourage compliance by giving colleges extra revenue for speedy completions.[24]

Engaged researchers would learn more about the roots of this reform effort over the next several years, as the reformers took on California. In 2010, the state legislature debated a performance-based funding measure. Teachers vehemently opposed replacing enrollment-based funding. The proposal drew so much flak that it was replaced by a bill that set up a Student Success Task Force to recommend ways to change community college education. The twenty-one-member body included just two students and five teachers, along with community college administrators and trustees and representatives of business and policy groups.

Echoing *A Nation at Risk*, the task force report declared that "California is at risk of losing its economic competitiveness due to an insufficient supply of highly skilled workers." But community colleges could fend off the crisis: "Due to their large scale and relatively low cost, community colleges nationwide have been identified as the most viable option capable of producing college graduates and certificate holders in the large numbers necessary to reverse current trends."

The twenty-two measures proposed by the task force increased state control over decisions that had been made locally. The proposals penalized part-time students and lifelong learners by sending them to the back of class enrollment lines, by requiring all students to have an education plan by the time they had taken thirty units (equivalent to two semesters of full-time study), and by instituting a quantitative measure of success, the "Student Success Scorecard."[25]

All the faculty organizations—the California Federation of Teachers (CFT; affiliated with the national AFT, which belongs to the AFL-CIO), the California Teachers Association (CTA; affiliated with the National Education Association [NEA]), the California Community College Independents (CCCI),[26] and FACCC, along with the statewide Academic Senate—raised loud concerns at a series of hearings on the task force proposals.[27]

"For the most part, the task force was a cover for the 'R' word, *rationing*—with limited funds, community colleges would need a policy excuse to do less," FACCC's Jonathan Lightman wrote. "Students who played in orchestras, enrolled in P.E., or who repeated courses became the stereotypes for our 'broken' system. Because of these 'non-serious' students, the argument went, *legitimate* students were precluded from enrolling in transfer, basic skills, or Career Technical Education programs."[28]

Committed teachers like Edgar Torres believed the task force approach negated the human connection at the core of learning. The very classes dismissed as "frills"—Diversity Studies, art, music, athletics—can be the keys that unlock education for at-risk students, Torres explained:

> At an inner-city school like we are, there are going to be many who dropped out of high school, and what are we going to do if we don't have these other alternatives to keep people going? We're recognizing that people often go to departments they identify with, at least initially, and our job is to serve as a retention center. These courses can become a foundation to move over into other areas that might be beneficial to them. . . . And I've been here long enough to see . . . students come through who never even expected they would make it, and something happened during their stay here where the ability to have confidence that they could learn just switched on inside them. I call it "the revolution that takes place in the heart."

City College Pushes Back

A solid bloc at City College of San Francisco united with statewide efforts challenging the task force agenda—students, student government, the college newspaper, faculty, administrators, and board members. Chancellor Don Griffin thundered a warning against "what should be called the Student Failure Task Force."

The school stayed out in front of the resistance right through the January 9, 2012, meeting when the task force presented its recommendations to the California Community Colleges Board of Governors. Fifty students and teachers from CCSF—student government leader Shanell Williams and Academic Senate president Karen Saginor among them—took the day off from their jobs or gave up a precious day of winter break to travel to the state capitol and testify against the task force proposals. "Our schools have been seriously defunded, but your recommendations speak to the fact that that doesn't matter. This is not about student success; this is about making the most disadvantaged students pay for an economic crisis that is not our fault," Williams told the BOG. "We need funding, not these recommendations. . . . Sixty percent of City College students will be impacted by this." In fact, even more would be affected than Williams suggested. More than 80 percent of City College students and close to 70 percent of community college students statewide were attending part-time.[29]

Despite the hours of impassioned testimony, the governors started voting to endorse the task force proposals as if they hadn't heard a word. Suddenly a voice called out, "Mic check!" And dozens responded, "Mic check!" Chants rang out: "Whose school? Our school! Whose education? Our education!" A dozen students clambered onto chairs and unrolled a banner emblazoned with "Keep the Community in Community College!" The Occupy-style call-and-response shattered decorum and rattled the board members, who hastily finished their roll call and fled the room.

But however hasty and uncomfortable, the deed had been done. The BOG had approved the task force report, and the state chancellor began implementing some of its measures as regulations. The state legislature packaged others as the Student Success Act, which became law in September 2012.

Enter the Accreditor

The Accrediting Commission for Community and Junior Colleges (ACCJC) was a vocal supporter of the Student Success Act. The commission is one of six regional bodies that are authorized by both federal and state governments to evaluate community colleges for educational quality and—a catch-all term—"institutional effectiveness." The ACCJC covers California, Hawaii, Guam, and American Samoa. It is a private entity, but it wields what is essentially the power of life and death over colleges. Institutions that are not accredited can neither disburse federal or state financial aid to students nor allow students to transfer credits.

ACCJC president Barbara Beno urged commission members to voice support for the task force report and the subsequent legislation, and the ACCJC was listed as a formal endorser of the Student Success Act.

A team from the ACCJC visited City College from March 11 to 15, 2012, as part of the regular reaccreditation process; schools get a comprehensive evaluation every six years. The evaluation in 2006 explicitly praised the school: "In general, the team found that the students and communities served by City College of San Francisco are well served by the talented and committed people who continue to work toward the excellence and ongoing improvement of this institution." Evaluators made eight recommendations for continued improvement.[30] After the March 2012 visit, the ACCJC team seemed to be pleased with the school's efforts to address those recommendations.

Still, the funding crisis, struggles over remediation policy, the Student Success Act, and the ACCJC visit were already weighing on faculty, administration, and trustees when Chancellor Griffin announced his sudden retirement because of a brain tumor.

Griffin Steps Down

The article on Chancellor Griffin's retirement in the *Guardsman* emphasized his concern for students: "He is the mastermind behind priority registration, minority retention programs, the student support program Puente, student equity, student diversity, and the modification of placement tests for student success."[31] The official goodbye came at the April 26, 2012, board of trustees meeting. Board president John Rizzo introduced a resolution commending the chancellor "on his forty years of service to us," and the audience jumped to its feet, clapping and cheering. The culinary students brought in a giant sheet cake, and for half an hour the meeting was transformed into a going away party.

"I see a larger group of people than I've ever seen in this room, and that's your legacy, Don," Trustee Milton Marks III said. Trustee Chris Jackson celebrated the way Griffin "prioritized the community in community college." He said that he once invited the chancellor to an event in Sunnydale Public Housing, really not expecting him to show. "But Griffin did come, and he said, 'If you want to come to City College, there's a place for you.' That was probably one of the few times anyone said there was a place for them anywhere but there in the projects," Jackson remembered.

When he was offered the mic, Griffin said, "City College has always done things differently, and we will continue to. Working for City College, being dedicated here, is a noble thing—faculty, staff, classified, administration, all of us. . . . It all comes back to the students . . . the reason I've been so stubborn on some of these issues is that they deeply affect our students."

Rude Transition

Griffin's sudden departure threw a curveball to the elected board of trustees, which had to hire his replacement.

California's community college districts cover specific geographic areas and elect their governing boards, as K–12 school districts do. The San Francisco Community College District governs City College, which is one district with many campuses. CCSF's board of trustees includes seven members elected citywide; students elect one nonvoting student trustee. Board members get a small monthly stipend ($500 in 2012) and access to district health insurance plans. State law tasks them with hiring the district chancellor, approving the budget, and setting broad policies for the district. In practice, they hold one or more public meetings per month, which often last five or six hours and run the gamut from high drama to grinding detail. They have multiple committee meetings as well and need to draw on or master specialized knowledge to make informed decisions on a host of subjects, including employee contracts, budgets, construction plans, and educational policies. San Franciscans tend to view the City College board as a kind of farm team for aspiring Democratic Party politicians, a stepping-stone on the path to the board of supervisors.

The team on the field when Griffin resigned was ethnically diverse, including two Asian Americans and two African Americans. The board's political interests ranged across the center of San Francisco's political spectrum: Chris Jackson was a policy analyst for the San Francisco Labor Council; John Rizzo was a leader in the Sierra Club; Anita Grier was a longtime administrator in the San Francisco Unified School District; relative newcomer Steve Ngo was close to the respected Black-led community organization Coleman Advocates and a combative, often long-winded ally in their equity campaigns.

"Usually a chancellor search takes six months," John Rizzo said. "We had two weeks." They decided to hire an interim chancellor while seeking someone to fill the position permanently.

Seven candidates answered the trustees' call for an interim chancellor, and they interviewed two. One was Dr. Pamila Fisher, the head of the same search firm they'd engaged to help them find applicants. Fisher had taught behavioral and social sciences at Modesto Community College before serving as vice chancellor for educational services and then chancellor of the Yosemite Community College District. She'd been president of the American Association of Women in Community Colleges and chair of the board of the American Association of Community Colleges (AACC), which calls itself "the primary advocacy organization for the nation's community colleges." (The Lumina and Gates Foundations poured more than $15 million into the AACC between 2004 and 2012.)[32] A special trustees meeting on April 29 took just nine minutes to hire Fisher to serve until October 31.

Fisher quickly disrupted collegial relations with the faculty. On her second day on the job, longtime department chairs Madeline Mueller (Music) and Darlene Alioto (Social Sciences) took her to lunch at the Pierre Coste Dining Room, run by CCSF's Culinary Arts program. "We always welcome people," Mueller said. "Pretty much her first words were, 'I don't really like you, because you're faculty and you're department chairs, but you should be administrators.'" Department chairs at City College are full-time tenured faculty members elected by their peers. They get some reassigned time and a modest pay bonus for handling a range of administrative tasks, and they have their own union, the Department Chairperson Council.[33] "Then she said, 'What I want you to be are deans, because I want to be able to fire you when you don't do what you're told to do.' To say 'I want you to be a dean so I can fire you,' that's—dumbnuts. That is so noncollegial. That was day two."

Fisher brushed aside collegiality in other ways as well. CCSF supplemented the legally required College Advisory Council meetings with expanded, informal "College Council" consultations.[34] The chancellor would call together senior administrators, deans and department chairs, the elected heads of the Academic and Classified Senates and the student council, and the faculty and staff unions, so the school's top leadership could get input on key issues. "The department chairs and the deans felt pretty comfortable speaking up in that environment. There was even some humor," said Karen Saginor, then president of the Academic Senate. "There were no explicit resolutions and decisions made, but it was clear that the chancellors and senior administrators got information they might not have had. . . . City College was such a large and complicated place that no one, not even the chancellor, knew what was going on all the time. She [Fisher] immediately stopped holding the College Council meetings. Like 'No! We're not going to have that meeting any more,' and she could do that." And while it was not legally possible to do the same with the College Advisory Council, Fisher suspended its meetings, and it did not meet after April 2012.

Fisher began ginning up a sense of impending catastrophe at her first trustees meeting, on May 10. "If you folks don't pass a true balanced budget with no game-playing, then I think that we're in jeopardy in terms of our fiscal solvency and in terms of intervention. The state chancellor's office clearly has the power to step in," Fisher said. "Everything's on the table."

Two tax proposals offered hope of financial relief: a statewide Millionaires Tax to fund education and a local parcel tax to support City College. While the Millionaires Tax proposed to tax the rich, as its name implied, the parcel tax was not progressive, taxing each lot in San Francisco an extra $79, regardless of whether the property was a mansion or an earthquake shack. In a special session, on May 31, the trustees unanimously approved placing the parcel tax on the November ballot. "Voters should know how the successful passage of the parcel tax might keep you from having to take these steps," Fisher said. "If we're looking at site closures, for example—and I use that one, because I know that's something the Accrediting Commission report's going to say—we need to talk about that issue."

The trustees accepted Fisher's suggestion that they seek advice from the state's Fiscal Crisis and Management Assistance Team (FCMAT).[35] Fisher described FCMAT as an outside neutral agency. She struck what would be a recurring theme, invoking the need to comply with the yet unreleased ACCJC report: "They [ACCJC] talked about our fiscal situation in the exit interviews; it's no secret. . . . This will help in terms of our response to them. What you do with it after that, of course, will weigh positively."

Only Trustee Chris Jackson resisted the proposal to bring in FCMAT. "The state chancellor's office vision of what community college should be is not necessarily the same one I share," he said. "Their budget implications also give me pause. They took a lot. That seems weird to me. It's like you take money out of my wallet and then say, 'Why are you broke?'"

Financial problems were old hat to CCSF, and the parcel tax promised relief. Griffin's retirement was a body blow, and Fisher's threats and maneuvers were alarming, but CCSF had survived before, flags still flying.

The July 4 holiday drew closer, and the campus was almost empty when the ACCJC published its ruling, setting in motion five years of struggle for the college and its mission.

CHAPTER TWO

The Sword Drops

July 2012

The Accrediting Commission for Community and Junior Colleges' July 2 letter to City College confirmed the dark hints Interim Chancellor Fisher had been dropping. The commission slapped CCSF with a "show cause" sanction, the harshest ruling short of closure. The college had to prove it deserved to stay open.

Shanell Williams was working for Jobs with Justice when she got a phone call from student trustee William Walker.[1] "He said, 'Oh, my god, Shanell, have you seen what's going on? The accrediting commission is sanctioning us, they want to shut us down.' I almost dropped the phone," Williams said. "I started shaking, because I had just been elected as student body president, and he was just elected as the trustee. We were just in disbelief, and I was, like, 'What are we going to do?'"

Accreditor Writes Prescription for Reform

City College had never been sanctioned by the ACCJC before. The commission bypassed two lesser sanctions, warning and probation, when it put the college on show cause. The ruling gave CCSF just nine months to remedy fourteen "deficiencies"; if these weren't corrected, the commission would terminate the school's accreditation, effectively shutting it down. Just in case, CCSF was to prepare a closure plan.

None of the fourteen deficiencies addressed the quality of education City College provided, and only two related to instruction at all. These faulted the school for not paying enough attention to measurable Student Learning Outcomes (SLOs). The remaining items directed the school to change its management and mission. It characterized City College as a mismanaged behemoth lumbering toward collapse. "The Commission is concerned about the institution's ability to successfully adapt to the changing resource environment facing public community colleges and believes that the College has not demonstrated, through its review of the institutional mission, adequate attention to the impact on quality as the resources have declined while broad breadth of its mission has been maintained."

Decoded: the ACCJC considered it a deficiency that CCSF did not accept slashed budgets as inevitable and continued to adhere to the open-access vision of California's 1960 Master Plan for Higher Education.

The commission also considered it a deficiency that CCSF faculty had one of the best contracts in the Bay Area. "These liabilities (pension, medical, and worker's compensation benefits) clearly are a threat to the financial stability of the college." The commission neglected to mention that faculty had not had a raise since 2007 and had already taken pay cuts to help keep classes open.

Attacking the school's shared governance system, the commission asserted that "leadership weaknesses at all levels, and established campus precedents for governance structures, decision-making priorities and processes, have kept City College of San Francisco from adapting to its changed and changing fiscal environment."[2]

The media amplified the ACCJC's harsh critique. On July 3, San Franciscans opened their morning *Chronicle* to the headline "City College of San Francisco on brink of closure." The lead added the spin: "The poorly run City College of San Francisco has eight months to prove it should stay in business, yet must 'make preparations for closure,' evaluators ordered Tuesday."[3] Less than two weeks later, the state's largest newspaper, the *Los Angeles Times*, joined the chorus:

> The report this month from the accreditation commission was scath-ing. It found that City College of San Francisco—at 90,000 students, the largest community college in the state and one of the largest in the nation—was riddled with problems, including paltry financial reserves, a dearth of leadership and a slow-moving style of demo-cratic governance.
>
> The 77-year-old school now must make a case for continuing to exist and craft a closure plan in case the onerous task of reform fails.[4]

AFT 2121 president Alisa Messer only found out about the show cause ruling when *Chronicle* education reporter Nanette Asimov called her for a reaction. "We knew that we were going to have a sanction of some kind but we weren't expecting that sanction," she said. "It was kind of a life-changing moment. I had a cold creeping feeling, kind of a sinking feeling, and then I got off and got really angry. There was no way we should have been on show cause." Messer wasn't altogether surprised, because members of CFT's statewide Community College Council had been sharing concerns about ACCJC for years. "We were very clear they weren't trustworthy or responsible people," Messer said. ACCJC president Barbara Beno in particular had a reputation for arrogance and vindictiveness that predated her service with the commission.[5]

We Are All City College

Messer and her union colleagues were also clear that they needed to get people together quickly to share the impact of the news and organize a response. AFT 2121 and the union for the classified staff, SEIU 1021, called an emergency meeting at the LGBT Center for July 9, just a week after the accreditor's bombshell hit. The flyer went out and the Facebook post went up. "I'd never seen anything light on fire on Facebook like that. It had thousands of shares," Messer said.

Shanell Williams arrived to find every seat filled in the large hall, people standing shoulder to shoulder around the edges, and dozens of people downstairs who couldn't squeeze in. "People were angry, yelling out 'What are we going to do?' just really furious. I started yelling too: 'We need to fight this! We gotta get organized. We need to figure out who this ACCJC is. . . . This is our city and we need to fight for our college!' I was just so pumped up, and people were yelling and screaming, all really pumped up. It was basically one massive speak-out, and we had leaders from all over the city there. It was super powerful." One after another, people got up to share what City College meant to them.

Only a handful of those who took the mic labeled the sanctions as a political attack. "The criticisms that the accreditation commission has leveled at City College are not valid," said Alex Schmauss of the International Socialist Organization (ISO). "Basically, they can be summed up in three points: 1) too much money goes to faculty and staff at City College; 2) there's not enough administration at City College; 3) there's too much democracy, the shared governance system doesn't work, [but] we should be defending all those things about City College. City College has been singled out because it has done well in a bad situation, and we need to continue and extend what we have been doing right."

A few pointed out that City did indeed need to change. "We are going to fix some things that have been broken for a long time, that needed to be fixed, but now they *have* to be fixed," said Angela Thomas from SEIU 1021. "Sometimes you don't deal with things till you have to. . . . And I can't wait until this time next year, when I have another microphone in my face, and I can honestly say, 'Look at what we've done. We are still here.'"

Anxious to channel their concern toward solutions that would help City College, many people talked about the two ballot initiatives that promised to help ease the school's finances: Proposition A, the San Francisco parcel tax that would guarantee eight years of support for CCSF, and California Proposition 30, the Millionaires Tax, a measure to raise education funds initiated and mainly carried by the CFT.

The meeting ended with a commitment to pull together behind the effort to pass the parcel tax. Over the next few months, the Proposition A campaign would draw together a broad coalition of students, faculty, unions, and community groups.

One of the people who would spend hours stumping for the measure was Kathe Burick, a part-time dance teacher and wholehearted union activist. Burick spent most of the July 9 meeting out in the lobby, working with a student to take photos of people who wrote snippets of their personal City College stories on butcher paper over the hashtag #iamcitycollege. The photos circulated on social media and became the first of many ways that AFT 2121 and the community coalition would mobilize San Francisco's love for the school to counter the media narrative. The logo for the campaign emerged soon after: a red heart on a yellow background overprinted with "We Are All City College," with versions in English, Spanish, Chinese, and Tagalog.

It soon became clear that the very nature of the school people loved was under attack, not only its existence but also its essence, and not only from the sanctions but from the bitter medicine Fisher prescribed as the only way to keep the school open.

CHAPTER THREE

Makeover: Crisis Is the New Normal

Summer–Fall 2012

When asked if she thought City College would survive, Interim Chancellor Fisher would say, "You'll survive, but you won't recognize yourselves." During her whirlwind six-month tenure Fisher brandished the threat of disaccreditation to impose radical changes to the school's mission, climate, and culture. To bolster her authority, she would repeat like a mantra, "I talk to Barbara Beno almost every day."

Within a week of the show cause letter, she had marshaled administrators, faculty, staff, and students into work groups for each area in which the accreditors dinged the college. The committees addressed everything from the school's governance structure to the Student Learning Outcomes required for every course. Advocates of SLOs say they improve accountability by using empirical data to refine courses and programs and improve student learning. To "do SLOs," faculty must identify three or four specific things that students should be able to know or be able to do by the end of a course, find a way of testing one of those things, look back at the end of the semester to see how many students achieved the outcome, and record all the data (in addition to recording the students' grades).

Some faculty appreciated the SLO process. Others detested SLOs, not only for the busy work they imposed with no appreciable benefit to learning but for the implication that education should best be evaluated quantitatively, with an approach like the "management by objectives" used to boost productivity on assembly lines. "SLOs imply that you don't teach for your students' sake anymore, but, as Pam Fisher explained (paraphrased but to the point), 'Employers will want to know exactly what a person can do when they complete your class,'" Kathe Burick said. "If somebody really gets something out of a class, a lot of times it's something you wouldn't even predict. For example, at the end of the semester I ask for a final paper addressing the three most helpful principles or techniques that make your tap dancing easier, more enjoyable, and more skilled, and one young person with ADD said, 'What I learned is if I stick with it, I can do anything.'"[1]

Like them or not, SLOs ranked among the Accrediting Commission's top concerns, and Fisher declared that SLOs would be a factor in teacher evaluations.

At that point, Academic Senate president Karen Saginor was focused on meeting ACCJC standards. Faculty bore particular responsibility for addressing SLOs, and Saginor felt something needed to be done to bring more information and urgency to the SLO discussion. She consulted with Department Chairperson Council president Darlene Alioto and AFT 2121 president Alisa Messer, and all three met with Fisher to urge her to cancel classes for a day and hold a special all-faculty meeting on SLOs, which she finally agreed to do.

On September 12, upwards of 1,200 teachers and counselors gathered in the gym at Ocean Campus for SLO training—the largest all-faculty meeting ever held at City College. Chancellor Fisher selected Bob Pacheco, a consultant from the Research and Planning Group, to anchor the event. Pacheco "set a tone of fear, saying that in the era of globalization, faculty had to prepare our students to compete with workers in Sri Lanka who make $2.25 an hour," Vicki Legion said. "He presented SLOs as the essential tool for modernizing. The 'proof' he gave was the commercial success of FedEx corporation, which evaluated employees with a goal-oriented checklist. As a cautionary tale he displayed the logos of about ten bankrupt corporations like Kodak that supposedly 'went the way of the dinosaurs' because they did not quickly adopt the equivalent of SLOs."

Pacheco's presentation "turned out to be quite helpful in opening the eyes of many faculty members to the possibility that just complying with SLO requirements (whether you liked them or not) was not going to fix our accreditation problem," Saginor said. "I think it helped build support for Alisa Messer's strategy of doing the SLO work *and* resisting the ACCJC through political and legal channels, a strategy that the Academic Senate also adopted at some point."

Shrinking the Mission

Barely a month after the show cause sanction was imposed, Fisher began pressing the board of trustees to approve a shrunken version of the school's mission. She advocated a narrowed "core mission" that echoed the just-enacted Student Success Act. This narrowed mission only addressed career and technical education certificates, transfer and associate degrees, and, after a fight, basic skills—lower-level English as a Second Language (ESL), representing roughly half of the college's students—and high school equivalency (GED) classes.

Cut out of the *primary mission* were "lifelong learning, life skills, and cultural enrichment," as well as "active engagement in the civic and social fabric of the community, citizenship preparation." The statement's last sentence made its purpose clear: "The mission statement drives institutional planning, decision-making and resource allocation." Narrower vision, smaller school.

Turning a Feature into a Bug: FCMAT Writes the Makeover Plan

At their August 23 meeting, after voting for the first time on the wizened mission statement, the CCSF trustees heard the report from the Fiscal Crisis Management and Assistance Team. Even before the sanctions, Fisher had pushed the trustees to request this allegedly neutral analysis of CCSF's fiscal problems.

FCMAT's representatives swept into the meeting to deliver their presentation, evaluation team chair Michelle Plumbtree in her flowered sweater and the men in their crisp suits. They announced that CCSF's budget was unsustainable, especially its labor contracts. The school had too many full-time faculty members and would have to make adjustments in employee costs. Their recommendations included ending health benefits for part-time faculty, reducing the number of full-time faculty, and eliminating subsidies for programs serving specific groups of students, such as the Disabled Students Programs and Services.[2] They scolded CCSF for running down its fund balance and not saving enough for future retiree health benefits. They also called for reducing staff (although the ACCJC had criticized staff levels as too low), eliminating or reducing the number of department chairs, and increasing the number of deans. They suggested eliminating some of the community sites where CCSF offered classes and evaluating "the cost effectiveness and service requirements of the college centers to determine the best future use for them." In closing, they declared that a crisis situation requires lots of decisive actions without wasting time on too much participation. They then swept out of the room without allowing questions.

In its written report, FCMAT distinguished itself from the ACCJC, yet cited it: "The Commission is concerned that CCSF is on the brink of insolvency." The charge of imminent insolvency blended misrepresentation with a strong shot of speculation. Reserves are calculated by taking the ending balance (revenue less expenses) plus other cash reserves or noncash assets in the general fund as a percentage of general fund expenditures for the year. As part of this fund balance, trustees can designate a separate board reserve, an extra pot of savings. FCMAT said that in 2011–2012 CCSF had reserves sinking below $2 million, about 1 percent—but that ignored the board reserve of $6.6 million. Adding the board fund would give the college a combined reserve of more than 4 percent even in that difficult year. FCMAT insisted repeatedly that the college should make draconian budget cuts, assuming Proposition A and Proposition 30 would fail and disregarding the energetic campaigns to pass them. In the end, the FCMAT analysts did conclude that the multiyear financial projections would be reasonable if the tax measures passed—but nobody paid attention to that part.

Instead, the report amped up fear. It urged the college to immediately request a special trustee, an official appointed by the state chancellor's office who would "advise" the elected trustees—and have veto power over their decisions.[3] It explicitly threatened the school with takeover if that didn't happen: "It [CCSF] must either make significant and ongoing budget adjustments or face the prospect of insolvency and possible state intervention. If the California community college Board of Governors determines that CCSF is not able to maintain its fiscal solvency under the current budget, the Board of Governors has the authority to appoint a special trustee to manage CCSF and restore fiscal solvency. . . . Because of its perilous fiscal condition and the charge it faces from the accreditation commission, it is urgent that CCSF act quickly."[4]

This followed a familiar script for students of austerity in education: cut funding, ask a nominally neutral body to analyze a district's finances, get a report calling for state takeover. But what FCMAT saw as bugs in the system, the unions proudly claimed as features.

"Our AFT national, state and local leaders are very proud of our local at CCSF because, through 35 years of collective bargaining, CCSF has emerged as the clear national leader in the fight for equity and respect for part-time faculty and for the protection and preservation of the college's fulltime faculty core," said Carl Friedlander, then chair of CFT's

Community College Council. "CCSF is admired throughout American higher education and has been appropriately honored for its extraordinary accomplishments in these areas."[5]

Interim Chancellor Fisher, however, rammed through big chunks of the FCMAT program in her remaining two months in office.

Shrinking the Footprint

Fisher harmonized with the *San Francisco Chronicle's* refrain, "CCSF is just too big." A month before the ACCJC ruling, the newspaper had run an article headlined, "S.F. City College can't afford all its campuses: Trustees may have to close sites to save money, academic standing." Reporter Nanette Asimov quoted Fisher's assertion: "Everything is on the table. [Closures are] a very legitimate question to be considering."[6]

With sanctions now in place, Fisher urged the board of trustees to close two neighborhood sites, put the school's administration building at 33 Gough Street on the market for long-term lease,[7] and cancel a pre-construction contract for the Performing Arts Education Center (PAEC), which had been approved and funded by San Francisco voters in two bond votes in 2001 and 2005. The PAEC, with its 650-seat theater and audio/video recording facilities, would give the school a sizeable auditorium for the first time. It would allow the college to expand its job training and degree offerings and to raise revenue by hosting performance festivals and events. It would provide a performance venue for community-based arts far south of the glittering San Francisco Ballet and Opera located in the Civic Center.

Two of the neighborhood sites the chancellor suggested closing focused on ESL. One was the only City College site in the mostly Asian Richmond neighborhood. The other, in the low-income immigrant-rich Visitacion Valley neighborhood, drew as many as two hundred students a night at peak enrollment. Both were running in the black, bringing in funds for the cash-strapped college.

Shrinking Democracy: Disciplining the Elected Board of Trustees

First the ACCJC and then FCMAT disparaged CCSF's management; the accreditor basically told the board to behave itself—"act in a manner consistent with its policies and bylaws." Undermined and under the gun, the board took up State Chancellor Jack Scott's proposal for a special trustee at its September 11 meeting. Board president John Rizzo introduced the plan and joined the chorus pressing City College to get "outside advice" to help solve its accreditation problems. Documents from the state chancellor's office counterposed the board's acceptance of a special trustee to the imposition of a "Special Trustee with Extraordinary Powers" who would supplant the board altogether. Cutting to the chase, trustee Natalie Berg summed up the input the board had gotten from FCMAT, the ACCJC, and multiple sources in the state chancellor's office. "[If] we don't take this action somebody will take it for us," Berg said. Trustee Chris Jackson was the lone opposing voice, saying that many people in the room disagreed, and that he hoped the board wouldn't just cede power to the special trustee.

"Reorganization": Disciplining the Administration

Citing the ACCJC's complaints that administration and governance at CCSF posed obstacles to meeting the standards, Fisher reorganized the vice chancellors by fiat. One of the first cuts was eliminating the position of Associate Vice Chancellor for Governmental Affairs that Leslie Smith used to advocate for more state funding. Fisher called eliminating Smith's position "concentrating on essential core services."

"[But] if the government is slitting your throat [or your budget], you want to have someone to say, 'Hey, stop, this is an educational institution, that's not going to work'," Kathe Burick said. She was there when Smith got the news: "She was going in to see Fisher. I forgot my coffee mug in Leslie's office, and went back later to get it. Leslie said, 'Fisher has basically forbidden me to do my job.' And Leslie retired within the month."

Disciplining the Faculty: Firing the Deans

California law specifies that community college faculty be organized in an Academic Senate run by faculty members elected by their peers and responsible for eleven areas, including curriculum and professional development. Although "the [ACCJC] standards talked very clearly about data-driven planning . . . in fact, what the ACCJC's people, Barbara Beno, really wanted was about decisions being clearly owned and made by the administration not by faculty," Karen Saginor said.

In a classic hostile takeover maneuver, Fisher fired about forty-five deans from schools, centers and administrative positions—all the deans who worked more directly with faculty and students—and had them reapply for their jobs. "She argued that the dean structure wasn't working properly. The deans were too close to the faculty, and they couldn't discipline them," African American Studies Department chair Tarik Farrar said, "In what sense did the faculty need to be disciplined? It suggests the structure wasn't authoritarian enough."

"They felt that anybody who was from within couldn't be in a leadership position, because they would compromise the mission, so that's why they wanted to change administrators," said Fred Chavaria, who declined to reapply for his position as dean of Social and Behavioral Sciences. "I had problems with the direction and could afford to have problems, because I had a pension already," he said; he went back to teaching classes and chairing the Administration of Justice Department.

From her second day on the job, Fisher had made no secret of her desire to hire and fire the department chairs. FCMAT gave her the ammunition she needed, with its recommendations to eliminate "redundancy" and consolidate departments. In perhaps her brashest move, Fisher proposed just that: collapsing sixty-one departments into seven schools, each headed by a dean who served at the pleasure of the chancellor.

"I was offered the chance to be the dean of this department," said Greg Keech, chair of English as a Second Language, CCSF's largest department, "but as chair I'm elected, and that matters to me. At City the chairs do what deans do at other colleges. We're experts in our disciplines elected to lead our departments. We do schedules and make assignments according to the AFT contract. Deans don't schedule, aren't necessarily experts in the discipline, and can't speak freely, because they're at-will employees. Elected chairs don't fit the top-down model. What Barbara Beno did allowed them to take over the administration. There's a noticeable pattern of bringing in new administrators and sidelining the ones with history here."

When Fisher summoned the department chairs to a meeting, Darlene Alioto had warned them of the plans afoot, and they were prepared to resist. The departments in the Diversity Collaborative were particularly concerned. Tarik Farrar attended for the Collaborative and stressed the difference these departments made in students' lives. Fisher interrupted him. "She said, 'I understand about these values, our values, our San Francisco values. . . . I understand about social justice, but we can't afford it anymore.' I was sitting right next to her and she actually said, 'We can't afford social justice anymore.' And I said, 'There's a concern on the part of the Diversity Departments, this idea that some departments have to be consolidated and others cease to exist,' and she said, 'There are too many small departments.' That's what African American Studies looked like at the time, because we were interdisciplinary. Most of our classes were under other departments. But she said, 'There are too many of them, so you are in our sights,' meaning you, collectively, the Diversity Departments were in the crosshairs."

Fisher's Farewell

At Fisher's last meeting with the board of trustees on October 25, she pulled out all the stops and hit a note of panic. As the *San Francisco Chronicle* reported: "'Without dramatic change, there won't be a college,' interim Chancellor Pamila Fisher scolded the trustees at 1:30 a.m. when she feared they might waver. 'Time is of the essence. The accrediting commission made it clear as recently as yesterday that they are concerned we are not moving quickly enough.'"[8]

Under this pressure, the trustees approved the appointment of Robert Agrella as special trustee; the retired president of Santa Rosa Junior College had been serving as a consultant since Fisher brought him on in August. They went along with the reorganization plan abolishing the elected department chairs, closing the Bernal Heights demonstration preschool that served two housing projects, and curtailing the hours for on-campus childcare. And they agreed in principle to require students to pay all fees in full to complete registration, whether or not financial aid checks had arrived, even at the risk of losing class enrollments.

At the end of this marathon meeting, trustees Rodrigo Santos and Steve Ngo moved to table a motion to award a contract for preconstruction services on the PAEC. The motion was only to table for a month, but as the crisis continued to deepen, the long-sought project was put on indefinite hold. San Francisco Mayor Ed Lee had appointed Santos after Milton Marks died; Ngo was also an ally of the mayor.

Taken together, the board's actions that night embodied the makeover of City College. "It was a *Shock Doctrine* attack," Alisa Messer said, referring to Naomi Klein's 2007 book that documented the ways natural and political crises can be exploited to undermine democracy and appropriate public goods for private profit.[9]

Fisher's contract expired on Halloween. Mayor Ed Lee officially proclaimed October 31, 2012, "Dr. Pamila Fisher Day" in San Francisco.[10]

Fear Becomes a Force

Fear and tension roiled the atmosphere at the school while all this was going on. "From the beginning of the crisis, I went into semi-permanent panic breathing, high in my chest," said Legion. I had a tape playing in my head: 'Okay, we have to figure out how to get out of this trap. Houdini is in the box under water, and there's just a few minutes left. . . . Think really hard. We need to get it right, or we're going down.'"

"One thing I noticed immediately [when the crisis hit] was a horrifying effect on morale, not just linked to the possible loss of jobs or the institution but something akin to PTSD," said CFT communications director Fred Glass, who worked closely with AFT 2121. "People who could come to a meeting, set an agenda, and do tasks would endlessly cycle on things they had no information about, in a whirlpool of confusion, despair, and paralysis internally. The first time I came to talk about a communications plan, we couldn't get through any item without twelve tangents."

Making matters worse, the CCSF administration pounced on anyone who dared hold up their head. Just after the show cause sanction, Alisa Messer and John Rizzo appeared on a popular talk show on one of the local NPR affiliates. "My goal was to make it really clear there was nothing wrong with the education [at CCSF]," Messer said. "John Rizzo was on and said something similar, and Interim Chancellor Pam Fisher sent an email to the trustees telling them it was dangerous to comment on accreditation."[11]

In that message, Fisher put the trustees on notice: "I also learned today that they [ACCJC] also have a policy prohibiting any official college representative of publicly criticizing the commission (which neither John [Rizzo] nor I did although others did). I always knew it was a bad idea but did not know it was prohibited. At next Tuesday's board meeting this will be especially critical. Not only will the meeting be broadcast live, the commission representatives will be in the audience."

That July 6 message had a chilling effect. "I started getting a much clearer picture of how afraid people were, and they were afraid for really good reasons. . . . And I was seeing how the media was saying, 'Of course, all these terrible things being said about the college are true,'" Messer said.

The fear rippled far beyond City College. "Even strong faculty unionists accustomed to crossing swords publicly with their own administration or reactionary politicians were at first deeply reluctant to publicly criticize the ACCJC, because they knew from their own experiences what damage that could do to their institutions," Fred Glass said. CFT Community College Council president Carl Friedlander spoke out at a special October 2012 Board of Governors meeting on City College, and named the fear, saying:

> I believe the Commission's decision to issue the most severe of sanctions to an institution, which, after its last accreditation cycle six years ago, received several recommendations but *no* sanction, was misguided. The Community College Board of Governors should understand that huge segments of the California Community College system believe, though reluctant to publicly express it, that the decisions of the ACCJC regarding institutional sanctions tend to be overly severe and even adversarial.[12]

Not So Fast: Students Resist the Steamroller

Meanwhile, students—not cowed by Fisher or the ACCJC—kept organizing. Eric Blanc and Micheál Madden started convening meetings in the Student Union. The group that gathered took the name Save CCSF Coalition and began the planning that led to the takeover of the September 11 board of trustees meeting to protest the appointment of the special trustee.

About fifty strong, they burst into the meeting, many wearing red T-shirts supporting the Chicago teachers who had just walked out on strike. Led by then Associated Students president Shanell Williams, they let loose with an Occupy-style mic check: "We reject the special trustee. No cuts! No fees! Education should be free!" Some trustees left the room, and the students moved to the trustees' table and sat down as though they were trustees. For a few minutes, they held the room and declared themselves a "people's board."

"We can stop this," said student organizer Eric Blanc. "If you take action, you can actually change what's going on. We can actually stop the accreditation process . . . and we can be an example. . . . Just as Chicago [the teachers' strike] is a critical test for K–12, CCSF is a critical test for community colleges." After about fifteen minutes, the students left the room, and the trustees came back and continued the meeting.

A San Francisco native born into a left-wing union family and a substitute teacher in the East Bay, Blanc had taken classes at City on and off over the years. He came up through Occupy Education and the movement against budget cuts at University of California, Berkeley in 2010–2011 and belonged to Socialist Organizer. He went with a couple of comrades to the big meeting in the Castro in July, and what they saw disturbed them. "It all happened extremely quickly, the big town hall. . . . We all went hoping to get more info, and came away thinking, 'Oh, my god, if these people are leading the resistance, we're in trouble,' because they seemed divorced from any fightback perspective. Besides the students and union reps, there were local politicians, nonprofit leaders. The message was vague, there was no sense of the attack on CCSF being part of broader program of austerity and privatization. The dominant line was, 'We need more information, we need to pass Prop A.' There was no questioning the legitimacy of the ACCJC," he said.

But for many people at the college and in the community, organizing for the Proposition A parcel tax offered a meaningful way to push back fear and respond to the crisis at hand.

CHAPTER FOUR

San Francisco Steps Up

Fall 2012

"**P**eople were walking around feeling like they were terrible people doing a terrible job at this terrible college. People felt terrible because that was how we were being made to feel by the media, by the interim administration, by the ACCJC," Alisa Messer said. "The only place we weren't getting that was the classroom—working with students was good—and on the doors [for Proposition A] where everybody had a good story about how much City College meant."

While the San Francisco media continued to run doom and gloom stories about what was wrong with CCSF, hundreds of AFT and SEIU volunteers and community supporters were ringing doorbells. In an election headlined by President Barack Obama's run for his second term, they hoped to sway voters on an array of issues.

These activists canvassed a city once again on the cusp of drastic change. San Francisco had become a key node in the global economy in the years following World War II, and the finance, administrative, and entertainment center of a regional economy powered by the tech industry. The economy of the internet revolution fed inequality, with sharp wage disparities between professional and service workers. It was also volatile, subject to booms and busts.

Geographer Richard Walker wrote:

> The Bay Area's urban landscape was in violent upheaval through the 1990s as a result of the New Economy boom and financial bubble. Real estate values shot up, and so did new buildings, at a markedly higher density than before. This came at a real cost in displacement of people and disarray in cultural life. The great urban beast arose and shook off many a poor soul like so many

fleas. By the time it settled down again, the region would never be the same.[1]

San Francisco, and the Bay Area as a whole, took by far the sharpest shock from the bursting of the dot-com bubble in 2000. It recovered and then was walloped again by the Great Recession in 2008. By 2012, another boom was building, encouraged by policy initiatives from San Francisco Mayor Ed Lee.

A lawyer who had started out helping tenants fight evictions, Lee spent most of his career in city government. The board of supervisors had appointed him to the mayor's office in 2011 to fill the remainder of Gavin Newsom's term, when Newsom was elected lieutenant governor. Former San Francisco mayor and State Assembly speaker Willie L. Brown Jr. claimed credit for tapping Lee for the job.[2] Brown was well-known for his real estate connections, and Lee too became known for his coziness with developers.

Lee backed a reduction in the amount of affordable housing developers would be required to build.[3] His administration looked the other way as Airbnb took thousands of apartments off the rental market, and pushed a 2011 ordinance that gave tech companies a massive tax break for locating in the neglected Mid-Market area of downtown San Francisco (known locally as the Twitter tax break). As the tech labor force rushed into the area, real estate moguls made a killing.

"The fight [over Lee's affordable housing initiative] indicated a new and powerful alliance had been formed: The tech sector had now linked with the market-rate developers in forming a new power source of substantial economic—and political contribution—power. Together they were overwhelmingly influential on the mayor and his staff," wrote veteran housing activist Calvin Welch.[4]

Rents began to skyrocket, almost doubling from 2010 to 2015.[5] Evictions increased almost as sharply, and working-class families were being displaced by high-paid employees of Google, Twitter, Yahoo, etc. CCSF student activist Win-Mon Kyi saw the Mission District neighborhood where her parents ran a small pizza shop change almost overnight, as small businesses were pushed out by spiraling rents.

Displacement was nothing new; it had accompanied the postwar transformation of San Francisco—and had been met by fierce resistance. Residents of the city's low-income communities and communities of color had been organizing to fight displacement and influence the course of development, starting with the African Americans battling redevelopment in the Fillmore District in the 1950s and continuing to the present.[6] San Francisco also had deeply rooted labor and LGBTQ movements.

Each of the city's major social movements had a history of electoral mobilization, and the political slant of its board of supervisors teetered on November's results. The board's progressive trio of Eric Mar, David Campos, and John Avalos were up for reelection. Former Harvey Milk LGBTQ Democratic Club president Rafael Mandelman—a cochair of the community meeting just after the show cause ruling—was running for the CCSF board of trustees.

In San Francisco, bluest of blue cities, the political drama hinges on the relative power of the progressive and centrist wings of the Democratic Party, and coziness to real estate interests defines their positions. The summer of 2012 saw corporate Democrats on the move. The local Democratic Party elected Mary Jung as chair. A lifelong party activist who had headed the local Clinton-Gore committee in 1996, Jung was hired in 2013 as chief lobbyist for the San Francisco Association of Realtors in a classic revolving-door career move. Other centrists scooped up most of the main roles in the party. Supervisor Mar, who would be first to champion City College in its crisis, had trouble getting the party to endorse his reelection bid.

The November 2012 California state ballot included the deceptive Paycheck Protection Act, Proposition 32, a frontal attack on the ability of unions to fund their work and politically mobilize their members, as well as the Millionaires Tax, Proposition 30, the latest in a series of proposals to raise education funds to fill the needs left in the wake of Proposition 13.

Unions Advocate Antidote to Austerity

The California Federation of Teachers had long fought for progressive taxation as the antidote to austerity budgets. In 2010, it anchored the March for California's Future, along with the American Federation of State, County and Municipal Employees. The three-hundred-mile, six-week march from Bakersfield to the State Capitol in Sacramento helped bring together a coalition of faith, labor, and community organizations. A year and a half before the Occupy movement exploded, marchers talked about income inequality, making scores of stops in the small cities and farming towns of central California. Union activists built a coalition that sponsored two ballot initiatives. Proposition 25, passed in November 2010, enabled the state legislature to pass a budget on a majority vote, thereby ending the gridlock-producing two-thirds requirement. In 2011, CFT proposed the Millionaires Tax, a tax increase on high incomes earmarked for education.

Governor Jerry Brown and the powerful California Business Roundtable opposed the original plan, and Brown's pressure peeled away all of the other unions who initially supported the proposal, leaving CFT standing alone. CFT, in coalition with three community-based networks (California Calls, the Courage Campaign, and the Alliance of Californians for Community Empowerment) pushed back and won the compromise that became Proposition 30. Brown wanted a narrative of "shared sacrifice" by residents and business, so the compromise measure included a small sales tax increase alongside an income-tax increase for high earners, the pointed moniker Millionaires Tax was deleted, and the Roundtable dropped their opposition.[7] Passage of Proposition 30 would forestall a looming $10 million cut in state revenue for CCSF, and add about $1 million in new revenue.

Proposition 30 joined Proposition A, the City College parcel tax, on the San Francisco ballot. If Proposition A passed, as Interim Chancellor Fisher acknowledged in her report to the ACCJC, "It would provide the College with an additional $14 million annually for the next eight years. If approved by San Francisco voters, this would mitigate many of the college's most immediate fiscal needs."[8]

Collaboration among unions was crucial to passing the parcel tax. SEIU 1021 represented the classified staff at the college, as well as thousands of other Bay Area public sector workers. It had a strong political staff and long experience, which it shared with AFT 2121. "We wouldn't have been able to do it without the larger local, without their political knowhow," Alisa Messer said. While most unions around the state focused on defeating Proposition 32, the San Francisco Labor Council put members in the street to campaign for the revenue measures as well.

During the campaign, Sheila Tully, president of the faculty union at San Francisco State, did weekends of street outreach in her westside Richmond District. She focused her outreach on Eric Mar's campaign for supervisor and on City College. She told Vicki Legion, "I spoke to about eight hundred people, and it was striking to me that every single person I spoke with used almost the same words: 'I *love* City College; it can't close! What can I do to help?'" But in the toxic atmosphere created by the ACCJC sanctions and the media echo chamber, even the commonsense fundraising measure drew a lot of skepticism.

Mayor Ed Lee tried to pull the parcel tax off the ballot, Alisa Messer said. "Before we got sanctioned, the trustees had gone to a meeting with the mayor to try to get his support for Prop A, and they got something noncommittal. But the story goes that on the way out the door they said, 'We just had an accreditation visit, and it will probably not be fully positive,' or something like that, and the mayor was furious that they hadn't led with that, especially once the decision came down. He thought the accreditation was far more important than any need for funding, and I'm told he used that as his excuse for a long time to be mad at the trustees— and the college."

Many City College faculty and staff who weren't skeptical were scared. "People were really scared the school would close if we made too much noise," AFT 2121 activist Kathe Burick said. "Two of my most intelligent, respected, caring colleagues pulled me aside for twenty-to-forty-minute conversations about how I should be quiet and step back, and [we could] get our accreditation first and then point out all the errors of the ACCJC."

"What you have to do in organizing is meet people where they are, listen to their fears, and try to show a little ray of hope or ray of light," said Burick, who got reassigned time through the union to work on Proposition A. "Prop A was the first big organizing tool. . . . It gave people something hopeful and reassuring," she said. Burick's transition from activist to organizer wasn't always comfortable. As she put it, "The internal organizing was a challenge for me too because I felt like, 'Am I talking to them because they're my friends or because I'm trying to get them to say something or do something?'" But she and other CCSF students, faculty, and supporters got out of their comfort zones and worked their hearts out for Proposition A; the AFT 2121 newsletter devoted a full page to its importance.[9]

Both Proposition A in San Francisco and Proposition 30 statewide won by comfortable margins. Their proponents were relieved and hopeful that having some financial breathing room would allow people to address other aspects of the ACCJC sanctions and increase the likelihood of them being dropped.

"The day after the election people on campus were walking on air, because 72 percent of San Franciscans had voted to help fund the college, even though they were being told terrible things about it," Alisa Messer said.

New Interim Chancellor Thelma Scott-Skillman was not impressed.

CHAPTER FIVE

From Scared to Mad

Fall 2012–Spring 2013

T he day after voters approved the parcel tax to support City College, new Interim Chancellor Thelma Scott-Skillman sent a vinegary email saying the projected $14 million in new revenue would change nothing. Pamila Fisher had brought Scott-Skillman out of retirement in August to serve as interim vice chancellor of student services, giving her an easy shot at promotion. Scott-Skillman had been the founding president of Folsom Lake College, a Northern California community college that had an enrollment of about 11,700 students when she left.[1]

Barely two weeks after Scott-Skillman took office, the administration presented AFT 2121 with a nasty package of contract proposals, including a 9 percent pay cut—despite the fact that the parcel tax would raise an estimated $14 million annually. (Negotiations between the community college district and the union had started in the spring of 2012.) "This felt like a punch in the gut," Alisa Messer said.

The administration's sour response to the Proposition A victory "shifted faculty from being scared to being mad," Tarik Farrar said. Injuries and insults had mounted. Deans got fired. "Reorganization" targeted department chairs and Diversity Studies. Never mind the site closures, the Student Learning Outcomes, the constant disrespect from administrators who knew nothing of CCSF's culture. All this came to a head at the end of the fall semester.

The Department Chairperson Council swiftly challenged the administration's proposal to mash sixty-one departments into seven schools. Its members assessed themselves monthly dues for the first time and hired a lawyer to help them with contract negotiations. The "reorganization" would strip authority from the chairs—elected by their peers, with frontline knowledge of their departments—and turn it over to deans of seven "schools" within the college. This posed a particular threat to Diversity Studies, because their identity and autonomy would be lost. "African American Studies, Latin American and Latino/a Studies, and Asian American Studies came out of social movements, as did LGBT and Women's Studies. The district wanted to put us under one department. We said every program had its different history, different issues. One person can't be an expert in it all," Latin American and Latino/a Studies chair Edgar Torres said.

Students jumped to the defense of Diversity Studies and sparked a postelection surge of action with a November 15 demonstration on Ocean Campus. A couple hundred people attended the noontime rally at Ram Plaza. Community allies of the Diversity Departments, students from San Francisco State University, University of California, Berkeley, and University of California, Davis joined CCSF students and faculty to oppose the administration's consolidation plan. Following on Fisher's dismissal of social justice as "no longer affordable," the demonstrators saw the plan as yet another move to dismantle the liberatory and community-serving programs that made CCSF precious to San Francisco.

The core of the student organizing group had grown to include Eric Blanc, Micheál Madden, Terence Yancey, and Sharon Shatterly from Socialist Organizer, student association leader Shanell Williams, and others newer to the work. One of those was Martín Madrigal, a vet who'd found his way to City after his fourth tour in Iraq. When show cause came down, Madrigal said, "*I* felt attacked. This was *my* school." Another was Lalo Gonzalez, who grew up in East Palo Alto, the majority Black and Latinx town across the freeway from the posh home of Stanford University. After college he'd signed up for the Marine Corps Officer Candidates School but left almost immediately, as it became clear to him that from a social justice perspective, he'd be joining the wrong team. Making a sharp left, he went to work with the Center for Third World Organizing, before returning to San Francisco at Blanc's urging.

The relationships and politics of the Bay Area's Occupy Public Education group laid the groundwork for the students' organizing, Blanc explained. "The political starting point for us was decades of attacks on public education—state, national, global. At the beginning of the crisis the dominant line was: 'If there's a crisis, it's City College's fault.' But we saw the crisis rooted in the political agenda of the state. The Student Success Act was a predecessor to the attacks at City College."

Save CCSF Coalition Forms

Seeking a way for faculty, staff, students, and community members to work together, two faculty members—Rick Baum from Political Science and Bob Price from Chemistry—called a meeting for November 12. The group that gathered became the Save CCSF Coalition, adopting the same name the student activists had been using since the beginning of the school year. While there was some criticism of faculty for "plagiarism," everyone agreed that such a vehicle was important, and the two organizing efforts soon merged. Students and faculty usually co-facilitated meetings.

The November 12 meeting drew lots of faculty but few staff. Though AFT 2121 and the City College chapter of SEIU 1021 cooperated on Proposition A and Proposition 30, long-simmering divisions between the staff and faculty unions widened during the crisis.

Some of the animosity dated back to 1998, when the staff went on strike. About three hundred faculty members honored the strike, and had their pay docked for their trouble. Many of them joined students and SEIU members in a spirited picket line that blocked the main entrance to Ocean Campus, but labor law barred AFT 2121 from officially authorizing a sympathy strike, and many other faculty went to work. Rancor from that incident festered among some in the staff, aggravated by what they saw as faculty elitism.

Staff at CCSF do all sorts of work that keeps the college running. They're custodians, library technicians, IT systems techs, campus police, financial aid workers, and administrative assistants. Their union contract covers more than seventy-five job classifications. At City, as at other colleges, these workers often don't get the respect they deserve.

Tehmina Khan worked as a writing tutor at CCSF for ten years before moving over to the English faculty. When she was a tutor, "There was this presumption on the part of some of the faculty, certainly not all, that they were the professionals, and I was the helper. Some instructors would ask how we could support the class, what we had to offer, others would just say, 'Do this, do that.' There were a few who really didn't care to have us in the classroom. Now I'm the same person doing similar work, but relationships with my colleagues who I knew before are different." Because the faculty was whiter than the staff, the disrespect could have an edge of racism.

The hard feelings worked both ways, AFT 2121 president emeritus Rodger Scott observed, "In the struggles between our local and theirs, neither side gets high marks. Faculty, including some union people, were unsympathetic to people they thought had less education and status, and SEIU folks were too quick to take umbrage. . . . There were sectarian views on both sides. We didn't have enough common goals and interests. . . . The administration didn't have to be too perceptive to see those differences and play us off against each other."

Shortly after the 1998 strike, Athena Steff was elected president of the City College SEIU chapter. She earned a reputation as a business unionist and pugnacious defender of her membership. When the crisis hit, she still held the post. She and other chapter leaders allied explicitly with the interim administrators, looking to them as the "adults in the room" who would advocate for them. At Pamila Fisher's last tumultuous meeting, SEIU members brought the outgoing chancellor flowers and a cake.[2]

Crossing a Threshold: Flex Day, January 2013

Continued attacks by the administration spurred Save CCSF's organizing. The December board of trustees meeting ran till nearly 2:00 a.m., as students gave emotional testimony against the administration's decision to cancel support for the A. Philip Randolph Institute's Southeast Shuttle that allowed students from the Bayview-Hunters Point neighborhood to get across gang territory to school safely. Tim Henderson, a recent graduate of the GED program at CCSF's Southeast Center, read a spoken word piece that concluded:

> GED students quarantined from all the promise of a classroom they were just beginning to be comfortable with, the room I finally graduated from, the van courageous to take us past war territory left empty. For us, what was one more opportunity is one more hurdle for us to jump, one more reason for us to stay home, to watch the confines of our boulevards envelop us whole. For the students you're leaving behind, please reconsider.

They didn't.

On December 20, new Interim Chancellor Scott-Skillman informed faculty they would be starting the new year with a pay cut. Instead of allocating Proposition A funds toward programs, services, and salaries, as the ballot language specified, Scott-Skillman put them toward "accreditation-related purposes." This included allocating nearly half the projected revenues to the school's reserve funds, inflating them far beyond the state recommendation.[3] As 2013 opened, approximately twenty-five part-time instructors and eighteen part-time counselors were cut, and thirty-four members of the classified staff got pink slips.[4]

Classified staff and teachers had accepted pay cuts and layoffs to meet the challenges of the financial crises that started in 2008. By 2012, "the [SEIU] union leadership stopped encouraging this. They said we couldn't afford more cuts, so this meant layoffs," said former Classified Senate president James Rogers, an information systems analyst with twenty years at City College. "At union meetings they would take the pulse of the membership on how to respond. In the first couple years, the consensus was let's just tighten belts. Not formal, a show of hands at the meeting." In late 2012, the district "asked for 5 percent in cost savings, so that meant 5 percent of the workforce laid off. We had months of negotiations. I was on the bargaining team. Half the bargaining team members got layoff notices."

Some staff members worked with the Save CCSF Coalition, but faculty and students took the lead in confronting the administration and the accreditor. "We decided we had to do something," Tarik Farrar said. "One man suggested we boycott the chancellor's speech at the beginning of the semester, and it caught on like wildfire." On the day before classes start each semester, the college holds a "Flex Day," a combination of administrative housekeeping and professional development, anchored by a speech from the chancellor. The action plan was hatched right at the end of fall semester, so most of the outreach needed to happen online and over the phone during the winter break.

Engineering professor Wynd Kaufmyn came back from her sabbatical and dove into the organizing. Bob Price had invited her to the first meeting of Save CCSF, because he knew she'd been an activist since her embrace of liberation theology drew her to Central America solidarity in the 1980s—but she'd never been active in the union or campus committees before. "This was the first time I worked on something that affected me in such a direct and personal way," Kaufmyn said. She remembers being at a family wedding, spending hours on the phone talking with people at the college. "Some people in my family still hold it against me."

The night before the January 11 Flex Day, Save CCSF activists gathered to refine their action plans. Tension ran high. Weak participation could leave people out on a limb. Yet they had to take the chance.

The next morning, faculty members went to the Diego Rivera Theater on Ocean Campus for the day's big meeting. At a signal—"Let's go!"—most people got up and walked out to join the picket line already moving outside. As the Brass Liberation Orchestra oompahed encouragement, the crowd grew till it overflowed the plaza in front of the theater. Chanting "Whose school? Our school!" and "They say cutback! We say fight back!" speakers demanded that Proposition A funds be used for classes and student services instead of paying consultants $1,000 a day.[5] "A thousand dollars a day! Every six days that's another class we could offer to our students," Shanell Williams said. "We are making history right here!"

This unity against the continuing high-handed behavior of the administration showed a qualitative change for the faculty. "We had a picket line of at least three hundred people, and we had a rally. That was the threshold we crossed that created the movement," Farrar said.

ACCJC: Seeing the Pattern, Seeking the Motive

People became more skeptical and willing to look at the ACCJC as the chaos at the school intensified—and eye-popping research by retired Los Angeles City College math teacher Marty Hittelman gave them a lot to look at.

Hittelman had served as president of both the California Federation of Teachers and its Community College Council. In 1991, he'd served on the Commission on Innovation, a forerunner of the Student Success Task Force. He had been following the ACCJC since 2001, when he took exception to their recommendation that accrediting standards be based on "quantified outcomes," a forerunner of SLOs. He inventoried the agency's arbitrary and capricious record in detail, basing his research on ACCJC publications, public sections of reports from the commission's visiting teams, confidential conversations with people on various campuses and visiting teams, and correspondence with ACCJC president Barbara Beno and with the CFT and the Community College Association of the California Teachers Association.

In 2008, while he was president of the CFT, Hittelman rebuked the commission for its "demands regarding SLOs, *because they intrude on negotiable evaluation criteria, and violate principles of academic freedom*" [emphasis in original]. Beno had threatened to disaccredit Solano Community College in 2009 if the school didn't adopt SLOs "regardless of collective bargaining."

Just before the 2012 election, Hittelman published the first iteration of his lengthy dossier *ACCJC Gone Wild*. It revealed that the ACCJC, one of six regional community college accrediting bodies, accounted for 89 percent of all sanctions issued against US community colleges from 2003 to 2008.[6] In January 2012, twenty-one California colleges came up for reaccreditation; fifteen of them (71 percent) were sanctioned. Two of those were placed on show cause. The same was true in June 2012, when CCSF was placed on show cause—fifteen out of twenty-one colleges up for review were sanctioned. Predictably, sanctioned colleges received negative publicity and their enrollment and revenue dropped, forcing class closures and layoffs.

The ACCJC not only issued far more and harsher sanctions than other accreditors, but the standards it applied had little to do with the quality of education. Instead, Hittelman said, "The ACCJC issues sanctions that are based on the successful performance of excessive documentation and data gathering, reviews of policy and procedures, and adherence to education practices that are not based on scientific studies."

Although the Accrediting Commission performed public functions, it maintained that, as a private agency, it could operate away from the public eye. "The ACCJC operations are cloaked in secrecy with all involved required to sign a pledge that they will not reveal the inner workings of the college visiting teams or how the ACCJC itself operates in determining what level of sanctions to impose," Hittelman said.[7] "Clearly, *the ACCJC has become a rogue agency*," he concluded [emphasis in original]. This theme would reverberate through the next several years. Hittelman's study of the ACCJC was foundational.

Others had a more disturbing analysis. "You *wish* it was a rogue agency," Tarik Farrar said. "It would be a lot easier to deal with."

The Research Committee
Inspired by the research unit of the Chicago Teachers Union (CTU), some Save CCSF activists formed the Research Committee and began working to discover the motives and context behind the pattern Hittelman laid out.

They started with research Vicki Legion had begun the moment the crisis hit. She was scheduled to have a two-week "staycation" when she heard about the death threat to the college. She dropped everything and googled for about twelve hours a day, fueled by endless cups of strong Lipton tea with milk. Legion's first stop was looking into officials who had been guiding the Accreditation Division in the US Department of

Education (DOE). It was easy to find clear evidence of what economists call "regulatory capture," which often operates through a "revolving door" of leaders moving between government posts and private industry, making industry-friendly rulings during their time in government, and then picking up handsome checks when they rotate out to private industry.[8] She quickly found a number of officials with deep ties to the for-profit colleges and student loan industry.[9]

Legion also looked into the 2006 Department of Education report *A Test of Leadership*, commonly referred to as the Spellings Report.[10] According to *Inside Higher Education*, the Spellings Commission "viewed the accreditation system as a potential lever for bringing about the broader changes they envision for higher ed, i.e. creating a market in education . . . at the core of the full court press on accreditors is a desire to have the agencies ratchet up the pressure they in turn place on colleges to measure (and prove) that their students are learning; and importantly to try to find ways to compare the institutions' success to one another," an explicit parallel to standardized testing in K–12.[11] The Spelling Report urged "the transformation of accreditation" to rely more on stricter enforcement policies and "learning assessments," such as SLOs.[12]

The Research Committee continued to explore the relationship of accreditation and privatization. In 2009, President Barack Obama appointed the CTU's nemesis Arne Duncan, a powerful promoter of charter schools, as secretary of education. Under Duncan, the DOE continued to pressure accreditors, leading even the ACCJC itself to complain. "The ACCJC newsletter of February 2011 says that standards have 'input from the US DOE that reflect congressional guidelines and expectations. . . . [T]hese federal requirements are increasingly more rigorous,'" the Research Committee found. For-profit colleges slid by with much softer scrutiny, though investigations by Congress and the General Accounting Office found fraud and abuse rampant in such schools.[13]

The Research Committee's February 2013 report "What Is the ACCJC? Facts and Analysis" was judicious and yet radical for that stage of the struggle. "We are not making a claim that the ACCJC has been the object of industry influence or regulatory capture by the career colleges, the student loan industry and other edu-corporations," the committee wrote. "Rather we are saying that—in view of the frequent occurrence of this problem in a money-soaked political system—this question deserves further investigation."[14]

Putting the Pieces Together

Save CCSF and AFT 2121 called a community meeting for February 6 at Mission Campus. They expected a modest turnout, but the response far surpassed their hopes. About three hundred people packed the multipurpose room at Mission Campus, representing students, faculty, and community. The organizers arranged for translation into Spanish and Cantonese to ensure that everyone could follow the packed agenda.

Seattle teachers were boycotting high-stakes testing that week, and one of their picket signs perched on the wall behind the speakers. The crowd erupted in cheers for a surprise guest, Spencer Coggs of the "Wisconsin 14," the Democratic state senators who left the state to break the quorum needed to pass Governor Scott Walker's bill stripping public workers' bargaining rights.

From the jump the students had linked the attack to austerity policies. The February 6 community meeting connected the attack on City College to the nationwide attack on public workers. The Save CCSF points of unity reflected this perspective:

1. Save CCSF as an affordable, accessible, and democratic community college.
2. Reverse cuts to classes, programs, and compensation. Use Proposition A funds as promised.
3. Fully fund CCSF and all public education by increasing taxes on the rich and corporations and by curbing military and prison spending. Stop privatization.
4. Stop the misuse of the accreditation process to impose austerity. Make the accreditation process transparent and democratic.
5. Keep CCSF diverse. Support student equity. Stop resegregation.
6. Stop union busting. Rescind staff and faculty layoffs.

The Meat and Potatoes of Student Organizing

Students were already planning a rally for February 21. Micheál Madden got up at the February 6 gathering and asked all the teachers present to sign in, so organizers could arrange to visit their classes. "We built all these things through classroom announcements. That was the meat and potatoes of student organizing," Madden said. The core group of organizers took shifts and circulated through the buildings, knocking on classroom doors and asking if they could have five minutes to talk. "It took hours and hours."

The mobilizing effort brought more than 150 people out to Ram Plaza at midday February 21. The sun made one of its rare winter visits to the Bay Area that day, and some protesters sported shirtsleeves. A bright orange banner proclaimed "Save City College of SF from the 1%. Education for the 99%." Speakers at the rally made common cause with student battles against privatization around the world—in Europe, in Puerto Rico, and in Chile, where students had occupied hundreds of schools in 2011 and joined with unions and social movement groups in the largest demonstrations in more than twenty years.

"If you remember the civil rights movement—when you know the real story, you know the vanguard of that movement were youth," Farrar said, bringing in history as he often did. "As I heard Micheál speaking earlier, what's happening in Europe, what's happening in Chile, what's happening in Puerto Rico is the same struggle that's being waged here. The significance of CCSF in the struggle is that it's the largest community college in the country. . . . If they can bring down CCSF, they can do it anywhere—they can do it everywhere."

At the end of the rally, about thirty students marched into Conlan Hall and asked to meet with Interim Chancellor Scott-Skillman. Several police officers blocked the stairs and told them she was away. Vice Chancellor of Administration and Finance Peter Goldstein spoke briefly to the crowd. "Without our accreditation, this college will not be able to exist in its current form," he said. "No matter how much we think the accreditation people might be wrong, they have the ability to make that happen."

The students refused to leave until they secured a meeting to discuss their demands: that the chancellor tell the trustees to reverse all cuts to classes, services, staff, and faculty, stop downsizing the mission of City College, and promote equity; hold town hall meetings at all the campuses to listen to students; make a public statement calling for Proposition A funds to be used as promised; and protest ACCJC's sanction of City College and call on the DOE to sanction the accreditor.

The workday ended, the building shut down, and the students stayed. Thus began the first occupation of a campus building in CCSF history—seemingly spontaneous but actually well-planned. Four TV trucks camped outside the building all night, continuously broadcasting news stories and pictures of the administration building festooned with banners and protest signs.

Wynd Kaufmyn, the only faculty member to stay inside for the entire occupation, remembers a low-key night highlighted by talking circles on the subject of "what City College means to me." Someone brought in a sound system, so there was music and dancing too; Shanell Williams had everyone bopping and singing along as she spun a rap, "We'll show cause to the show cause." Faculty brought bottled water and granola bars, and some collected bail money and kept watch outside. At around eight the next morning, tired and rumpled, the students were still singing, repurposing Woody Guthrie: "This school is your school, this school is my school . . . this school belongs to you and me."

A bit later, Chancellor Scott-Skillman arrived for work and agreed to meet with the students the following Monday—only to tell them none of their demands could be met. While the chancellor held the power gavel, the students had succeeded brilliantly in telling the story of the City College struggle to the whole Bay Area.

Save CCSF's First Big Public Action

Just over two weeks later, on March 14, Save CCSF's first big City Hall rally amplified the students' call. Save CCSF sponsored the rally, which was endorsed by AFT 2121, the San Francisco Labor Council, United Educators of San Francisco, which represents K–12 teachers, and the Mission Campus Associated Students. The action rippled and built through the city, starting with a 1:00 p.m. walkout at Ocean Campus that fed a 2:00 p.m. march from Mission Campus to the final rally in front of City Hall.

Conga drums and bells greeted the marchers as they arrived at Civic Center on a foggy, windy afternoon. The two emcees were Wynd Kaufmyn and Shanell Williams. Speaker after speaker lifted up the gifts that CCSF brought the city and demanded that the mayor and supervisors intervene to save the college.

After denouncing broad social priorities that put money into "wars and prisons and bank bailouts," Lalo Gonzalez got specific. "The interim chancellor has the audacity to call the students who are trying to save our school 'irresponsible.'. . . No. What's irresponsible is her reckless decision to lay off all part-time counselors, leaving students in the dark during the registration process," he said. "What's irresponsible is cutting funds for Disabled Students Programs and Services in the name of long-term stability. What's irresponsible is divesting from the Second Chance program, which provides formerly incarcerated students the necessary tools to become successful students. . . . We're here not to ask but to demand that the city elected officials pay attention to our demands."

Strong talk—but the response from city officials was still thin. Only Supervisor David Campos and Sheriff Ross Mirkarimi appeared at the rally. To understand why other city officials lay low, we need to take a pause and look back.

Fix City College: The SMAC Counter-Narrative

The crisis exposed persistent differences, not only between staff and faculty but also among other groups at the college. Students Making a Change (SMAC), a group of students of color, with their faculty advisors, had been organizing for educational equity. They embraced the ACCJC sanctions as leverage to win reforms for students of color at the school. Their slogan for the crisis was not "Save CCSF" but "Fix CCSF," because they saw that racist practices at the school produced inequities in education outcomes.

At that time, SMAC was a project of Coleman Advocates, a well-respected community group with Black leadership and a long track record of organizing on issues affecting children and youth. Coleman campaigned to close the achievement gap between African American, Latinx, and Pacific Islander high school students, on the one hand, and white and other Asian students, on the other. In spring 2008, Coleman won a San Francisco Board of Education resolution to align the high school graduation requirements across all city high schools to the "A–G" classes needed for admission to the state university system. Shortly after that, SMAC began organizing for an equity resolution at City College. Working with allies in the faculty and on the board of trustees, SMAC got the resolution adopted by the trustees in 2009 and organized equity hearings in 2010. After that, progress slowed.

SMAC sought to change the way students were placed in courses and shorten the remedial sequences for those who were deemed underprepared for college level work. Coleman and SMAC participated in a study with City College and the San Francisco Unified School District in 2010 that revealed problems with the tests City used to place incoming freshmen. "We were meticulous in analyzing the achievement gap," said Pecolia Manigo, then Coleman's education campaign director and a student at City College. A report mandated by the equity resolution documented unequal education outcomes for Black, Latinx, Pacific Islander, Filipino,

Southeast Asian, and Native American students. It found, for example, that they were between 19 and 21 percent less likely to transfer to four-year schools than were other Asian students or white students.

Their findings dovetailed with an emerging body of research that showed that placement tests often pushed students backward unnecessarily, and they found a champion in then chancellor Don Griffin. He pushed hard for what was called "multiple measures," meaning that other measures besides the placement tests (such as high school grade point average) could be used to assign students into credit-bearing classes earlier. This option existed on paper, but most students had no idea that placement test results could be challenged, and the process for doing so was obscure and time-consuming.

Once placed in remedial classes, students could spend two years or more before earning college credits, a discouraging situation that could derail their progress altogether.

Work to reform the placement protocol and accelerate course sequences moved forward at the deliberate pace of CCSF's shared governance process. Many faculty members supported SMAC's demands and worked hard to design new courses. Some worried that accelerated course work would simply water down education and leave students unprepared for university. Others feared that shortening sequences would cost faculty jobs and dragged their feet. Still others found both approaches wanting—acceleration with no new resources and keeping the long remedial sequences. Nonetheless, by spring 2012, the Math Department was ready to implement multiple measures, and the English Department proposed a pilot project.

Chancellor Griffin's last board of trustees meeting crackled with the tension between the SMAC students' passionate urgency and the English faculty's insistence on taking time to prepare a program that would work. The trustees passed a multiple measures resolution with a skillful compromise at that April 26, 2012, meeting, but the rancor lingered.

After the ACCJC sanction, SMAC organizers went through the show cause letter "with a lot of intentionality," Manigo said. Even though equity is not mentioned in the ACCJC report, many of the issues cited by the accreditor touched on the students' accumulated frustrations. For example, "There was a lot of conversation about the need for an upgrade to computer equipment and access. The system for online learning and the integration of registration and financial aid needed to be better," Manigo said. "I personally had a situation where my check was not disbursed on time due to a simple mistake within the Financial Aid Department, which delayed my success in my classes."

Calls to "save" City College—with no acknowledgement of the deficiencies—hit SMAC members as insulting, a denial of the realities they lived. SMAC aligned with the SEIU 1021 chapter and laid out their "Fix City College" agenda in a broadside:

> We call on the administration, Board of Trustees and faculty to follow the lead of SEIU 1021 in living and breathing City College's motto, "The truth shall set you free." This is *the* time to acknowledge CCSF's past—the achievement gap, inefficiencies and all—and be prepared to make the necessary changes for CCSF to become a better, higher quality, more just and equitable college.

Most difficult for organizers against the sanctions was the way in which SMAC characterized them as adversaries, resistant to change and, therefore, to improved equity: "Stop the resistance to change, and acknowledge the need for improving the college and student outcomes."[15]

In the broader community, the support for the sanctions by SMAC and, by implication, Coleman, a trusted community organization, confused and demoralized many potential allies. It stymied the influential labor-community organization Jobs with Justice, as well as San Francisco supervisor John Avalos, an outspoken social justice advocate who had a long history with Coleman. "I was trying to thread the needle," Avalos said. He saw the ACCJC sanctions as an attack on public goods and an expression of disaster capitalism. At the same time, he said, "the young people were well-spoken about what they needed. I felt they had valid issues, and that they saw the ACCJC ruling as an opening to air them."

The situation was "complex and disorienting and damaged our ability to move people together around this," Alisa Messer said. "Even within the labor movement there was a lot of tension. . . . We were going in different directions and had different ideas of what standing up for the college would be." A multitude of meetings ensued, with groups large and small trying to hash out a unified stance.

Save CCSF organizers tried another approach, seeking to put the controversy in a bigger frame. The militant and successful Chicago Teachers Union strike had ended just five months earlier. Hoping that lessons from Chicago could provide a new lens for looking at equity issues, they invited a CTU member to speak at the City Hall rally. CTU veteran Debbie Pope answered the call. "Our strike started in some small meetings, with some people who had a dream and a vision of what a union could be and how a union could be an ally to the community," Pope said, to loud cheers. "We didn't want a union that was just fighting for the interests of the teachers or the staff. We wanted a union that was fighting for the common interests of the teachers, the staff, the students, the parents, and the communities in our city, and that's what we've been working so hard to build, and I know that's what you guys are working so hard to build here."

Thinking far beyond the usual wages and working conditions, the CTU reframed the struggle as a "fight for the soul of public education." They had earned the Black and Latinx community's trust by showing up at scores of hearings to protest school closures. They fought for a decrease in high-stakes testing, smaller classes, more nurses and social workers, and more art, music, and gym classes in all schools. The CTU insisted: "Education unions have to stand up for the community before they can expect the community to back them up. . . . [We] spent two years doing that, and it's a key to our strike's success." Just weeks later, San Francisco activists would learn more lessons from the CTU that would cast the attacks on City College in a new light.

CHAPTER SIX

The Light at the End of the Tunnel Is an Oncoming Train

Spring 2013

C hicago teachers clearly linked their defense of public education to the broader fight against the galloping gentrification that was pushing Black and Latinx families out of the city. Such connections had received scant attention in the whirlwind of crisis at City College, but Save CCSF brought them forward. Following Chicago Teachers Union activist Debbie Pope's appearance at the City Hall rally, Vicki Legion and other coalition members organized a talk by Chicago scholar/activist Pauline Lipman, a professor at the University of Illinois at Chicago who works very closely with the CTU and the Journey for Justice Alliance. Several groups cosponsored the event; Teachers 4 Social Justice played the most active role, and one of its coordinators facilitated. Supervisor John Avalos attended the entire event.

In her presentation at the Filipino Community Center, Lipman explained how school officials in Chicago, the proving ground for K–12 education "reform," used low test scores as the rationale for closing more than 150 public schools, largely replacing them with charters. Students of color made up 99 percent of the student body in most of the closed schools.[1] Lipman had mapped the closures with neighborhoods targeted for gentrification because of their prime location near downtown Chicago. This revealed the close connection between education downsizing and real estate development. With the school closures, Black and Latinx neighborhoods lost important community anchors. Opening new charter schools, along with other steps like the demolition of large housing projects, made the neighborhoods more appealing to wealthier—and whiter—new arrivals.

Chicago's gentrification was part of its transformation into what Lipman called a "global city," a central marketplace for finance, information innovation, and production systems.[2] The global city is highly stratified: global capital floods its real estate market, and highly paid workers drive up prices, resulting in displacement. This description rang true to organizers in San Francisco, already one of the most unequal cities in the country and awash in venture capital and highly paid tech employees.[3]

As the crisis at CCSF intensified, the wave of displacement that would push students and their families out of the city was gathering force—and campus closures had been on the agenda since Pamila Fisher's first board of trustees meeting in 2012.

Drawing parallels with Chicago cast equity issues at City in a new light. Lipman emphasized the racist impact of school closures—so what did that say about threats to shut down a college whose students were generally working-class and mostly of color, and whose ESL programs filled such an important need in a city of immigrants? Significant actors were getting a bigger picture just in time for the board of supervisors' first vote on support for City College in its crisis.

First Timid Support from Supervisors

Since the Flex Day protest in January, Save CCSF and AFT 2121 members had been demanding that the administration "spend Proposition A money as the voters intended," rather than stuffing it into reserves and paying consultants. The rally at City Hall in March kicked off an effort to persuade the board of supervisors to pass a resolution backing them up. They turned to Supervisor Eric Mar to champion it.

Mar had just won reelection from District 1 in the predominantly Asian Richmond neighborhood of single-family homes. Along with Supervisors John Avalos and David Campos (representing the Latinx but rapidly gentrifying Mission District), he anchored the progressive end of the board of supervisors.

Mar had eager help to draft the resolution. "Alisa Messer and Allan Fisher from the union in particular were really great, and there were a number of other faculty members on the email list in drafting language," Mar said. But the CCSF administration opposed any input from elected officials. "From the chancellor and a few other key influential people, there was immediate pushback," Mar added.

The resolution calling for proper use of the Proposition A funds was presented to the board of supervisors' Budget and Finance Sub-Committee on April 17. It passed even though "people didn't want to touch it," said

Peter Lauterborn, Mar's aide at the time. Some were leery of meddling in CCSF's business, a point that Mar—a former school board member—could see. The community college district was, after all, a distinct entity with its own elected board.[4] Others were confused about the college's real challenges and the media miasma surrounding it.

CCSF administrators and some of the trustees did respond—with intense ire. "I particularly remember Steve Ngo. It would be only a slight exaggeration to say he yelled at me for an hour," Lauterborn said. "Ngo implied that if you pushed back against the accreditation attack, you didn't care about the achievement gap." Interim Chancellor Thelma Scott-Skillman and Special Trustee Robert Agrella also chewed out the supervisors. "We ask that you respect the college's need and responsibility to address our issues independent of outside political forces," they wrote in an April 18 letter. "Do not involve yourselves in the internal workings of CCSF and the actions necessary to retain institutional accreditation." The letter also scolded any CCSF trustees who may have talked to the supervisors.

By the time the resolution reached the full board on April 23, it had more cosponsors but was littered with amendments and changes. According to Supervisor Jane Kim, the process led to "agonizing discussions ... throughout the city. [CCSF] is an incredibly important institution, and [we didn't] want to come off that we as a city didn't care about City College [or weren't] working to make sure this institution remains viable."

The final version called on the CCSF administration and trustees "to use Proposition A funds as intended to preserve the quality and diversity of education that has served San Francisco well." It passed unanimously.

Union Stands Up and Fires Back at ACCJC

While the union was working with the coalition to secure support from the supervisors, internally it was thrashing through a stressful period. "Our members were all over the place. People were very scared, people were very mad, people wanted to fight back, and people wanted to be quiet. Lots of people were in different places, and some people were in all those places at once," Messer said.

She and other local leaders had been strategizing since the show cause order came down, often with other statewide union veterans. They tried to understand the regulatory process, where they needed to put pressure, and what resources they needed to tap, mobilize, or create. "Every time we tried to do a power map it dissolved. It was too weird and overcomplicated.

We tried to look at targets, but it was just too complicated, and we didn't know where all the power levers were," Messer said. At a national union meeting in the spring, she made an impassioned plea for help to AFT's national president Randi Weingarten. "Randi remembers that I was completely wild-eyed," said Messer. "But it became clear to her that it was not just a local in trouble but had much bigger implications—and she shifted some resources." AFT loaned organizer Alyssa Picard to the local, and CFT supported two organizing positions, one for community outreach and one for member organizing.

In weekly meetings with local, state, and national union staff and leaders, the puzzle began to come together. The strategy team learned that accreditors must be recognized by the US Department of Education. One lever available was the regulatory process, so, with the help of longtime CFT and AFT 2121 lawyer Robert Bezemek,[5] they decided to file a formal complaint against the ACCJC with the department—an expensive undertaking only possible with the backing of the state and national union federations.

Bezemek and his team worked closely with Marty Hittelman. They also, in Bezemek's words, "exhumed and digested" all the legal cases involving disputes between a college and an accreditor. The team developed a 280-page *Complaint and Third Party Comment* that spelled out the key issues that would inform the public critique of the ACCJC over the next four years. The complaint charged the commission with violations of due process, conflicts of interest, and failure to follow both its own regulations and state and federal laws.

Due Process Violations

The complaint contended that the ACCJC violated due process by retroactively changing its previous assessment of City College. The commission had reaffirmed CCSF's accreditation in 2006, noting no deficiencies and giving the school eight "recommendations for improvement." But in 2012, the commission rewrote the story. It claimed that the suggestions for improvement were in fact "deficiencies" that the college failed to correct—and then gave the school just eight months to remedy the problems.

The ACCJC also violated CCSF's due process rights by sending a team to the 2012 site visit that included far too few faculty members. Federal regulations stipulate that a proper accreditation process "involves all of the relevant constituencies in the review and affords them a meaningful opportunity to provide input into the review."[6] Thirteen out of the seventeen members on the team that evaluated City College in March 2012 were administrators, though administrators and managers made up only 3 percent of the community college workforce.[7]

The commission not only sent City College an unrepresentative team that produced administration-slanted results, it also violated its own procedures by not asking that team for a written, signed recommendation on the school's accreditation status. The team may have recommended a lower level of sanction, according to the complaint: "Evidence suggests that a recommendation of Warning was the oral consensus of the team. If Warning or Probation had been the recommendation, this would raise serious questions as to why the Commission chose to increase the sanction level."[8]

Conflicts of Interest

Federal law and the ACCJC's own policies commit it to avoiding "actual or apparent" conflicts of interest. This didn't stop Barbara Beno from naming her husband Peter Crabtree, a dean at Laney College in Oakland, to the visiting team that evaluated City College in 2012.

Estimating Benefit Costs

The ACCJC based its accusations of financial mismanagement against CCSF in part on the way the school funded its retiree health benefits. City College handled retiree benefits on a "pay as you go" basis, a policy that the state chancellor's office approved.[9] But the ACCJC invoked Governmental Accounting Standards Board (GASB) rule 45 to cast this routine practice as gross mismanagement. Rule 45 is simply a reporting requirement; it doesn't mandate that the entire liability be funded.[10] The ACCJC sanctioned CCSF (and other colleges) for not prefunding thirty years of benefits—recalling the way Congress required the Postal Service to prefund seventy-five years of retiree health benefits, thus driving the agency into debt and softening it up for privatization.[11]

Support for the Student Success Act

But the conflict that cut closest to the root of the CCSF crisis arose from ACCJC participation in the debate and lobbying on the Student Success Act. Commission President Barbara Beno gave full-throated support to the vision and provisions of the act. The complaint contended: "ACCJC picked sides in a contentious political dispute, involving legislation which would have affected the future of CCSF and other California community colleges. In doing so, it put itself in an awkward, untenable position. It concurrently oversaw the accreditation review of CCSF while being touted as and presenting itself as an opponent of the views and actions of CCSF, including its trustees, students, senate, faculty union, and faculty."[12]

Disrespect for Federal and State Law

Accreditation standards must be "widely accepted and in accordance with federal and state law." The complaint documented the ACCJC's practice of demanding that community college districts take unilateral action on issues that legally needed to be negotiated with unions representing faculty and staff. These included core issues such as evaluation methods and wage levels.

ACCJC Isn't Having It

Before the CFT could take its complaint against the ACCJC to the Department of Education, it had to try to file directly with the accreditor. On April 30, 2013, Alisa Messer, CFT executive director Dan Martin, and CFT communications director Fred Glass visited the ACCJC's office in a small tree-ringed complex in suburban Marin County.

"We took multiple file boxes of stuff, the complaint and all the background documentation," Messer said. "It was all very official. We tried to get them to sign [the complaint]; they threatened to call the police and kicked us out of the office. As we stepped outside, we heard the door lock and all the window shades went down."

Messer had been unsure about how the union's legal action would play with members and other groups at the college but was pleasantly surprised. "I remember being at the Asian Coalition dinner later that week, and they gave us flowers and said all kinds of nice things about AFT 2121, and an administrator stopped me in the bathroom and said, 'Thank you so much.' There was this sense of huge relief among folks at the college that there was some attempt to tell the truth," she said.

"The importance of that complaint can't be overstated, and it was damning from beginning to end," Tarik Farrar said. It confirmed information that had been circulating as rumor and suspicions that floated in a fog of fear. "What we had suspected, it was just clear: This was corrupt. It wasn't a fair, impartial, and professional assessment."

The union also developed an informational booklet—*What Does the Accreditation Report Say?*—to demystify the accreditation process and start conversations with members.[13] "The booklet asked questions and revealed the unfairness of how the standards were applied," Kathe Burick said. "It was another part of turning fearful minds toward courage."

Speedup: Working to Meet ACCJC Demands

Still, the work of addressing the ACCJC's demands rumbled on. Faculty members were "buckling down and serving on those damn committees, which were soul-sucking and tedious and worthless but necessary to meet accreditation standards," Wynd Kaufmyn said. Just after the show cause ruling, Interim Chancellor Pamila Fisher had organized work groups corresponding to each "unmet standard" cited by the ACCJC. These included "Effective Planning Processes," "Human Resources Components of Evaluation," and, of course, "Student Learning Outcomes." "The work groups were supposedly made up of all four main groups—faculty, staff, students, and administration—but it was the faculty who did a lot of the work," Kaufmyn said.

As president of the Academic Senate, Karen Saginor participated in several work groups. "My life was one meeting after another," she said.

The ACCJC also required many reports—two due in the first two months after show cause, and four due in March 2013, including the school's self-evaluation. More than two hundred faculty members commented on the latter, a multipart 140-page document. Saginor collected faculty input, then met with the administration to negotiate the final edits. "The faculty didn't end up with a document that we really liked and really agreed with," she said. "What ought to have been a joint process was driven and controlled by the chancellor's office."

Without saying so explicitly, she pointed to the destabilizing impact of firing the deans and having them reapply and of the effort to shove aside elected department chairs. The entire historical memory of City College leadership was about to be excised, raising the question of who would be left to manage one of the country's largest community colleges.[14]

When the ACCJC visiting team came to City College on April 4–5, the review of the school's progress on Student Learning Outcomes proved to be a high point. "Katryn Wiese, who had been the chair of Earth Sciences, created this online structure for reporting SLOs, to make it so we could do this effectively and efficiently," Tarik Farrar said. "And when the visiting team came, Katryn Wiese gave the presentation and showed them every-thing we had done, the structures and so forth. The ACCJC visiting team members who were at this presentation stood up when she was through, and they clapped, and they said to her, 'This could serve as a model for the entire state,' suggesting that we'd be a model other colleges would want to learn from."[15]

Many faculty members were cautiously optimistic. "All in all, members of the visiting team seemed quite interested in what we had to say, and often complimentary and supportive," ESL Department chair Greg Keech reported in the department newsletter. "But they are only information-gatherers. They will make their reports to Barbara Beno, the president of the ACCJC. . . . We will not know until late June. In the meantime, we will continue teaching and working together and serving students. We have a lot to be proud of, and I have a feeling we will still be here when this is all over."

Keech was right, but it would take far longer than he imagined at the time.

CHAPTER SEVEN

Takeover

July 2013

Wynd Kaufmyn sat at her desk in Science Hall, slogging through emails on a muggy afternoon. July 3, 2013, was her thirtieth wedding anniversary, and as soon as she had done enough, she was headed home for dinner with her husband.

The temperature hit eighty degrees that day, though the clouds never lifted—unusual summer weather for San Francisco. In the run-up to the Fourth of July holiday, the coup in Egypt topped news headlines. George Zimmerman was standing trial in Florida for the murder of Trayvon Martin, and some still clung to a faint hope for justice. San Francisco's tech boom was fueling an explosion of displacement, with evictions nearly double those of the year before.

Kaufmyn's phone rang. It was Alisa Messer with the news that the ACCJC was terminating City College's accreditation. This would shut down the school in a year. "I started crying and went into shock," Kaufmyn said. "I was in a daze for a few days."

Messer asked her if she could help respond to the press, and Kaufmyn turned to Tarik Farrar. He was home, hard at work on a manuscript he'd been trying to finish over the course of several summers. "Wynd called and said she was 'discombobulated,' because it was a shock to her. She said 'They're going to revoke our accreditation, and they're going to *Detroit* us.' She was talking about what happened in her hometown," which was put under emergency management. "I was not at all happy. My stomach just lurched," Farrar said, putting a hand to his middle.

Termination: The Letter

Barbara Beno's July 3 letter to Interim Chancellor Scott-Skillman minced no words and offered no comfort.

The Accrediting Commission for Community and Junior Colleges, Western Association of Schools and Colleges (ACCJC), at its meeting June 5–7, 2013 took action on the accreditation status of City College of San Francisco. . . . After careful consideration, the Commission acted to *terminate accreditation* effective *July 31, 2014* [emphasis in original]. . . . [E]leven of the fourteen recommendations [in the show cause letter] were not adequately addressed. . . . As noted above, the institution remains out of compliance with many Accreditation Standards.[1]

When schools lose accreditation they also lose federal and state funds and the ability to issue transfer credits; this letter was a death warrant for City College. Soon social media was filled with the news. Shock and sadness reverberated around the school. "I am in mourning. I feel like one of my oldest friends has died. I<3 CCSF," student JJ Narayan posted on Facebook when the ACCJC closure threat was announced. Six months earlier, Narayan had been depressed and miserable, working full-time at a pet store in the East Bay town of Moraga. But they happened to drive by the college during registration for the spring term and decided to enroll. About a month later, they found the Queer Resource Center, and life began to turn around.

Beno's termination letter was explicit. CCSF was not ready to remake itself to conform with the commission's requirements. The letter made little mention of the quality of education. Instead the ACCJC damned City College for failing to follow commission dictates around finance, governance, and compliance. Beno's letter dismissed the significance of new state and local funding measures giving the college substantial new revenue. It said, "City College of San Francisco has still not addressed, and appears to lack the capacity to address, the many financial and management deficiencies (Standard IIID) identified by the 2012 Evaluation Team Report."

The letter slammed the City College trustees, even though they had obediently attended board training sessions and agreed to be chaperoned by the special trustee. "The governing board has been unable to perform its appropriate roles . . . and its actions undermine the ability of the Chancellor to move expeditiously to make needed changes," Beno wrote.

The faculty was also a problem. "Significant divisions in the faculty and in the wider institution prevent the institution from responding effectively to requirements of accreditation and providing a sustained quality education."

The students, however, were the worst. "Active protests against the direction the college is taking, expressed at governing board meetings, and against the college leadership, indicate that not all constituencies are ready to follow college leadership to make needed changes in a timely manner," Beno wrote.

Thus was the crisis manufactured. The letter did inform City College of its right to request a review of the decision and to file an appeal. The officials who were installed to take over the college could then project themselves as being on a high-stakes rescue mission.

Beno was quick to congratulate State Chancellor Brice Harris. "Beautiful job," she said in an email to Harris sent at 5:30 p.m. on July 3. "Thanks for the video statement [released earlier], and for all the rest. I think generally the news is letting people know that the college may survive with the right leadership. I look forward to watching your efforts."[2]

The Formal Takeover

Chancellor Harris wasted no time jump-starting the formal takeover of CCSF. On July 7, he set the stage with an op-ed in the Sunday *San Francisco Chronicle* cosigned by Mayor Ed Lee.[3]

> What's needed now is a stronger hand, a single individual with the experience, trustworthiness and focus to turn City College around. Appointment of a special trustee, with appropriate powers, is the only way City College can quicken the pace of change and position itself for long-term viability. We know this decision will cause discomfort for many, but the alternative is the almost certain closure of one of America's great community colleges.

The next day, the California Community Colleges Board of Governors met in Sacramento. A concerned and increasingly defiant mix of CCSF trustees and faculty attended and found a new item on the agenda. Normally, the BOG could only appoint a "special trustee with extraordinary powers" to run a district in cases of gross fiscal mismanagement or insolvency. Neither of these applied to CCSF. The passage of Proposition A and Proposition 30 brought in new local and state revenues, and FCMAT had erred when it claimed the college had run out of reserves. But a proposed new "emergency regulation" would allow takeovers if needed "to maintain the accredited status of a college or to recover accredited status if it has been terminated."

The Hotheads Look Prescient

"Frankly, I'm outraged," newly elected City College trustee Rafael Mandelman said to kick off the public comment on this item. The elected board did everything suggested by the state chancellor's team, he said, "even when under attack by those who claimed the team was following a secret agenda to destroy or radically downsize the college." The trustees passed a budget with a large reserve and at that point the school seemed to have a future. Now, after "ACCJC's irresponsible and punitive announcement, that future is in doubt," and "the hotheads look prescient."

CFT Community College Council president Jim Mahler and Richard Hansen of California Community College Independents backed Mandelman up. State chancellor's office executive vice chancellor and general counsel Steve Bruckman grimaced and picked lint off his suit.

With no further discussion, the Board of Governors unanimously approved the change in regulations. Harris then presented the rationale for a state takeover. He ticked off the list of City College sins, speed-talking through his PowerPoint like an auctioneer: insolvency, dysfunction, too much money spent on personnel, too many full-time faculty members. He acknowledged the concerns about the ACCJC's practices but stressed the emergency at hand. "City College does not have the luxury of time to delay this decision or search for some other solution. We are at the end of the rope and need to act and act quickly."

The takeover proposal stirred a swarm of negative comments from the audience. When former Academic Senate president Karen Saginor stepped up to the microphone, she paused for a heartbeat, took a deep breath, and said, "The visiting team literally cheered our success! And yet . . .," she sat down, silently shaking her head. "City College faculty have literally moved mountains in the last year doing everything that needed to be done," Biology Department chair Simon Hanson said. "Yours really needs to be a thought-out decision. Look at the role of the ACCJC." City College trustee Anita Grier—one of two Black people in the room— called out the "authoritarian implications" of the proposed takeover. "Our collective judgment is invariably superior to individual judgment," she said. "Members of the board of trustees not only have a mandate from the people who elected us but also a moral and fiduciary responsibility to about 92,000 students, and more than 2,600 staff and faculty, and all the people of our progressive and diverse city."

Wynd Kaufmyn was home watching the livestream of the meeting. "This is so corrupt," she muttered. Her hometown Detroit had had an emergency manager imposed by Governor Rick Snyder four months earlier. Five other Michigan cities had already suffered state takeovers. Those and the takeover of City College fit a national pattern of coordinated state takeovers to thwart local Black and Latinx political power.

Takeover: The Back Story

The setup for state takeovers of city governments began in the 1960s and 1970s, with the intensification of white flight to the suburbs that had begun after World War II. Federal initiatives designed to pacify rebellious urban populations, like the War on Poverty and the Community Action Program, created direct relationships between the city governments of Black and Latinx majority cities and the federal government, bypassing state governments. The Nixon and Reagan administrations devolved these federal programs back to the states under the banner of "the New Federalism." Conservative state governments wasted no time curtailing programs, leaving the cities unable to respond to people's needs and expectations.

Local governments tried to keep going. They sold bonds. They outsourced services to private companies, hoping to trim costs. They spent beyond their starved budgets and hoped for the best. Then state governments charged cities with financial mismanagement and used their authority to install financial managers or supplant elected officials altogether. The New York State government imposed an Emergency Financial Control Board on New York City in 1975, trumping elected officials' budget authority and imposing austerity measures.[4] Cleveland was taken over in 1978, followed by Philadelphia in 1991. Takeovers became even more common after the Great Recession of 2008, hitting cities in New Jersey, Pennsylvania, and Michigan. By the time Detroit fell in 2013, nearly half of Michigan's Black residents had no elected local government.[5]

School districts suffered even more from the hijacking of resources and local control. The powerful conservative American Legislative Exchange Council had public education in its sights as early as 1985 and aggressively supported the Bush administration's No Child Left Behind policy, which emphasized high-stakes testing and school closures. Illinois upended the elected leadership of the Chicago Public Schools and put them under the mayor's office in 1995. This fed the wave of school closures in Black and Latinx communities that united parents with teachers during the 2012 Chicago teachers' strike. By 2013, more than one hundred school districts nationwide, 85 percent of them in Black or Latinx-majority districts, had been taken over by state officials. Their school boards were either rendered powerless or abolished altogether, as appointed "experts" fired principals and teachers and closed schools or replaced them with charters.[6]

California used financial problems as the excuse to take over Oakland's public schools in 2003. FCMAT had declared the Oakland school district insolvent in 2003, paving the way for a state takeover that was only lifted in 2009.[7] During the takeover, enrollment plummeted, maintenance of the physical plant degraded, and charter schools mushroomed. Ten years after the takeover, one in four Oakland students attended a charter school.

Once before, California had stripped local control from a community college. In 2005, the state took over Compton College in Los Angeles County. More than 95 percent of Compton's students were people of color.

Now it was about to happen again. After public comment and some hand-wringing by its members, the Board of Governors voted unanimously for the state takeover of City College. Harris immediately elevated Robert Agrella, who had been special trustee since October 2012, to Special Trustee with Extraordinary Powers. Agrella now had sole authority. The elected board of trustees had none. Brice Harris and Ed Lee underestimated the "discomfort" the takeover would stir. That would become clear the very next day.

CHAPTER EIGHT

All the Work Matters: Resistance Gets First Traction

Summer 2013

The July 9 rally at the US Department of Education's San Francisco office felt and sounded like a revival. Shanell Williams kicked it off: "We are not here to mourn; we are here to fight!" It was a call and response crowd: "We did everything we were told by the special trustee Bob Agrella, who has sole power over our college now and makes $1,000 a day"—boos— "Shame on him!" The crowd echoed "Shame! Shame! Shame!" "They want to steal our right to a quality affordable education. Are we going to let them?" "No! No! No!"

The crowd's favorite, State Assembly member and comedian Tom Ammiano, pointed upward: "Look in the sky—it's a bird! It's a plane! It's a SuperTrustee!" The crowd roared and clapped, and Ammiano turned serious. "They have not the right to say that the people we elected, whether we love them or not, are not our representatives. That is tyranny!" he yelled. "I served two years in Vietnam and the mantra then was, 'We destroyed the village to save it.' Well, fuck you! There's another agenda here. . . . City College is a success, City College is a treasure. . . . We have the highest achieving students, the best rate of return, the best everything. So. What. Is. The. Problem? Is it our politics?"[1] "In his role as the brave jester, Ammiano voiced what everyone was feeling but didn't feel safe in saying: 'Fuck you, ACCJC! City College means everything to us!'" Vicki Legion said.

The Last Straw
A year earlier when the Accrediting Commission slapped the show cause order on City College, people were stunned and fearful. When, now, after all their hard work, the ACCJC moved to close the school, they were furious. The Save CCSF Coalition had already been planning a march. As

soon as news of the termination broke, AFT 2121 began phoning all its members. "The office was abuzz with calling," Alisa Messer said.

On July 9, the crowd began massing in front of Downtown Campus at Fourth and Mission Streets at 4:00 p.m. With its tuba tooting and pink-haired drummers setting the pace, the Brass Liberation Orchestra added momentum to the boisterous chants that buoyed the crowd down Market Street: "Whose college? Our college!" "Education is our right. That is why we have to fight," and, of course, "Save City College!" By the time it reached the DOE's Civic Center office, it was four thousand strong. Unions and community groups joined CCSF students and faculty, and homemade signs sprouted everywhere. "If you looked down Market Street, you couldn't see an end to the march," Williams remembered. "You saw an uprising of San Franciscans saying, 'You're not going to take this away from us.'"

The termination letter jolted people who had been on the sidelines into action. Thea Matthews had just started studying at City College. "When the news dropped that City College may go down under, I just broke down and cried. . . . [T]he woman I am today is because of City College, the relationships, the bonds that people make there. It's a really magical space," Matthews said. "I was bawling my eyes out, I was, like, 'Oh, my God, what am I going to do?' I called my counselor, and she just said, 'You get up, and you fight. Don't let them take this from you. No, you take a stand, and you fight back!' And that was the turning point of 'Okay, time to get involved.'" So Matthews went to the march and linked up with the Save CCSF student organizers.

For Win-Mon Kyi, the march was her first mass protest. "It was beautiful, because we saw elders in wheelchairs, we saw families, we saw youth all along Market Street, totally packed. You could smell the kettlecorn being sold. . . . This was my first time hearing that what was happening at CCSF was part of a nationwide effort against neoliberalism." Inspired, she resolved to become part of the movement.

The day after the march, Save CCSF brought former CFT president and ACCJC expert Marty Hittelman to speak at their open meeting. Before a packed house at CCSF's Mission Campus, Hittelman forcefully argued that the ACCJC's extraordinary sanction rate was driven by a predetermined agenda, not a legitimate educational critique.

A week later, AFT 2121, with help from assembly member Ammiano, pulled together another packed community forum in a large auditorium at the California State Building that highlighted the college's deep roots in communities of color, with moving testimony from students and community members about programs ranging from certificates in health care interpreting and drug and alcohol counseling to post-prison support programs. To prepare for the forum, Alisa Messer said:

> We reached out to every department; we reached all over the place to pull faculty and students. It was about having the conversations to say, "We need to put out the importance of this college and what it does." That was a different narrative than a lot of the other conversations happening, and that had to be part of changing the narrative. . .
>
> For me, that felt like a watershed moment because we were continuing to shift the narrative in a really concrete way. I remember a young African American man and several of his friends who lived in [then supervisor, now mayor] London Breed's district, in District Five, who got up and talked about using their education to keep making change and making their neighborhoods better. I remember Fred Chavaria got up and talked about what City College had meant to him for many years as a [student, then a] faculty member, and now a department chair. There were several young women who'd been through Project SURVIVE and peer counseling around sexual assault who shared part of their stories. . . .[2] It had that effect of "What we do matters deeply and profoundly. We're all engaged in caring for this college, and this is what this college produces." We were very focused on keeping the community in community college.

At the forum, the Save CCSF Research Committee released its new discussion paper, "ACCJC, Accreditation Bullies for a Corporate Agenda." Linking the crisis to education reform for the first time in such a public way made them a bit nervous. "After all, the college was still shaking off just pure fear of the ACCJC," Vicki Legion said. The following Monday, they got the kind of surprise that any research committee lives for. A group of students had painted "ACCJC, Accreditation Bullies for a Corporate Agenda" on a bedsheet and were displaying the banner on the City Hall steps.

In the first weeks after the termination notice, organizers sought to capture people's energy, offering involvement as an antidote to despair. But the full weight of the moment crashed down on AFT 2121 in its contract talks.

Bargaining with Their Backs to the Wall

Three people sat across from the AFT 2121 bargaining team at their first session following the termination notice: the San Francisco Community College District's longtime employee relations officer, an attorney from a corporate law firm, and California Community Colleges executive vice chancellor and general counsel Steve Bruckman, who had played a key role in putting the takeover in place.

Since March 2012, contract talks between AFT 2121 and the district had been jolting along like a car with worn shocks on a rocky road. Faculty had not had a raise since 2007. They had even agreed to temporary pay cuts totaling 4.3 percent in the cooperative spirit of the bargaining that had brought union gains in better times.

Local 2121's contract expired in June 2012. The two sides agreed to a six-month extension, but bargaining only got gnarlier after the show cause order and the FCMAT report. FCMAT characterized three decades of union gains as threats to fiscal responsibility. Its report slammed City College for its high percentage of full-time teachers, as well as the health benefits and pay scale for part-timers.

Previous chancellors, though they didn't take part in negotiations, did talk with union leaders "off the record." Interim Chancellor Fisher had refused to say a word to a union representative without an attorney present.

By the new contract expiration date of December 31, 2012, the two sides were farther apart than ever. Interim Chancellor Scott-Skillman put coal in the faculty's Christmas stocking with her December 20 letter announcing that the district was imposing a 4.4 percent pay cut effective January 2, 2013, with another 5 percent scheduled for July. The union filed a grievance with the California Public Employment Relations Board and went back to bargaining.

The spring saw little progress. Then came the ACCJC termination letter and the state takeover. The takeover galvanized members. "People were upset and kept coming to the office to see what they could do to help," said AFT 2121 organizer Athena Waid. The local channeled some of that energy into ongoing community outreach and organizing and harnessed some to support the bargaining. It invited members and community supporters to come to bargaining sessions. The district wouldn't allow observers at the negotiating table, so the union asked people to come, sit in another room, and caucus with the negotiating team on breaks. The local also expanded the team; one of the new members was Jessica Buchsbaum, an ESL teacher at the Downtown Campus.

When she heard about the termination notice, Buchsbaum said, "My first thought was, 'What the heck?' and my second thought was 'Well, AFT 2121 will take care of it,' and then my third thought was 'Well, where's AFT 2121?'"—as if the union was someone else. She laughed sheepishly. "That was my moment of awakening." Still, she said, "Being a union activist was not on my to-do list." She was the mother of boys aged two and seven, and her mother had Parkinson's disease. "I was in a world of imminent crisis between my kids, my mother, and my job in 2013. Everything falling apart. The fact that it was this existential crisis really pushed me to get involved, because our family was dependent on the job." First, she helped organize the July 18 forum at the State Building, and then Alisa Messer invited her to be part of the bargaining team.

The union called for intensive negotiations in early August 2013, barely a month after the takeover. The negotiations took place in a small, musty, windowless room in the down-at-the-heel 33 Gough Street business office. Members turned out to bolster the negotiating team, hanging out in the next room to talk with the team during breaks—and being very visible to the administration negotiators. "I'm here to see with my own eyes what these guys are doing, and I want the people in the negotiations to know they have faculty, union, and community support," said Malaika Finkelstein, a part-time instructor in Disabled Students Programs and Services (DSPS) and another newly engaged Local 2121 member.

The bargaining sessions themselves were excruciating. "I still get the heebie-jeebies going in there. It smells so bad," Buchsbaum said. "It was super-emotional, full days—eight-hour, sometimes ten-hour days, and we were having to make these terrible decisions. They wanted to get rid of rehire rights, any kind of rights for part-timers, cut our pay by 10 to 12 percent. One of the hardest things I remember bargaining over was prescription drug co-pay reimbursements for full-timers. That benefit didn't affect very many people, but for people with a chronic illness, it was thousands and thousands of dollars a month . . . and we decided to let it go, because we decided it would be better to take a smaller pay cut for everyone. We were over a barrel. It was the low point of the whole thing. It was awful. I remember Alisa basically didn't eat the whole time. She would drink these tea things, but she couldn't put food in her mouth. . . .

Everyone who was at the bargaining table or supporting us felt brutalized by that process."

Some AFT 2121 members believed a strike could right the imbalance of power at the negotiating table. AFT organizer Alyssa Picard helped the local think through the problems with this strategy. "The local had a good activist base but not a wide reach," said Picard, a veteran of graduate student and adjunct faculty organizing who'd been deployed by AFT's national office to bolster Local 2121 in the crisis. "There were about seventy-five people whose commitment was a mile deep" but many more the union had never talked to, and members had sharp differences of opinion.

"There was the left flank, who thought militant action was needed and a right flank, whose initial posture was 'We need to figure out how to do the things ACCJC wants us to do.' It was a weird gamut and fractious situation inside the AFT," Picard said. She helped Local 2121 launch a serious internal reorganization. It reinvigorated its precinct representative structure to reach members on all the campuses and set out to talk with all its members. The tool it used to open the door was a petition to Special Trustee with Extraordinary Powers (STWEP) Robert Agrella; the content of the petition was less important than its value as a conversation-starter.

Just after the intensive negotiations wrapped up, CCSF supporters got their first bits of good news.

A Little Good News

State Chancellor Brice Harris—the man who had just implemented the takeover—addressed the CCSF faculty at the Flex Day assembly on August 13, 2013, the day before fall semester classes started. "I remember he gave this ridiculous speech about how he was working with us to save the college," Tarik Farrar said. As Harris was speaking, Alisa Messer checked her email and learned that the DOE had upheld key elements in the CFT/AFT complaint against the accreditor.

The DOE agreed with the union that appointing Barbara Beno's husband to the visiting team created the appearance of conflict of interest, and that the team didn't include enough faculty members. The department also found fault with the ACCJC evaluation process. The commission made several "recommendations" when it reaccredited City College in 2006. "Recommendations" are strong suggestions but don't carry sanctions. In 2012, the commission switched its story. It said the "recommendations" meant the college was not complying with accreditation standards and deserved sanctions for its deficiencies. The DOE called this bait-and-switch a violation of due process. The commission failed to notify the college of deficiencies, then sanctioned it for not addressing them.

The DOE could have taken action against the ACCJC right away. Instead, it gave the commission a year to correct the issues pointed out in the letter. The department's finding also sidestepped important issues the union included in the complaint: the questions of political agenda, the retiree health benefit prepayment, and anti-union bias. But, still, it held out the first hope that the apparently all-powerful agency could be challenged.

As the wheels of the regulatory process began to grind, student activists again took direct action to highlight the high stakes in the fight.

Students Sit In at City Hall: "Where's Ed Lee?"

Student activists had been trying to get a meeting with Mayor Ed Lee since the state takeover seven weeks earlier. "They [the mayor's office] systematically ignored us," Eric Blanc said. The students carefully prepared to escalate their request. When they started talking civil disobedience, they made the risks quite clear.

Students new to the work stepped up to help plan and carry out the August 20 action; others who'd already been involved took more leadership. The protest began with a rally in front of San Francisco City Hall. "A number of people were outside supporters of City College students," said Windsong, who'd come to Save CCSF from Occupy SF.

> We had passed the bullhorn around and talked about ourselves and our involvement, and it was just really cool to hear other people's stories. That's one of the inspiring things about rallies. Different characters stuck in my mind . . . elders, a mother who talked about how taking classes had helped her. There was a big presence from VIDA [Voices of Immigrants Demonstrating Achievement] with the undocumented perspective and that was incredibly inspiring. There were other people who were City College alums and had moved on to [San Francisco] State and were now doing organizing at State, and they were talking about the importance of Diversity Studies. A lot of people were shouting out to the Diversity Studies Departments how learning about their cultural background really empowered them as people.

As the rally ended, students filtered into City Hall in ones and twos. Someone even managed to smuggle in a banner. "We went to bring the rally inside, because 'we deserve for you [the mayor] to hear us,'" said Thea Matthews. This was one of her first protests. The attack on City College politicized her, she said, because she lived it. "I learned that . . . what I'm living in this present moment, what I'm being impacted by, is political and is connected, inherently connected, to the systemic infrastructure of this society, the systemic lines of oppression, and it's not just some macro-level bullshit in the ether."

The students planted themselves in front of Mayor Lee's office and hung their banner over the wrought-iron railing facing the marble stair-case that sweeps up from the lobby to the second floor. They came in just before the end of the workday, and their last request for a meeting with the mayor went unheeded. "We were really conscious that we weren't putting anybody—in particular [people] without papers or who had priors—at risk," Blanc said. "We did a forum and [during the action we] made a lot of announcements suggesting that people leave if any of these things applied to them. We knew it was politically important not to put people at risk without their having full knowledge."

In the measured language of their press release, the Save CCSF Student Committee said the mayor "has the political and moral responsibility as the leader of San Francisco to throw his weight behind the effort to overturn the ACCJC attacks on City College." Once inside, they sent their chant ricocheting off the building's dome: "Where's Ed Lee? Where's Ed Lee?" They held the space until almost midnight. In between chanting and singing, they played "the type of games that you would play at camp, silly ice-breaker type things," Blanc said. "I remember being pretty goofy, and it being a funny contrast between this lighthearted almost festival type spirit of the occupation, with the periodic police announcements that we were going to be arrested." Around midnight the police finally carried out their arrest threats. They ticketed and discharged the students right there in City Hall.

Standing, daring, and laughing together forged strong bonds among the new and the more seasoned activists. "Everybody came out of that as friends. You made friends in an intense way overnight. It's hard to imagine in any other context that happening so rapidly," Blanc said. While the sit-in solidified the student core, a surprise announcement from Sacramento let ACCJC know that the state legislature was paying attention.

"I Have Never Met with a More Arrogant, Condescending, or Dismissive Individual"

State Senator Jim Nielsen (R-Yuba City), a longtime right-wing stalwart, represents rural north central California. Lifelong liberal Senator Jim Beall (D-San Jose) has spent his career advocating for affordable housing, better transportation, and support for foster youth. But after being lobbied by the CFT and California Community College Independents, this odd couple coauthored a letter requesting that the Joint Legislative Audit Committee formally ask the California State Auditor's office to look into the ACCJC.

Senator Beall led off their August 21, 2013, presentation to the committee. Bald and broad-shouldered, Beall rose to the mic to declare ACCJC a "monopoly. . . . The stakes are high and the commission's power is absolute," he said. "We believe it is imperative that the commission be audited by the state auditor."

Senator Nielsen spoke from his seat, a shock of iron-gray hair vibrating with indignation. He stressed that the audit request would apply to community colleges around the state. Complaints from various schools, ACCJC's lack of accountability, and the DOE complaint had thrown up red flags for him, he said. He and Senator Beall had met with Barbara Beno. Of that meeting, Nielsen said:

> In all my career, in my *thousands* of meetings with agencies and individuals, representatives, secretaries, etc., I have never dealt with a more arrogant, condescending, and dismissive individual. . . . That attitude in such a senior person raises huge red flags for me. . . . And we had asked for lots of information, Senator Beall and I. We had previously and formally asked for it, and we asked for it in this meeting. Three days after [our] meeting with these individuals from the ACCJC, President Beno released a commission statement—I have a copy of it here—directing members of the evaluation team to shred confidential documents, personal notes, evaluation team reports, committee reports, and evidentiary documents. Shredding of documents! Talk about red flags. Ladies and gentlemen, that certainly is one. What have they got to hide?[3]

The audit request passed the committee by a 10–1 vote, with three abstentions.

The next day would give City College's defenders their strongest encouragement yet, with City Attorney Dennis Herrera's announcement that his office was suing the ACCJC to keep City College open.

The People v. ACCJC

Ever since CCSF's crisis began, people had been coming to San Francisco City Attorney Dennis Herrera asking what he could do. "There were a lot of conversations happening," Alisa Messer said. "I don't know everybody who talked to Herrera, but I know Tom Ammiano talked to Herrera. [Newly elected City College trustee] Rafael Mandelman got a meeting with him."

In the beginning, Herrera didn't see much of a legal hook. "People approached me more as a politician than as a lawyer," he said.

San Francisco is one of only eleven California cities that elects its top lawyer, and voters have favored aggressive advocates. Herrera won his first term in 2001. In 2004, he filed the first suit defending lesbian and gay couples' right to marry, and his office litigated on the issue until the Supreme Court upheld marriage equality in 2013. When he heard the ACCJC planned to close the school, he was "outraged," Herrera said. "I was outraged by what I perceived to be just sort of a go along, get along approach by some elected officials and regulators. Instead of focusing on the importance of City College and how we could keep it open and serve San Franciscans, they took it almost as a fait accompli. Considering the history of this office and its independence and the ability we have to use the power of the law to fight injustice, I felt we had a real opportunity if we could find the right legal hook." He called on the "complex and special" litigation team to investigate.

"None of us knew anything," said Sara Eisenberg, the deputy city attorney who led the City College work. "We started with Google. We start with Google more often than we admit. We got our hands on the ACCJC reports, articles, AFT 2121's complaint to the Department of Education, just read everything we could find to get the picture of the facts on the ground. We dug in, and the more we dug, the more we saw there was lots we could work with." About seven weeks of research convinced the team they had a strong case.

At an August 22, 2013, press conference, Herrera—with Eisenberg standing just behind him—announced that his office was suing the ACCJC in state Superior Court on behalf of the people of California. *People of the State of California ex rel. Dennis Herrera v. Accrediting Commission for Community and Junior Colleges, et al.* charged the ACCJC with bias and flawed process. "The accreditor withdrew accreditation in retaliation for City College having embraced and advocated a different vision for California's community colleges than the ACCJC," Herrera said at the news conference.

In quick strokes the complaint painted a picture of City College, its commitment to open access, and its strong role in opposing the Student Success Task Force and the proposals that flowed from it. The case exposed the corporate roots of the "student success" agenda and the ACCJC's aggressive advocacy for it, which put it in direct conflict with City College. The complaint contended: "By evaluating City College while embroiled in a public political fight over the proper mission, vision and role of community colleges in California, and in specific ways detailed below, the ACCJC violated both its own conflict of interest policy . . . as well as California's Unfair Competition Law, Business and Professions Code Section 17200 et seq, which prohibits unfair, unlawful and fraudulent business acts and practices." Citing the Department of Education's findings, the complaint also objected to the lack of academics on the ACCJC visiting teams, the appointment of Barbara Beno's husband to the 2012 team, and the commission's failure to distinguish between "noncompliance with accreditation standards" and "areas of improvement."

The suit sought to overturn the show cause and termination decisions against City College and to block the ACCJC "from engaging in accreditation evaluations at any of California's 112 community colleges in a manner that violates applicable federal or state law."[4]

The filing brought immediate blowback. "I remember the beef with the mayor's office," Herrera said. "They called me down there and were, like, 'Who's your client?' My client? The people of the State of California. I don't need to represent the City and County. It's a 17200 action, I can do what I want. . . . We got into it. We got into it hard."

The *San Francisco Chronicle* blistered Herrera for filing the suit. Its editorial titled "Off Target" charged him with "playing with fire."

"When you have a losing argument, change the subject," the August 23 editorial began. "That's been the approach of certain City College defenders who want the [*sic*] attack an accreditation commission instead of the serious problems it has identified. Now City Attorney Dennis Herrera has put his imprimatur and legal muscle behind this dubious tack of distraction that is raising the risk of a shutdown."[5]

People kept emailing the editorial to Sara Eisenberg. She was sitting at her desk biting her nails when Herrera rang. "In some really colorful language, he said, 'Forget those guys, we're doing the right thing; you're doing a great job, keep going,'" Eisenberg said.

Herrera also heard from CCSF administrators. "In the beginning it's fair to say that there were folks there who thought that our litigation would impede ongoing political and other issues at City College," Herrera said. "There was a feeling I was taking one side, on behalf of teachers, labor, against administrators and others that were trying to impose reforms on City College to get it on better financial footing . . . where I was just focused on keeping the place open and making sure the ACCJC was playing by the rules," he said.

Having the city attorney act on such a strong critique of the ACCJC sent the loudest signal yet that the activists defending City College might prevail.

An email tipped Tarik Farrar off to Herrera's press conference, and he pulled a news site up on his computer. "I just sat there and started crying," Farrar said. He likened it to the climactic moment in the third *Lord of the Rings* movie. "Minas Tirith is under siege and the army was coming from Mordor, and its forces have broken the wall. . . . It seems all is lost, and then you hear this horn off in the distance ('da-nuh, da-nuh,' he hummed softly), and there were the riders of Rohan, all massed on the hill. The battle wasn't over by any means, but somebody with some strength and determination [had arrived]. Ed Lee had been doing nothing but criticize, and here's Dennis Herrera. I guess when that happened I felt, 'We're going to be okay.'"

CHAPTER NINE

Takeover Speeds Makeover, Resistance Builds

Fall 2013

For as long as anyone could remember, City College class schedules for each semester had been mailed to every household in San Francisco. But the interim administrators had failed to provide schedules for spring 2013—and Women's Studies professor Leslie Simon stumbled across boxes of the fall 2013 booklets languishing on the loading dock in the basement of Cloud Hall. She and other faculty volunteers began a guerilla-type distribution effort. "I was friendly with the guys working on the loading dock. They let me use the hand truck to put boxes in my car," Simon said. "We worked hard, schlepping those heavy boxes." The volunteers called themselves the Branch Brigade, because they started by taking the schedules to San Francisco Public Library branches. Soon they were also visiting laundromats, coffee shops, and community-based organizations, and tabling at street fairs and BART stations.

A full-fledged volunteer outreach campaign evolved, launched by Simon, Susan Lopez, and Danny Halford. They asked the administration for space to use as a home base—and, to their surprise, got a small office at Mission Campus.

Despite the outreach efforts and the heartening news of the City Attorney's suit, the fall semester opened under a cloud. Confusion abounded in the community. Outreach volunteers would run into students who asked them how they were coping since City College closed.[1] Enrollment for the semester dropped to 50,955, down 12.19 percent from fall 2012, accelerating the downward spiral of lower enrollment/class cuts/ lower state revenue. The *San Francisco Chronicle* kept up its drumbeat of disaster: "City College's accreditation loss stuns students"; "CCSF students race to finish classes—or withdraw"; "S.F. City College bonds downgraded amid woes."[2]

National media picked up the story. In September the *Washington Monthly*, influential for its rankings of US colleges, published a long hit piece headlined "America's Worst Community Colleges: The San Francisco Bay Area's economy may be high tech, but its community colleges are the bottom of the barrel." The article repeated the "mismanagement" and "too much democracy" mantras of FCMAT and the ACCJC and cited a Community College Student Engagement ranking funded by major players in the education reform movement, including the Gates Foundation.[3]

"This Is Not My Fault; This Is Not Your Fault"

The bad stories hit close to home for faculty. "There were all these voices saying it [the crisis] was our fault," said Karen Saginor. Typically, the AFT 2121 president got a few minutes on the agenda at the faculty meeting that started the semester. That fall, Alisa Messer addressed the demoralization head on. "Alisa got up and said, 'I want everyone in this auditorium to say out loud: *this is not my fault*. And now I want you to turn to the people on either side of you and say: *this is not your fault*,'" Saginor reported. "Our administration was telling us it was our fault, the newspaper was telling us it was our fault, the ACCJC, of course, was telling us it was our fault, even things where it was obvious it was an administration problem the faculty had no control over, there were still all these voices trying to blame the faculty. Even though we knew it wasn't our fault, it still was demoralizing, and you internalize it. Having so many faculty together in one room and getting us to make that affirmation, to stop blaming ourselves, was really very powerful." They would need to hold onto that affirmation as they pushed through their first semester under takeover.

"It felt like an occupation," Wynd Kaufmyn said. "That's a bit of a stretch, but it did feel like we'd been taken over by aliens. We didn't have a voice anymore. We didn't have the collaborative relationship with administration we used to have. Faculty and administration always clash but at City College there was a lot of respect and collegiality, and that was just gone. . . . It didn't shut us up, but nobody listened to us anymore. . . . It was always tense and distrustful."

The ACCJC's July 3 termination letter found City College out of compliance with eleven of fourteen accreditation standards, but allowed CCSF to appeal the decision and request a review. This meant that work groups continued to review and revise piles of policies and procedures on areas ranging from the college's governance to its use of software. And despite the visiting team's effusive response to the work done on Student Learning Outcomes, the letter found fault with those too, so all the faculty had to redouble their work. "Faculty meetings were like a bad acid trip, with everyone pledging allegiance to the SLOs," Vicki Legion said.

Noncredit ESL instructors had a particularly hard time. "On the state level noncredit is always viewed as unimportant, but it is important, and it is rigorous," said ESL Teacher Resource Center coordinator Vivian Ikeda.

> We worked with testing, curriculum, reports to show our department was on course. Along with [department chair] Greg [Keech], we went through each standard and wrote about what we were doing to meet them. We were all good with the ACCJC evaluation team except for one stupid minor thing; the ACCJC said we were supposed to put the SLOs in English on the first-day handouts we prepared (even for lowest-level classes). . . . We were used to teaching refugees, nonliterate immigrants, and immigrants with no other resources. A list of objectives in a language and writing system totally foreign to many would add more confusion to the already anxiety-filled situation of arriving in a new country. The ACCJC rep told us that "students could take the papers home and find someone to translate" the objectives to them. My job was to interpret standards and give them to the faculty. It was insulting to everyone's intelligence. Did I hate it? Yes. Did it have to be done? Yes.

But while the faculty kept working hard to meet the ACCJC standards, it wasn't always clear that the administration was pulling in the same direction. At this point, Karen Saginor was the first vice president of the Academic Senate. In a report to the senate in late October, she assessed the progress the college was making on the "Road Map to Accreditation," the college's plan to comply with the ACCJC standards. "I am very glad to see that the majority of items on the Road Map are progressing well," Saginor wrote, but given the ACCJC's harshness toward City College, she still had serious concerns. The new director of the Office of Research and Planning had already been reassigned; the vacancy in that position, plus ongoing shortages of IT staff, could slow work on many plan items that depended on data. Some action items were completely stalled, and the administration had made little progress on the criticisms in the FCMAT report. "The FCMAT items are a high priority for meeting accreditation standards, and many of them are complex and difficult. In the Road Map, items in this area appear to be six weeks behind the expected end dates."[4]

About this time, Saginor started to say, "I can't answer 'why' questions about the administration. Sometimes there seemed to be a desire to cause harm; sometimes there was just incompetence." She adopted as something of a mantra, "I would be happier if I didn't attribute anything to malice that could be attributed to incompetence."

The statewide Academic Senate for community colleges issued a flurry of resolutions asking the ACCJC to be more consistent in its language and more transparent in its actions. Although there is no evidence that the ACCJC changed in response to these resolutions, they reflected the growing perception that there was something wrong with ACCJC practice.

"Board" Actions: Agrella Holds Meetings with Himself

The corridor-facing windows in the big meeting room in the Multi-Use Building on Ocean Campus were covered with white paper. No official video was taken of the monthly meetings at which STWEP Robert Agrella announced his decisions as board decisions. He continued to install administrators who would be compliant with the new regime, hiring, reclassifying, or moving almost a dozen deans and vice chancellors. With the college facing the biggest crisis in its history, top posts were filled with people "who had to ask where the bathroom was," Vicki Legion said.

In October, Agrella hired Arthur Q. Tyler as the new permanent chancellor, the third chancellor in less than two years. Tyler had served as a special trustee at Compton Community College while it was under state takeover; he had also worked as chancellor of Sacramento City College and of a college in Houston, Texas.[5] Music Department chair Madeline Mueller was on the hiring committee. "Agrella told us, 'Interview anything that breathes, and I will choose who I want,'" she said. Four candidates were considered, and Tyler was hired.

With the hostile takeover in place, Agrella continued to administer shock treatment to the school.

Scuttling the PAEC

One recommendation of the FCMAT report had been to halt new construction. "We really believe you should hold off on any new projects till you have a plan for deferred maintenance," said FCMAT analyst Michelle

Plumbtree to the board of trustees just before the termination letter came from the ACCJC.

In September, Agrella returned $38 million in state funds slated for the Performing Arts Education Center (PAEC) at the Ocean campus. The campus, in a city with a legacy of creative performance reaching back to the Gold Rush, enrolled approximately 4,500 music and theater students but lacked professional production equipment and practice rooms, and its aging theater had only 286 seats. Cancelling construction of the PAEC put a hold on the school's programs and plans to offer more professional level technical training in the performing arts. "We can't expand the program into job training opportunities," board of trustees president John Rizzo said. "The theater we have was always inadequate from the start. It's old, and it's showing its age." Moreover, San Francisco voters had twice approved bonds to build the center. That money "cannot be used for other CCSF projects, no matter how worthy, unless they were voted for already," Madeline Mueller said. "It should be decided by the bond oversight committee."

Chancellor Brice Harris approved of Agrella's decision to scuttle the PAEC, calling CCSF art and performance programs "peripheral" to its mission, ignoring both the professional training value of the center and its value to the arts-loving San Francisco community.[6] Arthur Tyler, the new chancellor, supported Agrella's decision to use funds voted for the PAEC to do maintenance on the Ocean campus's aging infrastructure.

Pay Up or You're Out

In October, the administration announced that the college would drop students from classes if they hadn't paid their fees in full at registration, beginning the following semester. A November 8 email sent to everyone with an active CCSF application encouraged students to work out a payment plan with the Nelnet company. (Nelnet had overbilled the US government hundreds of millions of dollars for student loan servicing.)[7] Nelnet posters urging students to "invest in yourself" appeared all over campus. The *Guardsman* ran a big red back-page ad with the same message, announcing the "schedule for dropping for nonpayment." Students who registered in January before classes started would automatically be dropped in one day if they hadn't paid—even if their financial aid checks had not arrived.[8]

The *San Francisco Chronicle* reported that eighteen thousand students had been warned that they were at risk for being dropped:

"Now, when spring registration begins on Nov. 12, students who can't pay for classes right away will be offered a payment schedule for an additional $18 fee," said Faye Naples, City College's new vice chancellor for student development. . . . Current and former students who owe past registration fees are being offered a six- or twelve-month payment plan. . . . "Our students know that we are in a serious transition to right-size the college," Naples said.[9]

When You Walk Through the Storm, Hold Your Head Up High

In the midst of gloom and chaos, the press of compliance tasks and the daily work of teaching and learning, students, faculty, and community members churned up a whirl of activity in defense of City College.

When Agrella announced the pay-up-front policy, students reacted immediately. The policy was a direct threat, particularly to undocumented students who had to pay out-of-state tuition unless they met the strict criteria of the "California Dream Act," AB 540.[10]

The Save CCSF student committee cosponsored a November 12 teach-in on the payment policy with VIDA, a student organization supporting undocumented students. Their leaders had ties to Students Making a Change. "It was a first for bringing people together and having people directly impacted by the problem in ownership," Lalo Gonzalez said. That cooperation didn't last, so after the forum Gonzalez worked with Itzel Calvo to start a City College chapter of Movimiento Estudiantil Chicanx de Aztlán (MEChA), a national organization with roots in the student movement of the late 1960s. The first meeting of MEChA de CCSF drew about fifteen people.

AFT 2121 Tells It to the Judge and Takes the Show on the Road

AFT 2121 stepped up its legal/regulatory challenges to the accreditor, as well as efforts to broaden and deepen support for City College.

CFT's lawyer Robert Bezemek worked with the local union to file a separate lawsuit against the ACCJC a month after the City Attorney sued. Both suits relied heavily on the information the union amassed for its complaint to the Department of Education, charging the ACCJC with conflicts of interest and failures of due process. The CFT/AFT 2121 suit also alleged that the commission sanctioned City College for faculty and students exercising their First Amendment rights, citing the sections in the termination letter that faulted the school for "acrimony," protests, and resistance to change. The case contended that the ACCJC decided prematurely to disaccredit CCSF; by the commission's own rules, the meeting on termination should have taken place in June 2014. The lawyers pointed out the flaw at the heart of the sanctions: Federal regulations specify "the only purpose of the accreditation process is to assure positive educational outcomes for the students who attend the accredited institution. . . . In 2012 and 2013, the ACCJC found no educational programs offered by the CCSF to be deficient with respect to the achievement of their educational objectives. . . . the ACCJC's primary complaint was that the CCSF did not do what it told it to do in regard to several administrative matters."[11]

The state federation also helped organize outreach to community college locals around the state and trained speakers for what they called "the road show." Whenever possible, road show teams included students and a member of the board of trustees (most often Rafael Mandelman) alongside faculty. They talked to locals in neighboring counties but also ranged as far as Los Angeles and San Diego. "The teams got excellent reception around the state," said CFT's Fred Glass, who did the speaker training. "Everyone understood this could happen to them. At some colleges, only thirty people came out, at others, two hundred. Faculty would bring their classes."

AFT 2121 members who took part could also take heart from hearing about experiences of others with Barbara Beno and the commission. "We were hearing these things from school after school. Nothing was inconsistent," Tarik Farrar said.

The statewide road show was one piece. AFT 2121 also looked for ways to engage San Franciscans. "We wanted to get the word out any way we could that there was a plan in place to fight it [the closure], people could get involved, and we weren't going to just say, 'Okay, we're closed now,'" AFT 2121's community organizer Athena Waid said. "We asked students, faculty, and community members to support our college by signing a postcard to Mayor Lee, asking him to step up and more publicly speak out against the ACCJC and protect City College."

With flyers in three languages declaring, "San Francisco would be spooky without our City College," the local rallied supporters for a Halloween march to City Hall. Marchers delivered nearly six thousand postcards to the mayor, and a delegation of students, faculty, and community leaders went in and met with the mayor's higher education advisor Hydra Mendoza. "It didn't do much to sway Mayor Lee," Waid said, "but it really helped to engage community around this and to help us further the conversation about what City College means to San Francisco, and that we're going to keep fighting for this, because it's our community college."

The mayor had been conspicuously silent since he and State Chancellor Harris published their op-ed supporting the takeover. A public records act request by the *San Francisco Examiner* revealed continuing close communication between Lee and Harris.[12] The mayor's office had convened an Education Task Force, but even the supervisors weren't in the loop, according to Supervisor Eric Mar. Hydra Mendoza zipped her lip when Mar's staff asked for information.

Other elected officials unhesitatingly stepped up for the college in these dramatic months. Their efforts, like the City Attorney's suit, put new information before the public and helped shift the narrative.

Elected Officials Use Their Megaphone

Supervisor Mar asked the board of supervisors' Budget and Legislative Analyst to spell out the price San Francisco would pay if CCSF closed: lost jobs, opportunities, options, skilled workers, and revenues.

Nearly 2,500 people who work for City College would lose their jobs if the school closed, according to the analyst's report.[13] San Francisco employers rely on City College for skilled workers in key sectors of the local economy, including health care, hospitality, and construction. "City College graduates qualified for jobs in fields in which there were more job openings than graduates," the report said. And the school brought a total of $306,778,329 in federal and state revenues into the city in 2011–2012.

Students would suffer the most, especially ESL students, who had limited access to other programs. The report cited figures from the US Bureau of Labor Statistics and the Census Bureau that showed a dramatic loss in earning power for workers who couldn't speak English.

The study also highlighted the price students would have to pay if they turned to the private for-profit colleges for their career and technical education: $395–$765 per semester unit at the for-profits, compared to, at most, $46 per unit at City, with almost half of CCSF students qualified for fee waivers. The report included a dramatic graph showing that programs at for-profit colleges cost seventeen times as much as similar programs at City College.

A few state and federal officials stepped up early as well, including State Assembly member Tom Ammiano, who had defended the school so colorfully at the big July rally, and US Representatives Jackie Speier and Anna Eshoo—two legislators who had graduated from community colleges. Speier represented a bit of San Francisco and most of San Mateo County; Eshoo's district ran from San Mateo County south to Santa Cruz.

Early in November, AFT 2121 organized a forum with Representatives Speier and Eshoo, Assembly member Ammiano, State Senator Jim Beall, CFT president Joshua Pechthalt, San Mateo Community College District chancellor Ron Galatolo, student leader Shanell Williams, and Alisa Messer from AFT 2121. Speier and Eshoo insisted on holding the forum at Ocean Campus. "It was kind of a big deal that we had it at City College. They [the administration] didn't want to, but they couldn't say no. These things are highly positioned and strategic in terms of moving the conversation. The whole college came out . . . and it was still in a period when people were very nervous," Messer said.

To the full house, Speier attacked the ACCJC and promised support for CCSF from the federal level. Beall reminded people that the legislature was auditing the ACCJC. Barbara Beno declined to attend. Chancellor Ron Galatolo was an outspoken critic of the ACCJC, even though his district had three fully accredited colleges: "Our entire community college system is and has been under attack for an extended period of time," Galatolo said. "The only plausible explanation for City's massive enrollment decline is due to the severe overzealous actions taken by the ACCJC. Simply: the punishment does not fit the crime."[14]

All This Work and a Contract Fight Too

While AFT 2121 continued to organize on many fronts, its contract fight dragged on. After the summer's intensive negotiations, the CCSF administration declared impasse, a legal step that sends the two sides to mediation. As it did with bargaining, the local invited members into the mediation sessions. Around thirty of them joined the ten-member negotiating team at the first mediation in late September. After two more sessions, the union leadership decided to ask the members to take a meager deal so the local could focus on fighting to keep the college from closing. "The union's strategy was 'we've got to end this negotiations thing, because we only have so much bandwidth, and we have to move to make sure that the college doesn't get closed completely or carved down to a shadow of its former self,'" Jessica Buchsbaum said. "We had to run a ratification vote. We wanted to be really sure it was a strong vote as the beginning of a show of our own strength."

The member engagement the local had started building over the summer bore fruit with a record-high turnout and an 82.5 percent "yes" vote. The contract only restored a fraction of the pay cut the faculty had suffered since 2007, but it protected pro rata pay for part-timers and retained most health care benefits in the face of administration attempts to shift more of the health care costs to faculty.

Save CCSF Coalition in Disorder, but the Work Goes On

After the huge July march and the forum with Marty Hittelman, Save CCSF foundered on some of the contradictions almost baked into coalition work. Because they draw together people from a wide array of backgrounds and perspectives to work on a particular campaign, coalitions are vulnerable to differences over strategy and work style. Save CCSF organized mass community meetings and protests for several months with its mix of faculty, students, and community members, many with histories in various corners of the left—but by late summer the stress and hectic pace of the work ignited differences among the members.

Some, notably the conveners of the group, identified political differences, expressing dismay at what they saw as top-down work styles and pandering to elected officials. Others saw it differently. "It wasn't a question of political differences. It was what we called, back in the day, 'methods of work,'" Tarik Farrar said. "Three or four women were actually doing the work, doing the leaflets, even taking notes, taking minutes. . . . In terms of the sexism and misogyny, the dimensions are that so much of the work has fallen on literally a handful of women," and these women were subject to criticism and attack. "There really was misogyny and disrespect," Wynd Kaufmyn said. "I wish that the men in the group were a little more aware. . . . We had this one meeting where each of the women, five or six of us, made a presentation, and the men just didn't get it."

The coalition lacked group agreements on dynamics and how to handle them based on an understanding that we are the products of the society we are trying to change. So the coordinating committee disbanded, but various groups kept working using the name.

"After that we were working on projects, but we did them without a coordinating committee, in small groups," Kaufmyn said. One group organized around a creative plan to press another lever in the accreditation process. After corresponding with the director of the DOE's Accreditation Division, Kaufmyn got the idea to intervene in the process at the federal level. Seven students and six faculty members traveled to Washington, DC, in December to give public comment to the National Advisory Committee on Institutional Quality and Integrity (NACIQI), which advises the DOE's accreditation staff. There are eighteen NACIQI members, six each appointed by the House, the Senate, and the administration.

"They sit around a big table. They have their agenda. . . . I do think people were listening," Kaufmyn said of the NACIQI meeting. "They don't often get people doing public comments on accreditation proceedings. . . . I actually think we were very eloquent and persuasive. I remember one of the NACIQI members, Jill Derby, after we were all done and they started their own discussions, said, 'If we don't listen to these voices, we put ourselves at peril.' And the students were, of course, really compelling." AFT's national higher education director Craig Smith also appeared at the hearing, lending the federation's weight to the call to strip the ACCJC of its status as a recognized accreditor.

Stopping the Clock: Filing for an Injunction

After the City Attorney's Office filed its suit against the ACCJC in late August, the ACCJC's legal team unrolled a shuffle-and-stall strategy. First it tried to get the case moved to federal court. Then it stonewalled the city's motions for discovery, refusing to produce information pertinent to the case. Meanwhile, the clock kept ticking.

On November 25, the City Attorney filed for a preliminary injunction to keep City College open until the lawsuit could be settled. "Suddenly we were coming up on the spring enrollment deadline. Because of all this noise going on . . . the enrollment numbers were going down. Understandably, students and prospective students were afraid," said Deputy City Attorney Sara Eisenberg, who led the team. "At that point we realized we needed to do something quickly, because justice moves slowly; court cases can take a long time."[15]

The weeks between Thanksgiving and Christmas were incredibly busy, as Eisenberg and her colleagues collected testimony from dozens of teachers and students to help make the case for the injunction. "There was a lot of work from a lot of people," Eisenberg said, and what seemed like "never-ending nights" for the legal team.

Speaking in front of a packed courtroom the day after Christmas, the City Attorney's Office argued for a preliminary injunction to keep CCSF open.

Just three days later—on the first workday of 2014—the judge ruled.

CHAPTER TEN

Whose School? Whose City?

Winter–Spring 2014

Hundreds of teachers, students, and community supporters filled the courtroom the day after Christmas, and again four days later, as Judge Curtis E.A. Karnow heard motions in the City College cases. He took on the City Attorney's motion for an injunction, a similar request from the CFT and AFT 2121, and two motions from the ACCJC. One of the ACCJC's motions alleged that the unions' suit violated the commission's free speech rights, calling it a SLAPP suit, a strategic lawsuit against public participation.[1]

Judge Karnow rebuffed both the unions and the ACCJC. However, recognizing that the closure of City College would have a "catastrophic" impact on students, faculty, and the city, the judge granted the City Attorney's motion for a preliminary injunction to keep the school open until the lawsuit was settled. "Without accreditation, the College would almost certainly close and about 80,000 students would lose their educational opportunities or hope to transfer elsewhere; and for many of them the transfer option is not realistic. The impact on the teachers, faculty and the City would be incalculable in both senses of the term: The impact cannot be calculated, and it would be extreme," the judge wrote in his January 2 ruling.[2]

"This is just a reprieve," Deputy City Attorney Sara Eisenberg explained to *Guardsman* reporters and other City College students a month later. Perched on a desk in a City College journalism classroom, Eisenberg broke down what led up to the injunction and what it meant.[3] The injunction acts "to press the hold button, keep the situation exactly as it is until the court makes a decision." When the judge considered the injunction, he had to weigh both the merits of the City Attorney's case and the harm that could come of closing the college. His decision signaled that the city had a strong case and might well win at trial; public support fed his assessment of harm. "Having a packed courthouse filled with people who care enough to come out the day after Christmas and show our support influenced the judge to make him realize this is a really serious issue," Eisenberg said.

Welcome though the injunction was, Judge Karnow stopped short of granting all the relief requested by the City Attorney's Office and AFT 2121. "While the judge could—and indeed, we think should—have gone farther in his injunction, directing the ACCJC to rescind and re-do its evaluation of CCSF . . . there is no doubt that this is a tremendous win for City College," Alisa Messer wrote in her January 4 "President's Message" to the local. "Yet another important independent voice has corroborated that the process leading up to the show cause sanction and disaccreditation was unfair and likely illegal."[4]

The ACCJC ducked media interviews after Judge Karnow ruled. State Chancellor Brice Harris opined in a letter to Herrera that "court intervention is not necessary to keep City College open," and expressed his full confidence that the ACCJC "will acknowledge the college's progress in the coming months." The letter ticked off several steps taken by Special Trustee with Extraordinary Powers Robert Agrella that, in the chancellor's mind, signified progress. These included scuttling the Performing Arts Education Center and contracting "with a firm to recoup several million dollars in unpaid student fees, putting the school in compliance with state law, bringing in much-needed revenue, and ensuring equitable treatment of all students."[5]

Downsizing for Some

The injunction protected City College from closure for the moment, but, as Harris made clear, downsizing the school's physical footprint, as well as its the student body, was proceeding apace.

Interim Chancellor Pamila Fisher had put campus closures on the agenda, saying they would indicate a new consciousness of frugality that would appeal to the ACCJC. Early on, the elected trustees had voted to close two campuses and several neighborhood sites.

In January 2013, the board had voted to hire CBRE "for expert advice on real estate matters, including how to leverage the CCSF building at 33 Gough," compensation to be set later; "leverage" in this case meant sell or lease. CBRE billed itself as the world's largest commercial real estate company and had a well-documented history of profiting off the sale of

US Post Office buildings. (Richard Blum, husband of US Senator Dianne Feinstein [D-CA], served for many years as chairman of CBRE's board of directors.)[6] A year after bringing CBRE on board, STWEP Agrella set the fee for the firm's services to City College at 3 percent, the maximum allowed by the board resolution.

The pay-up-front policy lauded by State Chancellor Harris booted 2,259 students out of classes at the beginning of the semester. Close to half of them didn't reenroll, according to CCSF's own figures.[7] The policy cost the school revenue, because it would've gotten as much as $4,565 in apportionment per student from the state while students snared by the policy owed an average of $256.[8] While seemingly counterproductive from the point of view of maximizing college revenue, the policy was part of a culture shift to "running education like a business."

Cancellation of more than one hundred classes provoked sharp outcry from students and teachers alike. Protestors delivered an eighty-foot-long petition bearing 2,500 signatures to administrators on January 29. Faculty members were earning 4 percent less than what they made in 2007, and their numbers had plunged by 285 since fall 2011; staff had been furloughed or laid off, and student workers were paid $1.74 per hour less than San Francisco's minimum wage.

But STWEP Agrella was systematically fattening the school's reserves, hiring consultants, and inflating top administrative salaries. Hundreds of people rallied in the rain February 14 to protest hiring of new top-tier administrators at "exponential" rates. The first of these contracts was signed December 10, 2013, the day after AFT 2121 members reluctantly ratified a concessionary contract.[9]

The new hires included vice chancellors of finance, academic affairs, and student services, as well as a chief technology officer. Agrella also created a new position, president of campuses and centers, and Chancellor Tyler brought in Virginia Parras, a colleague from Houston Community College in Texas, to fill it. The new administrators earned 178 percent more than fulltime faculty members and an average $25,000 per year more than previous vice chancellors—when the school faced loss of its accreditation in part over allegations of fiscal mismanagement.[10]

The Agrella administration diverted $6.3 million into the school's reserves when $3.2 million would have met the state-recommended 5 percent set-aside. Agrella and Tyler signed off on a $13.5 million contract to Ellucian for information management services.[11]

James Rogers, longtime information technology specialist, talked about the decision to outsource IT to Ellucian. "The help desk had been cut from four-and-a-half people to just me, and I was Classified Senate president too. I handled password changes and desktop support for 2,500 people. A couple weeks later, Tyler brought in Ellucian to do a general survey on our process—Banner, the help desk, etc. Then we hear that the college will contract with them for the help desk and programming, five years for $13.5 million. The Ellucian contract included $750,000 for the help desk. That would buy a call center so people could call in and open service tickets 24/7, with a capacity of fifty thousand tickets. We don't get even half those. For that money we could have hired back everyone who was laid off and have $300,000 left over. They asked me to do student calls for no extra money, but there was $750,000 for Ellucian."

Although the ACCJC faulted City College for having too many administrators in temporary positions, Agrella and Tyler relied heavily on consultants and outsourcing. Business professor Carole Meagher noted, "He [Agrella] brought a consultant in who was updating our policies and procedures. We seem to have a lot of consultants doing things that should be done by a permanent person." But to the Save CCSF Research Committee, the whole package of program and salary cuts, outsourcing, and privatization paralleled what had happened with K–12 education reform and reflected the corporate roots of the new vision for community colleges.

One of the earliest projects of the Research Committee had been studying the parallels between education reform in K–12—where it had started decades earlier—and education reform in the community colleges. The parallels were unmistakable. The committee put forward the idea that "corporate education reform has jumped the fence from K–12 to the community colleges"—and its work would play a role in meeting one of the gnarliest organizing challenges faced by those working to save CCSF.

Mending Rifts

The San Francisco branch of Jobs with Justice (JWJ), a national labor-community coalition, served as a hub connecting grassroots community groups—mainly based in communities of color—with the city's progressive unions. But it had been holding back from the City College organizing, because its members had disparate views of the crisis. Notably, the respected Black-led community organization Coleman Advocates sponsored Students Making a Change at City College, and SMAC and its faculty advisors believed the ACCJC sanction could open a path to improvements for students of color at the school.

San Francisco JWJ had just come together in 2010, after a bitter conflict between unions and community groups over a development project. "This is one of the important things we do," said Conny Ford, a member of the JWJ executive board and a vice president of the San Francisco Labor Council. "We provide a table for differences to be struggled through, and we did this with the unions and community groups working on City College." After a few discussions of the City College situation in its executive board, JWJ convened a bigger meeting. Coleman staff and members were there, and students from SMAC, along with leaders of SEIU 1021's City College chapter and representatives from the larger local, AFT 2121 members and leaders, and activists with JWJ.

Discussion grew loud and heated. Coleman members, many of them parents of City College students, vented years of frustration with drawn-out remediation sequences and racist behavior by some teachers. City College members of SEIU 1021 stood along the wall looking down at those seated around the table and added their grievances. AFT 2121 caught the flak. But what many referred to as "that awful meeting" did lead to a series of more productive conversations among Coleman staff, SMAC, AFT 2121, and JWJ. "Through a long and intentional process, we really struggled to build our relationships, to not dismiss students' concerns but to hear out their legitimate critiques about CCSF and the racism they faced from faculty and the institution. And we also recognized what was at risk if City College closed, and the people who would be harmed the most would be the low-income students of color," said Emily Ja-Ming Lee, then political director of the Chinese Progressive Association (CPA).

As the hard conversations inched forward, Vicki Legion and Allan Fisher from the Save CCSF Research Committee were also meeting with the JWJ board and leaders to share what they were learning about the parallels between corporate education reform in K–12 and in the community colleges—what people began to call "the bigger picture."

In spring 2013, Teachers 4 Social Justice and several other organizations had sponsored a forum with Chicago scholar/activist Pauline Lipman, who linked education reform to the gentrification that was displacing Black and Latinx families in her city. Lipman also highlighted the parallels with the crisis at City College and San Francisco.

Over the next several months the Research Committee deepened its understanding. They showed the systemic roots of problems faced by students of color—not only at City College but throughout the state. Community colleges get far less funding per student than do the colleges in the California State University or University of California systems and serve far more students of color, students who've moved through public school systems marked by deep inequality. One study found that K–12 public schools in California that serve 90 percent or more nonwhite students spend $4,380 per student per year less than schools serving 90 percent or more white students. This amounts to more than $3 million a year for the average-sized public school.[12] The problem goes far deeper than "bad teachers" or "racist teachers." CCSF, far from being a uniquely dreadful school, was an exceptionally high performer in a system that had been disinvested. Among California's seventy-two community college districts, San Francisco ranked near the top for students successfully completing ESL classes and had the sixth highest rate of students transferring to four-year universities.[13]

The privatization agenda in K–12 showed in the move to divert money to privately owned charter schools, educational technology, and testing companies. In the community colleges, privatization involves: downsizing public community colleges, which gives for-profit colleges new room to grow; more outsourcing to private contractors; promoting full-time attendance. Community college was affordable not only because of low fees, but because students could attend part-time while working. The push for students to take a full-time fifteen-unit load would drive them straight into the debt trap set by the student loan industry.

As in K–12, where the foundation started by Microsoft's Bill Gates had a major influence on policy, corporate-linked foundations played a key role in developing the education reform project at the community college level. The most important was Lumina, created in 2001 with money and personnel from the dominant student loan company in the United States, the Student Loan Marketing Corporation, nicknamed "Sallie Mae." Lumina in turn helped craft and fund the development of the "student success agenda," defining success as "a degree or credential of economic value." Both California's Student Success Task Force and the ACCJC had received Lumina funding, but the ACCJC's ties to the "success" agenda only became widely known with the San Francisco City Attorney's lawsuit.

Having the big picture supported the hard work of relationship-building at the JWJ table. "We were learning that ultimately we had one big enemy who was trying to destroy the college," Conny Ford said. JWJ drafted points of unity on City College and engaged deeply with the fight for the school. It mobilized members for every demonstration and public hearing and worked hard behind the scenes.

Meanwhile, students organizing with Save CCSF were building for a confrontation with the college administration over its pay-up-front policy, which the students labeled "the racist payment policy."

Democracy for None: Police Violence at a Student Demonstration

The Save CCSF Student Committee called a demonstration to press their request for a meeting with STWEP Agrella and demand an end to the payment policy. Micheál Madden was between jobs at that point, so he and Eric Blanc blocked out a week and a half for making classroom announcements to build the action. "Because teachers were angry, there was more leeway to come into the classes," Madden said.

STWEP Agrella and Chancellor Tyler took the unprecedented steps of closing Conlan Hall, a public building, and calling out the San Francisco police to enforce the closure.

Students rallied briefly on March 13, then marched around Ocean Campus to gather their forces. They approached Conlan Hall two hundred strong, behind a banner demanding "End the Dictatorship, End the Payment Policy" and the red flag of the new CCSF chapter of Movimiento Estudiantil Chicanx de Aztlán (MEChA). A compatriot inside Conlan opened a door, and the crowd attempted to push past the police to enter. Officers shoved them away with batons and bare hands. Screams filled the air, punctuated by shouts of "What are you doing? What are you doing?" One officer pried a student off the door outside and pushed him over. He landed on his butt.

Windsong stood by the door, chanting and clutching the lead banner, until an officer slammed her to the ground. "My adrenaline was so high, I barely noticed it," she said. Some of the officers formed a line across the front of the building, with batons in strike position, shouting at students to back up. "You're hurting us!" one woman yelled. Otto Pippenger, a student and reporter for the *Guardsman*, made a run for the door. An officer tackled him, then stood over him while three others moved in and pummeled his back with their fists. They yanked him upright, pushed him into the building and carried him up the stairs belly down, like a sack of potatoes. Then they arrested him for battery on emergency personnel and resisting arrest. He was taken to the hospital with broken wrists and a concussion, and then to jail.

Student Dimitrios Philliou went around the back of the building and walked in an open door. Police stopped him and told him the building was closed to the public. He argued, then asked to leave. The two officers tackled him, twisted his arm, pepper-sprayed him in the face and tore off his shirt. Philliou narrated the entire encounter to another *Guardsman* reporter as he was being restrained and loaded in a police car. "I just want to have a conversation with our special trustee Bob Agrella. Come talk to us like a real human. I just want to see our elected board of trustees back in power. And I would like to see SF police officers not macing students for just trying to speak to their administrators," Philliou said as he was being led away. He was charged with "misdemeanor returning to school, which was described as trespassing by the San Francisco Sheriff's Department," according to the *San Francisco Bay Guardian*.[14]

About eighteen students made it into Conlan Hall and began a sit-in. A few dozen kept vigil outside. San Francisco supervisor David Campos came down to show solidarity with the students. Alisa Messer updated students on what happened with Dimitrios Philliou.

Once inside, "The first thing we did was regroup, calm down," Madden said. "We started phoning press and sending press announcements and spreading the word the occupation was staying overnight," he said. The occupiers were a varied crew. "There were undocumented folks, LGBTQ folks, folks from Associated Students. It was cold, and a lot of us weren't prepared. We made makeshift blankets out of signs, worked on home-work. There was a little organizing, a little getting to know each other," Martín Madrigal said.

Student, faculty, and community supporters came down with hot drinks, food, and sleeping bags for the students outside in the raw and windy night, but no food was allowed inside. Five CCSF police officers stayed inside with the students but made no arrests. Through the glass walls of the Conlan lobby, students outside and inside the building could see each other and chant back and forth: "Inside or outside, we're all on the same side."

At the vigil outside, students and faculty circled up and talked about why they were there. The moment politicized new activists, like

JJ Narayan. Student organizers visited the Queer Resource Center when the vigil started. Narayan went down and joined the vigil, and that was the moment that the issues hit home for them. "We were sitting around outside in a circle and talking about what City College meant to us. Five or six of us said, 'City College saved my life, literally.'"

The occupation lasted until 8:00 a.m. Campus police denied the protesters food to the end; several media outlets captured Save CCSF member Chris Hanson trying to deliver a bag of McDonald's breakfast sandwiches to the students and being rebuffed. That morning saw another small demonstration at the jail, when Otto Pippenger was released. Well into the night, Supervisor John Avalos had been jawboning the police and the DA, arguing for Otto's release. Messer and other AFT 2121 leaders, including then vice president Nancy Mackowsky, gathered money to post bail for Pippenger and Philliou and drove down to the jail to help them get out. Philliou was cited and released; Pippenger was held on $23,000 bail. His bail bond was paid by several AFT 2121 members out of their own pockets.

The Conlan Hall protest was the "coming out party" for the MEChA chapter, Madrigal said. Lalo Gonzalez and Itzel Calvo had founded the chapter after the failed attempt at making common cause with VIDA over the payment policy in November. Working with MEChA students from University of California, Berkeley and CCSF faculty member Marco Mojica, they built a core of students committed to advocating for everyone in the Latinx community, documented and undocumented. "We brought our flag. It was red, and all the writing was in black stencil: '*CCSF no se vende. Se ama y se defiende*' (CCSF is not for sale. We love you and defend you). The MEChA eagle was in black ink with a Zapatista woman in a circle in the center," Madrigal said, tearing up.

Students carried the fervor of the sit-in to the San Francisco Board of Supervisors later in the morning. Media coverage of the police attack helped pack the chamber, as the Neighborhood Services Committee passed a resolution demanding the return of CCSF's elected trustees. The measure, introduced by Supervisor Campos and cosponsored by eight of his eleven colleagues, was unanimously approved by the full board the following week.

Chancellor Tyler, feeling the blowback, issued an email a week later announcing his intention to pursue an independent inquiry into the March 13 events and to form a task force on "campus climate." He also ordered Conlan Hall closed again before a vigil protesting police violence organized by the Save CCSF student committee.

The Conlan Hall protest grabbed the headlines, but another event that day also highlighted San Francisco's stake in CCSF's fate. Members of CPA and AFT 2121 held a rally at CCSF's Chinatown/North Beach Campus,[15] then gave public comment at a forum organized by the college administration to discuss its proposed "Education Master Plan."

CPA's youth group, Youth MOJO, had decided to organize in support of City College the previous summer. Like so many others, they were jolted by the ACCJC's intention to shut the school. "We come from low-income families. City College is the only affordable option for many people in our community. If City College were to close or lose accreditation it would hit communities of color the hardest. Cuts to public education in San Francisco affect us directly," they wrote in a flyer describing their work. Over the summer and fall, Youth MOJO members surveyed nearly five hundred members of San Francisco's Chinese community to learn what City College meant to them. Ninety-five percent of those who answered appreciated CCSF for serving both credit and noncredit students with a range of educational goals, from transfer to learning life and job skills. Half said they didn't know where they would go if City closed.

Behind a colorful banner painted with "Keep the community in CCSF" in English and Chinese, CPA youth and other community allies joined AFT 2121 members at the March 13 rally. Speakers exhorted the administration to bring student and community voices into the planning process and ensure that the new plan embraced all the parts of the CCSF mission. "We're worried about the impact [of the new plan] on immigrant communities, on free English as a Second Language classes, on vocational training," CPA's Emily Ja-Ming Lee told the *San Francisco Bay Guardian*.[16]

San Francisco: Rising Inequality, Police Violence

The toxic pattern of rising inequity and police violence on display at City College in early 2014 also showed in San Francisco as a whole. Takeaway contracts pinched teachers and staff, while the payment policy threw thousands of low-income students out of school or into debt. The most vulnerable, the students who depended on CCSF's community-serving programs, feared for their future at the school.

The neighborhood around the rundown administration building at 33 Gough Street was transforming from trashy to trendy, thanks to the

"Twitter tax break," which exempted companies from city payroll taxes if they located in the Mid-Market area. Since the exemption passed in 2011, fourteen companies, most of them in tech, had opened offices in the area. Chic restaurants and a fancy apartment building followed.[17] The tech boom fueled spikes in rent and a widening income gap.[18] A study by the San Francisco Human Services Agency found that San Francisco had the biggest and fastest growing income gap of any California county and the highest proportion of very wealthy people in the country. Low- and very low–income San Francisco families were far more likely to be people of color than white.[19]

"Google buses" came to symbolize inequality and the displacement of longtime city residents that came with it. The outsized gleaming buses with tinted windows pulled up to public bus stops, ferrying tech employees from their high-rent apartments in San Francisco to jobs in Silicon Valley. The Google buses created a large-scale, completely private, luxury transportation system, while San Francisco's underfunded public transportation system coughed along, with low-income passengers packed like sardines on the buses serving the Mission, Chinatown, and the city's southeast neighborhoods. Activist groups blocked Google buses at stops with bodies and scooters, got on and asked to ride, and, in one case, vomited on a bus windshield.

Alex Nieto Killed by Gentrification

On March 21, 2014—a week after the occupation of Conlan Hall—San Francisco police shot and killed Alex Nieto, a City College student and lifelong San Franciscan. Nieto was eating a burrito before work at the top of Bernal Hill, dressed for his job as a security guard, holstered Taser at his side. A newcomer to the neighborhood called 911 and reported "suspicious behavior." Four policemen rushed to the scene and barraged Nieto with fifty-four bullets. They said they thought his Taser was a gun.

"That was particularly difficult for me," Martín Madrigal said, bowing his head. "He was a young, bright Chicano student, a positive role model."

The son of Mexican immigrants, Nieto attended preschool at a City College childcare center, one of the centers closed in the early phases of downsizing. He spent his life in the Mission District and Bernal Heights. As a teen and young man, he volunteered with youth organizations, including Coleman Advocates. He aspired to be a probation officer and was mere units away from graduation; he had been a practicing Buddhist for several years when he was murdered.

Save CCSF printed and distributed posters of Alex, which were posted on many classroom bulletin boards. The student committee called a small demonstration and built an altar with candles between two of the main classroom buildings on Ocean Campus. Alex Nieto's murder by San Francisco police shifted MEChA's orientation. "We began to link up the issue of police violence to the cuts to the classes and the payment policy, as part of a larger attack on people in the Mission and Latinos in general," Lalo Gonzalez said. "We established the connection between defending your home from eviction and defending your classes from a similar kind of attack."

The students' bold action fed AFT 2121's political organizing, which had gained major ground since Judge Karnow's injunction.

CHAPTER ELEVEN

They Can't Stop. We Won't Stop.

2014

C ity College of San Francisco's Chinatown/North Beach Campus rises proudly at 828 Kearny Street, its fourteen stories of windows gleaming. Across from the elevator in the lobby is a wall filled with plaques thanking the individuals and groups who helped fund its construction. Former chancellor Don Q. Griffin is on the list, along with the Building and Construction Trades Council. The biggest donors have special red squares with gold letters. Thirty years of community organizing built a coalition of close to one hundred organizations that brought the building into being over the objections of powerful developers. It sits on the edge of San Francisco's poorest, most overcrowded Chinese neighborhood, one of the first stops for new immigrants to the United States.

"Building the Chinatown Campus was important partly because it would help change the material conditions for the community and partly because it helped change the narrative of education equity for Chinese Americans," said Vincent Pan, co-executive director of Chinese for Affirmative Action (CAA). "There are more Asian Americans at City College of San Francisco than at all eight Ivy League colleges put together. . . . This is the first first-rate college campus in a Chinatown anywhere in the US."

The strength of CCSF's roots throughout San Francisco's communities visibly moved US Representative Nancy Pelosi when she came to the Chinatown/North Beach Campus for her first public comment on the City College crisis at a January 6, 2014, press conference. AFT 2121 had begun to lobby the veteran congresswoman from San Francisco—then serving as House minority leader—in fall 2012. AFT 2121's Alisa Messer and Save CCSF's lobby committee organized numerous meetings with Representative Pelosi and her team over more than a year. (Reportedly, Pelosi's office didn't always appreciate the outreach.) Some of these meetings included representatives from the broader San Francisco labor movement and CAA. US Representatives Anna Eshoo and Jackie Speier from nearby San Mateo County, who had taken more public positions, also helped sway the minority leader. AFT president Randi Weingarten came to San Francisco and insisted on meeting with her with local union representatives. "Sometimes you have to organize your elected officials and figure out what people to bring together to move them," Messer said.

Pelosi held her news conference just days after Judge Karnow issued his injunction; the ruling not only kept CCSF open but also bolstered the legitimacy of the school's fight. The lineup at the Chinatown event included representatives of CAA, which had been a major force for building the Chinatown Campus, along with speakers from the (still powerless) elected board of trustees and the San Francisco Board of Supervisors. Pelosi paid lukewarm respects to City College and opened up the floor to the other speakers.

"We are on hallowed ground," San Francisco Supervisor David Chiu said, acknowledging the work that brought the Chinatown Campus into being and noting that it was built close to the site of the historic I-Hotel, where aging Filipino immigrants had fought eviction for nearly a decade, with mass community support, before the sheriff drove them out in 1977. Fred Chavaria told his own City College story: he went to City and then San Francisco State on the GI Bill and got a PhD, ending up back at City as faculty and then department chair for Administration of Justice.

"Jenny Lam came out and was strong," said her coworker Vincent Pan. "She said, 'This is about people's lives, not a technical thing.' Everyone applauded loudly, and Pelosi 'associated herself' with the remarks. This was a turning point that made clear that this was a huge concern, not just in the Asian community." People also applauded City Attorney Dennis Herrera, the unions, and the prospect of stabilization funds for the school coming through the state legislature.

Closing the press conference, Pelosi proffered notably more animated support for the school than she had at the start. She assured her listeners that there would be "close scrutiny" of how the Accrediting Commission does what it does and "why the Department of Education doesn't do more." She specifically associated herself with Jackie Speier and Anna Eshoo, who had spoken at a CCSF forum two months earlier, saying, "This is a commitment of the California delegation."[1] Sidestepping questions on why she hadn't spoken up earlier, Pelosi declined to directly confront the ACCJC or the special trustee. Still, the support of a major national Democratic Party figure represented a significant change in the weight of opinion and a breakthrough for CCSF's resistance forces.

Mark Leno represented San Francisco in the California State Senate and chaired the Senate Budget Committee. He championed CFT-sponsored legislation to provide "stabilization funding" to help City College through the accreditation crisis. State funds are tied to enrollment, and the ACCJC sanctions caused a sharp enrollment drop, so this infusion of resources was a huge boon. At first, Leno's bill included language that tied the funds to CCSF's keeping the special trustee, in a nod to the school's critics. Lobbying by AFT 2121 and the San Francisco Labor Council persuaded Leno to take this out. But when the funding passed later in the year as part of the higher education budget, a new condition had been added: City would only get the third year of funding if FCMAT approved.

CFT also worked with allies in the state legislature on other bills that would address the CCSF crisis and keep it in the public eye. Assembly member Rob Bonta offered the "Fair Accreditation Practices Act." Assembly members Tom Ammiano and Phil Ting addressed the takeover directly with a bill that would prohibit the Board of Governors from "usurping, transferring or limiting in any way" the powers of locally elected community college boards.

Hard work was building up political support from local, state, and national figures. Although the elected officials couldn't impact the accreditation process directly, their attention helped build pressure on the entities that could: the Board of Governors, which selects the accreditor for California community colleges, and the Department of Education, which authorizes accreditors.

Sometimes You Have to Read the Fine Print

CFT and AFT 2121 had filed a complaint against the ACCJC with the DOE in June 2013. The DOE upheld some sections of that complaint in August 2013, and in January 2014 renewed the ACCJC's recognition as the accreditor for just one year instead of the customary five. The department's decision was a kind of "show cause" sanction for the ACCJC itself. The commission got a year to comply with all of DOE's standards. If it didn't, "the Department may be compelled to limit, suspend or terminate ACCJC's recognition."[2]

Facing mounting pressure to give City College more time to meet the ACCJC's demands, the president and vice president of the commission claimed in an April 12 op-ed in the *San Francisco Chronicle* that they could not change their deadlines: "Any change to the two-year rule would require Congress to enact a new law."

The two-year rule, frequently invoked during the crisis, was an obscure sentence in hundreds of pages of accreditation regulations. The DOE elevated its importance in 2006, implying that the accreditation agencies had been toothless. The rule said that colleges were to have no more than two years to correct deficiencies before sanctions kicked in.

The first time CCSF was sanctioned was July 2012, and the commission issued the termination letter after only one year, in July 2013. Challenged to justify their sanction, the ACCJC leadership changed their story, declaring that the two years ran from 2006–2008, after CCSF was reaccredited with "recommendations for improvement." ACCJC tried to retroactively paint those recommendations as "deficiencies." In other words, they moved the goal posts. The DOE wasn't having it, as it had explained in August in its response to the CFT/AFT complaint. Neither was Nancy Pelosi.

Pelosi followed through on her promise to do something concrete for CCSF. On May 9, she wrote on congressional letterhead asking the DOE specifically whether their regulations prevented the commission from revising the deadlines faced by CCSF. The response came in just five days. The ACCJC "has the authority to reconsider or rescind its termination decision so as to provide the institution with additional time to come into compliance within the two-year time frame, if such period has not run out, or to provide an extension for good cause," wrote Lynn Mahaffie, a senior accrediting director with the DOE.[3]

Pelosi's challenge to Beno became a public spat in the *San Francisco Chronicle*:

> The letter to Pelosi confirms what a spokeswoman for US Education Secretary Arne Duncan told the *Chronicle* last week: that the commission can extend its deadline.
>
> "This letter from the Department of Education responding to my inquiry proves that the (commission) retains the flexibility to grant CCSF an extension for good cause, despite their previous claims to the contrary," Pelosi said in a statement.
>
> "For the [commission] to refuse to allow good-cause extension— even after this clarification from the Department of Education, even after all the monumental progress City College has made along its

Roadmap to Success—would be destructive, irresponsible, and could be viewed as a political act."[4]

It was clear that the ACCJC was losing its uncritical ally in the media. The release of the state auditor's report confirmed that.

The Audit Damns ACCJC

On June 26, 2014, State Auditor Elaine Howle released the report the legislature had requested a year earlier. Howle and her team echoed what Marty Hittelman said two years before: ACCJC applied sanctions inconsistently. This showed clearly in the amount of time it gave institutions to correct deficiencies. Some schools got as much as five years, while CCSF got less than a year. They noted the commission's lack of transparency and the DOE criticisms of apparent conflicts of interest and suggested that these shortcomings "are weakening the accreditation of California's community colleges." They recommended that the state chancellor's office begin looking for another accreditor.

The *Chronicle* reported:

> Perhaps most damning to the future of the commission is the finding that California has other accrediting options for its 112 community colleges rather than relying on the Accrediting Commission for Community and Junior Colleges for accountability.
>
> "We can either find a new accreditor or we can reform this accreditor, but we need changes," said state Sen. Jim Beall, who had requested the audit the previous summer with Sen. Jim Nielsen.
>
> Commission President Barbara Beno hit back just as hard, clearly irritated that the audit was essentially a referendum on the commission's decision to revoke City College's accreditation, now delayed. Beno accuses the audit team of defaming her agency. . .
>
> "[T]here is no indication from the report that any of the members of the team had the experience or competence to express opinions regarding matters of accreditation," Beno wrote to Elaine Howle, the state auditor, in a response included in the 74-page audit. Howle's point-by-point refutation of Beno's letter is also included.[5]

Parsing the fine print and reading the correspondence between the DOE, the ACCJC, and City College led Karen Saginor back to the heart of the problem: "Although ACCJC's written directives to CCSF have mostly focused on requiring CCSF to conform to ACCJC standards as they are written, informal directives from ACCJC leadership, mostly conveyed through written subtexts and through oral channels, have sent coded messages that the only CCSF that will please the leaders of ACCJC is a college with a narrow mission and a very top-down power structure."

In defense of their vision of City College, faculty, students, and community allies kept showing up: at Board of Governors meetings, at board of supervisors meetings, at meetings of the Labor Council, even at the June meeting of the ACCJC itself, which deigned to admit only twenty members of the public (infuriating the *San Francisco Chronicle* reporter, who was among the excluded).

CFT coordinated a statewide protest at the capitol in Sacramento on June 6. Hundreds of teachers and students from as far away as San Diego rallied to demand that the ACCJC grant City College's appeal of the termination decision. The turnout and the passionate speeches testified to the organizing CFT had started as soon as the crisis broke. "As the majority organization of faculty in the California community colleges, we saw it as crucial to push our locals to be actively involved in the exposure of the agency's rogue behavior," said former CFT communications director Fred Glass. CFT's Community College Council kept the City College struggle on its agenda from September 2012 on, and CFT furnished a variety of educational materials for locals to use. Ten campuses had heard directly from the City College "road show" teams. Organizing, political, legal, and media efforts all aimed "to make Beno and the ACCJC as toxic as possible—as poisonous as they actually were—in the public eye so that their actions could be neutralized and rolled back," Glass said.

It was working.

ACCJC Invents a New Status—Activists Call BS

On June 11, the ACCJC announced what looked like a brand-new exit route from accreditation hell. A new status, "restoration," would give City College two more years to come into compliance—but the school would have to hit 100 percent on every standard or face immediate closure, with no appeal.[6]

"Disaccreditation is the capital punishment of the higher education system," CFT president Joshua Pechthalt and recently elected AFT 2121 president Tim Killikelly wrote in a joint public comment. "If we were dealing not with a college but with a policy aimed at a prisoner convicted of murder and awaiting appeal, then under a criminal law version of what ACCJC has proposed, the prisoner would be expected to surrender their right of appeal in exchange for the opportunity for a commission to determine, in secret, if he has been 'rehabilitated.' In this analogy, the prisoner would have to give up his right to appeal. Even worse, if he were denied 'rehabilitation' status, the prisoner would be summarily executed, without any right of appeal."[7] They went on to point out that the new status was not necessary, since the ACCJC could extend the time for CCSF to respond based on their own rules.

Before looking closely at the new policy, supporters of City College might have been tempted to welcome it. "Not so fast," warned Alvin Ja, a Save CCSF ally, crackerjack researcher, and retired bus driver. "It would only be natural for supporters of CCSF to breathe a sigh of relief because of a respite provided by the newly announced Restoration Status. But the announcement of ACCJC's graciousness and generosity of giving CCSF more time to meet 100 percent of accreditation standards is a wolf in sheep's clothing. The Commission only did it to save itself from total isolation and discredit. . . . It would be foolish to trust an incorrigible accrediting agency to save CCSF. The fight is not over. The successful maiming (Takeover and Downsizing) and attempted murder (Termination sanction) must be punished! Can't stop. Won't stop!"[8]

Even the *San Francisco Chronicle* saw the pitfalls when it reported that the CCSF administration had applied for the new status.

> This week, college leaders asked the Accrediting Commission for Community and Junior Colleges to grant it restoration status, an invention created by the commission in June after federal officials pressured it to come up with a way to give City College more time to comply with accrediting standards and avoid closing its doors to nearly 80,000 students.
>
> City College "is participating in this process because it simply has no other administrative option at this time," Chancellor Art Tyler wrote the commission, adding that the college "submits this (request) with serious reservations."[9]

Two days after proposing the newly invented restoration status, an ACCJC panel (whose membership was secret) rejected CCSF's appeal of the termination decision, saying *"the decision [termination of accreditation] was made due to years of inaction by CCSF to address serious deficiencies [that] severely impacted academic quality and the operational sustainability of the college."*[10]

The ACCJC was still in power, but Chancellor Brice Harris was worried about the crescendo of criticism of the commission—so worried, in fact, that in a June 20 letter to Beno, he detailed the

> increasing involvement of the California Legislature, expressions of concern by California community college CEOs, and a soon-to-be-released Legislative Audit that will be extremely critical of ACCJC; there is limited time for the Commission to claim a victory and preserve its role as the regional accreditor for California community colleges . . . . [T]he Commission is in trouble, and we need to work together to find a solution.[11]

Beno fired back:

> I am writing this letter to express strong concerns regarding communications from your office that appear to politicize the imminent decisions of the ACCJC regarding the accreditation of CCSF. The communications can be read as predicting, if not threatening, possible political retaliation against ACCJC. . . . We request that you disavow any intent to support such efforts to influence the ACCJC decision.[12]

The ACCJC's credibility, already strained, would be shredded as the trial of the City Attorney's suit put its machinations on public view—and exposed the political agenda behind its attacks.

CHAPTER TWELVE

ACCJC on Trial

October 2014

O n October 27, 2014, an hour before the trial of the City Attorney's lawsuit began, about one hundred boisterous demonstrators took over one lane of the street in front of the San Francisco Superior Court building before going inside to help pack the courtroom. Judge Curtis Karnow had recently rejected the sixth attempt by the ACCJC to stall or derail the suit, so the City Attorney's legal team was feeling positive. Their case charged the commission with violating federal and state laws, as well as its own regulations: the agency failed to provide due process and fair procedures and to avoid conflicts of interest.

"We file on cases on behalf of the people, but normally the people don't come out and show us their support," said Deputy City Attorney Sara Eisenberg, the lead on the case. "People would come up to me every day and tell me how important City College was to them and why they were there. It absolutely kept us motivated and inspired and ready to fight the good fight."

The two sides looked the part. The audience was the City College of San Francisco (CCSF) community in all its diversity and disarray. "ACCJC had two law firms, dozens of lawyers . . . and they were almost exclusively older white men. Our legal team definitely was not. City Attorney Dennis Herrera is Latino, Yvonne Meré is Latina, we had two white gay men, me— and our token straight white guy, but he's vegan," Eisenberg said.

The City Attorney's office framed its lawsuit narrowly but clearly saw it as part of educating the public and demonstrating that the ACCJC was a political actor. Deputy City Attorney Meré made that known in her opening argument:

> The People will present evidence that Barbara Beno was not only a vocal supporter of the Student Success Task Force herself but that

she knew that individual colleges, the same colleges the ACCJC was charged with evaluating, were sensitive to the recommendations of the Task Force.

In December of 2011, Dr. Beno sent a letter to the Chair of the Student Success Task Force announcing her personal support for its recommendations. A month later, in January of 2012, Dr. Beno called upon ACCJC Commissioner Barry Russell to give a presentation on the Task Force and asked that the Commission voice its formal support.[1]

The city's first witness was AFT 2121's former president Alisa Messer, who reminded the court and the community of the role CCSF played in opposing the so-called Student Success Act for its narrowing of the college's mission. Meré then introduced the first conflict of interest charge: that ACCJC president Barbara Beno's husband, Peter Crabtree, served on the ACCJC evaluation team for City College. "It strained credulity to think that there was no conversation at the dinner table or anywhere else" about City College, Messer said.[2]

On the afternoon of the first day, California Community Colleges chancellor Brice Harris, who had ordered the imposition of the Special Trustee with Extraordinary Powers in 2013, confirmed that CCSF ranked high among community colleges for its academic achievements, including transfer to four-year institutions. Under questioning by Meré, Harris declared that he proposed the takeover because Barbara Beno told him it was the only chance for CCSF to stay open.

From the trial transcript:

Q. So once the ACCJC voted to terminate City College's accreditation, did you take any steps to assist the college?
A. I did.
Q. And what were those steps?
A. I went forward to the Board of Governors with a recommendation that the State exercise a takeover of City College.
Q. And why did you do that?
A. Because I believed at the time that was the only way to find a pathway forward to retaining the accreditation of the college.
Q. Before going to the Board of Governors, did you have a conversation with someone from the ACCJC?

A. I did.

Q. And who did you speak with?

A. Barbara Beno.

Q. And what did Dr. Beno tell you?

A. She at the time said she was fearful the college could lose its accreditation and that she believed the State takeover was really the only way the college would have a chance to retain its accreditation.[3]

Dr. Beno herself held power over CCSF's accreditation, so exactly who or what was she afraid of? Meré didn't ask, and Harris didn't volunteer. Under later questioning, he added, "Today I believe the college does not deserve to have its accreditation terminated, and that, in fact, to do so would be a tragedy to this community, but, most importantly, to students enrolled."

Former vice chancellor of finance and administration Peter Goldstein, who had more than twenty years of experience with CCSF's finances, detailed the funding cuts the school had suffered and the ways it cut costs. He also debunked the oft-repeated assertion that CCSF was running a deficit in 2011. Because the state was late with its apportionment payment, there was an apparent "deficit" on paper for a month in 2011, which disappeared once the state paid what CCSF was owed.

Beginning in 2009, Goldstein explained, the state cut "apportionment" funding to community colleges; it cut the amount per student and capped the number of students it would pay for. Also, Goldstein explained, the payments were frequently late, which showed on the books as a negative.

From the transcript:

Q. So When the books closed on 2010–11, and there was a negative $17 million, did that mean that City College was unable to pay its bills?

A. No, it did not.

Q. Did that mean that City College was at risk of a financial break?

A. No, it did not.

Q. In November of 2012, prior to the time that ACCJC terminated City College, did City College receive good financial news?

A. I would say great financial news.

Q. And what was that?

A. There was both a statewide ballot measure and a local ballot measure that had a very direct impact on the college.

Q. Can you tell me about the statewide ballot measure?

A. I believe it was Prop. 30, and it essentially ended the threat of continuing State reductions and apportionment funding and funding
for student services, which was quite a relief to the college to no
longer have to experience these continuing cuts, not a restoration
but just the end of the cuts.

And then locally, Prop. A, a parcel tax dedicated just to—to
Community College Districts, passed, and that would allow the
college to gain $15 to $16 million a year in revenue."[4]

The ACCJC lawyers kept up their argument that CCSF was sanctioned
for financial mismanagement. Ignoring Goldstein's debunking of the
"deficit" claim, they focused on the FCMAT report requested by Pamila
Fisher in 2012, with its controversial claims that CCSF bordered on insolvency and, in particular, on the accounting method used to estimate the
liability for retirement benefits.

Looking back over the day's events, AFT 2121 president Tim Killikelly
said, "The basic issue in this case is fairness. Is it fair to close down a college
of 80,000 people, the educational quality of which is not in question?
We hope the trial that began today will help create a fair and transparent
accreditation process for City College of San Francisco and all the community colleges in California. That's why we're here today."[5]

"Dramatic Testimony Shakes Up City College of San Francisco Trial"

Days two and three of the trial starred ACCJC President Barbara Beno.
Under persistent examination by the city's attorneys, Beno became their
best witness. She repeatedly denied that she had discussed the case with
her husband, so having him on the evaluation team posed no conflict
of interest. She insisted that she didn't even know that CCSF opposed
the Student Success Task Force while she and ACCJC commissioners
were lobbying for it. But she had to admit that she had made substantial changes to the visiting team's report. Where it found on the basis of
scores of meetings and reports that City College had met several standards,
Beno simply changed the verdict to "did not meet." She even deleted the
team's comment, "The college had demonstrated a high level of dedica-
tion, passion and enthusiasm to address the issues."

"Beno was on the stand for more than two hours, and, at times, it felt
as if Deputy City Attorney Ron Flynn was a dentist pulling a painful and

deeply impacted molar. Over and over, Beno resisted answering the questions. Over and over, she ducked and diverted and tried to avoid the key admission," Tim Redmond wrote at 48hills.org, a San Francisco investigative journalism website.[6]

Even the *San Francisco Chronicle*, which had relentlessly characterized City College as badly managed and almost insolvent, had to report on the second day: "The president of the commission trying to revoke accreditation from City College of San Francisco admitted in court Tuesday that she had edited out language in the report favorable to the college and that the college was denied a chance to defend itself as required." The headline read "Dramatic Testimony Shakes Up City College of San Francisco Trial."[7]

Standing Room Only

From beginning to end of the trial, supporters of City College showed up at court in force. Members of community organizations, including Jobs with Justice, the Chinese Progressive Association, and Young Workers United, turned out; so did former State Assembly member Tom Ammiano, Supervisors David Campos and Eric Mar, and San Francisco Labor Council vice president Conny Ford—alongside scores of CCSF faculty and students. "It was electrifying entering the hall and seeing all these people who cared so much about City College," said Allan Fisher, a past president of AFT 2121 and a Save CCSF stalwart. "The large courtroom was so packed that you couldn't get in without waiting in the hallway for someone to leave."

And the drama continued. Dr. Sandra Serrano, chair of the commission's visiting team, confirmed that the 2012 team had suggested warning or probation for CCSF, not show cause, and that Beno had substantially altered the report, specifically changing the evaluation of three standards from "met" to "not met." The city's attorneys also questioned the ACCJC about the result of the CFT/AFT complaint to the Department of Education, in which the department admonished the ACCJC for "perceived conflicts of interest" and renewed its recognition as accreditor for only one year instead of the customary five.

The final witness in the trial was Steven Kinsella, at the time chair of the ACCJC. Kinsella reiterated the assertion—made by the ACCJC in its 2012 show cause report and repeated by FCMAT—that CCSF faced financial disaster, because 92 percent of its expenditures went to salaries and benefits. To supporters this showed that the college unions had made CCSF a good place to work. When asked about union involvement, Kinsella, clearly caught off guard, said that he thought unions "had a tremendous amount of influence," and that they were engaged in "an attack on the ACCJC's actions." Under questioning by Deputy City Attorney Ron Flynn, Kinsella stubbornly denied that the cash infusions from Proposition A and Proposition 30 made any difference in City College finances.

From the transcript:

Q: Did you understand that San Francisco voters had passed a—a parcel tax that was going to give City College $15 million a year beginning on July 1, 2013?
A: Yes, I was aware of that.
Q: Okay. You did not consider that an improvement of money coming to City College?
A: That just stemmed the acceleration of deficits. It didn't improve the financial condition of the organization.
Q: Was it an improvement in their financial situation?
A: By itself I would say no.

And so it went, back and forth about six times.[8]

Judge Karnow wanted to put closing arguments off for the new year, but as he conferred with the lawyers Sara Eisenberg pointed to her very pregnant belly. The judge nodded and agreed to hear the arguments on December 9.

In the closing arguments, ACCJC attorneys kept returning to "restoration status" as a more appropriate path for CCSF, until Judge Karnow interrupted to ask for clarification. Wasn't it true, he asked, that there are two differences between "restoration status" and the remedy sought by the People: that under restoration status, rather than the "substantial compliance" with standards usually required, the college had to come into "complete compliance," and failure to do so could result in immediate termination of accreditation? And that under normal rules, there were appeals built into the process, while with restoration status there would be no possibility for appeal? "The judge's question heartened the crowd, as it demonstrated the judge's full awareness of the disingenuousness of the ACCJC's argument," CFT's Fred Glass reported. "In fact, the entire presentation was rife with inaccuracies, such as the casual assertion by the ACCJC attorney that 'upwards of 30 percent of City College's students live outside San Francisco.' This was meant to show that closing City College would cause no harm to the students, because they could go elsewhere. I turned to an ESL instructor and asked her, 'How many of your students live outside San Francisco?' She thought for a moment and lifted up one finger."[9]

Karnow said he would issue a ruling the following month. As he left the courtroom, the audience burst into applause and crowded around the city's lawyers. CFT president Joshua Pechthalt, who had flown up from Los Angeles for the day, said:

> The judge can now right a terrible wrong. He can't undo the damage that the ACCJC has already done to City College, its faculty, the thousands of students that have left, and the community that relies on the college. But he can restore a fair process for City College's accreditation, and let ACCJC know that they are not above the law.

Sara Eisenberg's daughter Samantha was born on New Year's Eve, and the last session of the trial was held amid a burst of actions in defense of City College. More than fifty people rallied at the state Board of Governors' November meeting in Sacramento, calling for an end to the takeover and the return of power to CCSF's elected trustees. US Representative Jackie Speier spoke at a forum on Ocean Campus. Student organizers held teach-ins and mobilized singing, dancing flash mobs, demanding an end to the Special Trustee with Extraordinary Powers and defending Diversity Studies. At the last trustees meeting of the year—traditionally quick and quiet, in light of the approaching holidays—more than one hundred people showed up to speak against the latest version of the administration's reorganization scheme.

Amid the excitement of the trial and the flurry of activity, daily life at the college rolled on. Final exams started just three days after the gavel came down on closing arguments. Classes ended just a little over a week after that. Teachers at the Civic Center Campus did their traditional end-of-semester cleanup—and put extra energy into it. The 104-year-old building at 750 Eddy Street housed mostly ESL classes. Since City College took over the building in 1973, the school had put down deep roots in the Tenderloin, one of San Francisco's most diverse and poorest neighborhoods. Word spread among immigrants from China, Vietnam, Yemen, Ethiopia, and more than two dozen other countries that this was where you went to learn English. "We always cleaned up, but that year we cleaned like we'd never cleaned before," said Denise Selleck, who's taught ESL at City College for twenty-seven years. Teachers tidied their classrooms, scrubbed sinks, and cleaned the refrigerator in the break room. Two of them, Kelli Crow and Jenny Hammer, spent three hours polishing the brass railings on the staircase. When the cleaning was done, they gathered in the library for a potluck. Campus dean Carl Jew joined them. "He told us how wonderful we were, what a great team we were . . . he talked about our future together," Selleck said.

That future, it turned out, would be short.

CHAPTER THIRTEEN

Central City Rising

Winter–Spring 2015

C hancellor Art Tyler turned the January 2015 Flex Day meeting into a corporate-style pep rally, with mandatory attendance for some eight hundred faculty from all ten campuses. The meeting was held in the Ocean Campus gym on the Friday before classes were to start, with rock music blaring and large smiley face posters positioned on both sides of the stage—an otherworldly counterpoint to the dismal morale among faculty. The gym was drafty, the bleachers were hard, the sound system scratchy. Tyler rattled on and compared himself to Martin Luther King Jr. After the big gathering, the faculty broke out by departments. English as a Second Language (ESL), the largest department, further broke out by campuses.

Rick Kappra, the coordinator for Civic Center Campus, expected to lead their meeting as faculty prepared for classes to begin on the next working day. "When I got to the door of the classroom, our campus dean [Carl Jew] was standing there. He grabbed my hand and shook it very firmly and said, 'Prepare yourself.' I looked in and I could see the chancellor was inside sitting on a desk, talking to some people. We went inside; he [Chancellor Tyler] completely ignored us, and I was thinking, 'Why is he here? And who are these other people in the room?' And we looked at each other and sat down, and he started talking to us. He said, 'The good news is you will all continue to get paid,' and then told us that our building [750 Eddy Street] had been found unsafe, so we would be holding classes at Gough Street. They needed time to prepare—the rooms at Gough were used as storage—so there would be three weeks when we weren't teaching, and then classes would resume. We were in shock."

AFT 2121 secretary Jessica Buchsbaum was in a room down the hall meeting with her ESL colleagues from the Downtown Campus. Up popped a text from her good friend Audrey Wallace, who'd just started teaching at Civic Center. Buchsbaum bolted out of her meeting and ran down the hall, texting the rest of the union officers as she went. "I got to the door and there's Art Tyler and Virginia Parras walking out," Buchsbaum said. "Both were dressed to the nines, as usual, Parras in a pink Chanel knock-off suit and matching stiletto heels. I go in, and there's Carl Jew standing in the front of the room and he's looking grey, and I turned, and there were my dear ones, the teachers who helped me figure out a lesson plan on my first day of teaching, and their faces are drawn, and their eyes are wide open, and they're starting to ask questions like 'How are we going to let the students know about this?' These are students who may not know a single word of English yet, who may or may not be literate. They don't have computer skills. We may or may not have a working phone number for them. They're supposed to arrive at class, and the building will be closed." About two thousand students took classes at 750 Eddy Street, most learning the foundations of English in noncredit ESL classes.

Deep Roots, Old Foundations

Before 750 Eddy Street became a campus of City College, it was an elementary school and then an adult education center for the San Francisco Unified School District. Built in 1911, the three-story building has huge windows that open and close, large rooms with ample closets, wide staircases with curved banisters. On the other hand, there was no hot water, and "there were loose cords, it needed painting, there was a hodgepodge of castoff furniture in the work room, but the building supported our needs . . . students felt at home there," said Beth Ericson, who taught there for almost thirty years. "That building had a soul."

In its early years, the Tenderloin site was called the Alemany Campus, named for Bishop Joseph Alemany, who, in 1856, taught the first ESL class in San Francisco to Gaelic-speaking Irish immigrants. Teachers at the campus had also taught students who came with the first wave of boat people from Vietnam in 1978 and had developed a method for teaching ESL by talking about what was going on in the world. The campus became a leader in ESL teaching. A few faculty members started Alemany Press in 1980, which published ESL books for seventeen years, many by CCSF faculty members. The teachers organized and lobbied to change the name to Civic Center Campus in 2009, ending confusion about a campus located nowhere near Alemany Boulevard.

The neighborhood around the campus had morphed over the years from the city's red-light district to one of the most diverse and affordable areas in San Francisco. Neighborhood organizing in the 1980s won zoning restrictions that kept out luxury high-rises, and nonprofit housing developers bought up land when it was still relatively cheap. Waves of immigrants from Southeast Asia joined the Greek, Arab, Indian, Filipino, African American, and LGBTQ residents of the neighborhood. By 2015, it was also home to a large number of Latinx families displaced from the Mission.

Sunny Ngo left South Vietnam in 1978 aboard a forty-two-foot boat with her brother, her parents, and 139 other people. Two years later, she reached San Francisco. A week after she arrived, a friend brought her to Eddy Street. A year later, she started working in the campus counseling office. By 2015, she was the dean's assistant, handling many of the day-to-day details that kept things running. Most students found out about the school the same way she had, Ngo said. "In the early years when a lot of refugees arrived, those were Grandpa and Grandma, and later those grandpas and grandmas sponsored their children. When the children came, Grandpa and Grandma brought the children to school and saw me and talked to me, 'Look, they just came,' [so I] introduced them to teachers. . . . And later the grandchildren came, and Grandma brought them and said, 'Here are my granddaughters, grandsons, remember my daughter and my sons a couple years ago?'"

For many of the new arrivals, the campus was the first friendly space they would find in their new country.

First Responders

ESL teachers were resources and counselors for the students. "They'd come up and tell you their problems," said Kevin Cross, who'd taught ESL at Civic Center for twenty-one years. "They'd get a phone call from their doctor or some government agency, and they couldn't understand it, so [he pantomimed handing over a phone], 'Here, listen, teacher.' So you'd have to listen and be able to distill it down to 'You need to call, or you don't need to call, and this is the number.' I've called, I've gone to the hospital, because somebody got knifed as he was walking in the Mission. We've gone to marriages. We've gone to funerals. That's what we do."

Faculty at 750 Eddy Street had developed strong bonds among themselves. Most of the full-timers had worked together for more than twenty years. They engaged in the broader City College community as well. Several had served in the Academic Senate, some in the union. Many participated in the protests for more education funding and against the Student Success Act that set the stage for the accreditation crisis—and in the response to the crisis itself.

At the end of the Flex Day meeting where they learned of the campus closure, faculty members exchanged private emails, so they could plan more securely. Over the weekend, they met at the AFT 2121 office. How could they inform their students and ease the blow of the closure? Dean Carl Jew told them not to show up at school on the first day of classes, but they unanimously rejected that directive. They made their own handout to give students. One side bore a simple message in English, Chinese, Vietnamese, and Russian: "The building at 750 Eddy Street is unsafe. School will open on Monday, February 2, 2015 at 33 *Gough Street.*" The other side showed maps with directions for how to get from 750 Eddy to 33 Gough on foot and on the bus—a twenty-minute journey. By phone, email, and Facebook messages they recruited higher level students to come help translate into the thirty-three different languages spoken by the beginning students.

On Monday, January 12, teachers gathered outside 750 Eddy to meet the students who would start arriving early in the morning. The dean denied their request to set up tables in the parking lot, so the teachers counseled the baffled students standing on the sidewalk in the raw January fog. Eventually, they were allowed to use part of the first floor but congestion in the cramped hallway contributed to the chaos.

Students were angry, sad, confused, disbelieving. Teachers tried to reassure them that classes would start soon and close by. They also asked more advanced students (ones they thought would understand) to sign a letter to the board of trustees. "We protest the surprise closure of our school . . . and demand to be included in plans for our school," it said in part. Sally Winn, another veteran teacher, drafted the message and presented the letter to the board of trustees at their next meeting. "I wanted them to see what the signatures of our students looked like. They're not beautiful. They're struggling to form letters," Winn said.

A few teachers left Eddy Street to join AFT 2121 president Tim Killikelly and secretary Jessica Buchsbaum and staff, ESL chair Greg Keech, and Academic Senate president Lillian Marrujo-Duck in a meeting with Chancellor Tyler and other top administrators.

Why Now?

They met in the chancellor's "bunker," as many teachers called the bungalow on Ocean Campus that Tyler had appropriated for his office. The chancellor kept them waiting. When the meeting finally convened, AFT 2121 president Killikelly took the administration to task for their lack of transparency and failure to work cooperatively with the faculty. "We need to know who is saying that this building is not safe and needs to be closed now, and on what basis you made that decision, particularly in the way the decision was made at the last moment. If it's true that the documentation you sent me was the basis for the decision, we should've been discussing this last semester."

Tyler punted, saying that they'd been looking for alternative locations since November. General Counsel Steve Bruckman backed him up, saying they'd engaged real estate agents to help.

The Eddy Street building had been known to have structural issues ever since City College acquired it from the school district in 1973. It is made of brick, the type of building most vulnerable to earthquake damage. The City of San Francisco had red-tagged the building in 2000. In 1999, 2003, and 2007, the college made plans for seismic repairs at Eddy Street but didn't follow through.

"Why would you not, over the course of eight weeks, turn to the experts in the location, in the neighborhood, in the classes, in the languages being spoken, in the students' needs—why did you decide—repeatedly, as you've said—that you would choose not to communicate?" Academic Senate President Marrujo-Duck asked. "Because I didn't have a solution," Tyler responded, sticking to his guns. After more sparring, Tyler finally agreed to consult faculty on the Gough Street move and negotiate over schedule changes that would be needed due to the semester starting three weeks late.

The Academic Senate Executive Council spent much of its January 14 meeting on the Civic Center situation. Chancellor Tyler and President Parras had gone to a state budget meeting, leaving two other administrators to take the heat. Under sharp questioning from the Senate, both admitted that none of the reports and correspondence received by the college recommended an emergency closure. This was the administration's decision. The Senate minutes note: "This is the exact reason why we need AB 1725 [California legislation that requires consultation with the Academic Senate]. Had the senior administration made a decision to bring in the ESL faculty and the department chair this chaos could have been thwarted. This is a tight-knit community, and we could have had help from others."

AFT 2121 called a rally and press conference for Friday, January 16. The shock of the campus closure propelled nearly three hundred people into the streets. Civic Center students and faculty, bolstered by colleagues from other campuses, massed at 750 Eddy and marched to City Hall. In signs and impromptu speeches, they denounced the top-down decision to close the campus and demanded a return of democracy. "We Are All Civic Center," the union declared on its web page, echoing the slogan that united people from the beginning of the accreditation crisis, "We Are All City College."

The Gough Street Quake

Teachers continued preparing to move to Gough Street, despite their concerns about working conditions there. While Eddy Street was a beautiful, light-filled space, classes at Gough would be in basement rooms with beige walls, linoleum floors, and fluorescent lighting. The basement already housed a few offices, including that of ESL Resource Center coordinator Vivian Ikeda. The part of the basement not used for office space was piled high with storage. It wasn't clear how all the students would fit.

"They'd painted, partitioned, hauled out crap, looked into renting portapotties that they'd keep in the parking lot. The lack of planning was like you're having a party for two hundred people, and you have no paper plates," said Venette Cook, an ESL teacher with twenty-nine years at Civic Center.

Ikeda would step into the hallways and talk to the workers. Progress didn't look good. Then one day she found the hall almost deserted. She asked the lone worker, "What is going on?"

"We were told to stop working."

"Why?"

"I don't know, they just said stop working. Gotta go. Bye!"

Around 9:00 p.m. on Wednesday, January 28, Civic Center faculty got an email from administration summoning them to a meeting at Ocean Campus the next day at 10:00 a.m. A 9:00 p.m. notice for a 10:00 a.m. meeting? About a dozen faculty members turned on a dime and showed up the next morning, bolstered by the AFT 2121 officers and the Academic Senate's Marrujo-Duck. They got there ahead of the administrators and took the seats in the front of the room.

"The administration came in with the suits, Tyler and Parras and some other suits. There were chairs set up in the front of the room, and they went to sit down there," said Kevin Cross. "Jessica Buchsbaum said, 'No, those are for us.' It was totally on the terms of the teachers."

Then the chancellor announced that Gough Street also had seismic issues and would need to be closed. "Since 1973, two years after we acquired the building, we have been noncompliant. That was not known to me or my staff." He went on to blame past facilities staff and the fact that "our records are in boxes instead of a retrieval system" for the late discovery. Faculty pressed for clarity on why the sudden closure was needed, why the administrators had once again failed to consult them, and why boxes were still being moved from Civic Center to Gough. About a half-hour in, AFT 2121 secretary Buchsbaum directly addressed Virginia Parras. "I'd actually like to direct my question to Virginia Parras, who I believe is the president of our colleges and centers. You've been mostly silent, and I believe this issue really belongs under your purview. . . . We hear promises from all of you to share documentation, to share decision-making. What guarantee can you possibly offer at this point that any of us can trust that any of you will honor your promises?" Parras fielded a few questions before Tyler stepped in.

Buchsbaum wasn't having it. "Are you speaking for President Parras, Chancellor Tyler?" she asked.

"In this point, yes, I am," he said.

"Why is that, sir?" Buchsbaum queried.

"Because everybody in this audience except Trustee Agrella works for me," he replied.

For more than an hour and a half, faculty members upbraided the administrators for shutting them out of the process and for taking drastic action that would wreak havoc on their students. The meeting ended with formation of a task force that was to include teachers, students, and administrators. Planning for how to immediately relocate classes was dumped on Vice Chancellor Susan Lamb. She gathered ESL Department chair Greg Keech and a few of the campus deans and ESL coordinators. They figured out how to disperse classes between the Mission and Chinatown Campuses.

What was to be the first day of classes at Gough Street was far more organized than January 12 at Eddy Street, if no less traumatic. The prospect of having to leave their neighborhood and schlep to the Mission or

Chinatown on the bus dismayed many students. "I had students who came to Gough Street, and they came and hugged me and cried right there. We were crying," Sunny Ngo said. "The first day of the semester we had told them we would be teaching them at Gough Street, and they thought, 'Oh, not too far,' but when we told students we can't teach them there either, they cried. They came and hugged me. When would they see me again? It was like the end of the world, no more school."

With students dispersed to more distant and unfamiliar campuses, enrollment dropped like a rock. Teachers reported some classes as small as six people.

Venette Cook taught in an office training program, part of the vocational ESL track, as did Vivian Ikeda. The two of them, with Denise Selleck, organized a mailing to Eddy Street students as an office exercise, because communication from the administration was so lacking. "The students wrote the letter, we addressed the envelopes, and we sat around the tables and did it," Cook said. "It was the spring semester, Lunar New Year's coming, and there's a pattern of students being rather intermittent until after Lunar New Year. They would come back to Eddy Street, and it would be all closed down, and it was rather quickly starting to look like a homeless encampment, and it would be confusing. It seems like in this day and age it should have been easy to communicate." City College lacked advanced communications tools, "and we have less service for the non-credit students in every which way you can think of. The letter project was great, because the students saw how committed we were, how an office handled things like that. That's fine, but it shouldn't have been the only thing. . . . [The administration] would just say, 'There's no budget for that. Find the money!' The chancellor went to China to recruit students. . . . Why is there money for that, and there's not money for postage stamps to mail the students a letter?" Cook asked.

Central City Comes Together

With the dispersal of students to the Mission and Chinatown Campuses, it looked like CCSF might lose its presence in the Tenderloin for good, stripping ESL classes from the neighborhood so many immigrants called home. AFT 2121 put staff organizer Athena Waid on the case. She started out talking to some of the union's longstanding allies in Jobs with Justice. James Tracy of Community Housing Partnership (CHP) sat on the JWJ board. CHP owned seventeen affordable buildings in the Tenderloin, and

Tracy was a veteran of San Francisco's anti-displacement struggles. "Let's go talk to some people," he said, and introduced Waid to key organizations in the Tenderloin. She pulled together teams of faculty and students, and they began visiting the community groups.

"We framed it as an equity issue: We needed to keep a campus in the Tenderloin," Waid said. "We discovered a lot of feeling in the community that City wasn't good at checking in on community needs. We said this could be an opportunity to make it better." Some groups jumped on right away, like La Voz Latina, an organizing project of the Tenderloin Housing Clinic. "Within a day or two [of the closure] people were coming here: 'What do I do? I've been going to this campus for many years, what do I do?'" said Kelly Guajardo, program manager at La Voz. "We meet a lot of people who are new here, and they just take intensive courses for a few months, just to have some basic competency, and it opens doors. It's hard for me to spell it all out, because it's everything; it's how do you take the bus, how do you navigate this transit system, how do you apply for jobs, read postings, apply for housing. Everything's in English. . . . So it's the difference between being able to thrive and have some self-determination and relying on interpretation which is often really flawed."

Within a few weeks, the Central City Coalition for Public Education (3CPE) took shape, with CHP, the Vietnamese Youth Development Center, Young Workers United, and the Chinatown Community Development Center joining La Voz and Glide Memorial United Methodist Church, a famous social justice church in the Tenderloin. "We built trust among coalition members by going to each other's meetings and helping with events," Vivian Ikeda said. Coalition meetings and facilitation rotated among the different organizing groups.

Early on, James Tracy approached the office of Jane Kim, the San Francisco supervisor for District 6, which included the Tenderloin. Kim's aide Bobbie Lopez challenged him to show that the community cared, saying that if they could get four hundred people in the streets, the supervisor would take it on. 3CPE put together a petition that asked Kim to sponsor a resolution urging the City College administration to immediately find a new campus in the central city area. They translated it into six languages and collected more than two thousand signatures.

Around six hundred people answered the call to protest at City Hall on March 5, and they reflected the spectrum of the neighborhood itself. Old, young, and in between, they carried the 3CPE organizations' banners and their own handmade signs: "Don't Displace Our Dreams," "Don't Cancel Our Future," *Devuelveme Mi Escuela* (Give me back my school), and more. Supervisors Eric Mar and David Campos, Assembly member Tom Ammiano, and Tenderloin neighborhood activists took the podium. Jane Kim paid close attention. "I remember the look on her face when United Playaz came up to speak," Athena Waid said. United Playaz works to provide a bridge to keep young men out of gangs, and many of its members go through City College's Second Chance program for formerly incarcerated students. "She was definitely impressed," Waid said. After the rally, 3CPE members went inside to present the petitions to Kim, who posed for a photo op.

"Anytime you can get six hundred people from a neighborhood slandered as a collection of calamities, it shows another face of the Tenderloin the press doesn't get," Tracy said. Six days later, Supervisor Kim introduced a resolution that urged the City College administration to present a construction plan for a prompt retrofit of 750 Eddy Street and find a temporary location in the Tenderloin/Central City for the displaced classes. The next day, Glide Church hosted a community forum.

When Supervisor Kim's resolution came up for a vote, several speakers from 3CPE groups reminded the board how much the campus meant to the community. Yen Dinh from the Vietnamese Youth Development Center spoke to the experience of "many, many newcomers, who, like my family, came here in the 1980s." Derrick Brown of CHP appreciated the computer access and training for better jobs. Anakh Sul Rama, also of CHP, brought up the SRO residents and families with children who need the campus to be nearby. Speaking for AFT 2121, Alisa Messer thanked the supervisors "for their continuing vigilance and leadership to hold the whole community accountable to be sure City College is here for all of our students for another eighty years."

Supervisor Julie Christensen, recently appointed to the board by Mayor Lee, kicked off the discussion by saying, "This situation is distressing not only because of the abrupt closing, but because there was apparently a great deal of foreknowledge that this was going to happen and little action to prevent it or mitigate and no notice to the students." Supervisor Norman Yee called it "outrageous. This wouldn't have happened to any other campus." He and Christensen, along with John Avalos, joined the original trio of Jane Kim, Eric Mar, and David Campos in sponsoring the resolution, which passed unanimously.

Back on Campus

The task force created out of the January 29 emergency meeting didn't convene until March 6. Administrators, faculty, classified staff, and students were all represented, but "the meeting did not begin with an overview of the scope and purpose" of the group, Venette Cook observed in her notes. She, Jenny Hammer, and Beth Ericson attended for the Civic Center faculty. The task force met weekly in March and April, with faculty consistently trying to pin down the administration on the details of a possible temporary location and on a timeline for the Eddy Street retrofit. "It was a constant frustration," Cook said. "Just tell us the truth and we'll deal with it. But we were in this accreditation spiral, and Art Tyler was clearly there to earn a salary and not make decisions."

The Civic Center faculty got no help from the state honchos either. Beth Ericson gave public comment at the Board of Governors meeting. She swallowed her discomfort and did what she had to do. "I stood up and said it was unprecedented; I'd never heard of anything like this, where a community college campus is just closed willy-nilly," she remembered. The chancellor and the board "looked kind of uncomfortable, and then they went on to other business. . . . They've got a lot of nerve to act like that was nothing," she said.

The Central City Coalition hit the streets again on May 6, this time holding the "Tenderloin Free School" in Boedekker Park. Classes included workplace rights, how to grow plants in an SRO, how to get a driver's license under AB 60 (the recently passed law that allowed undocumented Californians to get licenses), an ESL teach-in, and Vietnamese-American history. "If you won't find us a place to hold classes, we will hold them in the park," Waid said.

Unbeknown to the organizers, and even to the faculty on the task force, the administration had issued a press release the day before, announcing that they would rent space from the Art Institute of California at 1170 Market Street, on the edge of the Tenderloin. When the news did surface, the allies who worked so hard to make it happen enjoyed a brief moment of victory and vindication. "If we hadn't made all the noise we made, we wouldn't exist as an entity right now. There would be no Civic Center," Venette Cook said.

An unusual constellation of factors lined up to make the win possible, according to James Tracy. "The foremost was that City College of San Francisco, still reeling from its accreditation crisis, needed to preserve political goodwill with members of the city's board of supervisors. It was a rare moment in organizing when bad publicity, together with the mobilization of sympathetic politicians, actually amounted to real leverage."

STWEP Robert Agrella slipped out of town at the end of January, his departure announced only by a tweet from State Chancellor Brice Harris. Guy Lease assumed the STWEP role. He demoted Chancellor Tyler to head of facilities in early June and assigned him to an office in a corner of the moldy Gough Street basement. Vice Chancellor of Academic Affairs Susan Lamb became the new interim chancellor and fired Virginia Parras within a week.

Over the summer, 3CPE's focus shifted to outreach. The campaign to save the Civic Center Campus taught AFT 2121 they needed to listen as well as talk, so the work included a survey of 304 Tenderloin residents to find out how City College could better meet their needs. More than a third were students, faculty, or staff or had a friend or family member at City. More than two-thirds said the most important offerings at the school were "classes for personal improvement," including ESL and computer skills. When asked what else would encourage them to come, they highlighted a range of options, including job training (114), nonprofit building management (109), training for employers (100), Red Cross safety classes (99), and ethnic studies (97).

Besides doing the survey, the coalition held a mid-summer "registration fair" in a Tenderloin park and passed out flyers all over the neighborhood. "The Farmers' Market [Heart of the City Farmers' Market in Civic Center Plaza] was great, and let us set up a table. I saw former students, and they didn't know where the school was, and I said, 'It's right there,'" said Rick Kappra.

Despite the outreach efforts, class sizes hovered around seven to ten that first semester on Market Street, according to Kappra. "Before the move, it was between eighteen and twenty-two on average; in the diaspora, we were down to five or six, though there were a few classes that were healthy, a few that were over twenty."

Compounding the enrollment losses at Civic Center, another 1,400 students were robo-dropped under the pay-up-front policy and didn't return.[1] Faculty ranks had been thinned by close to four hundred since the accreditation crisis hit, and the school was seeing its physical footprint downsized as well.

Realizing that the 1170 Market Street site would only be temporary, 3CPE organizers kept pressing for updates and a timeline on the restoration of 750 Eddy. They presented the survey results to the trustees in September but got little response to their efforts at follow-up. Some administrative workers carried on at 33 Gough Street, despite its being declared unsafe for students—and the fact that STWEP Agrella had already put the building on the real estate market early in 2014.

The sudden and seemingly careless closing of 750 Eddy Street was "confusing, yes, and students were worried," said Kelly Guajardo of La Voz. "Is this part of a larger plan of just shutting it down? They're just going to take it and chip away, chip away, chip away. . . . It's in the trend of taking resources away from the most vulnerable, doing it in this way that's careful enough, it's not obvious or overt, but, in fact, it's huge." But for the moment, the alliance of City College teachers and their union and students and their community had halted the erosion—and the relationships they formed in the process would prove pivotal a year later.

CHAPTER FOURTEEN

How Can We Keep Winning and Still Be Losing?

2015

On weekdays, thousands of teachers, staff, and students park their cars on the windswept parking lot next to Ocean Campus.[1] On weekends the lot has been repurposed as a practice space for a motorcycle safety class and the marching band from Archbishop Riordan High School and as a venue for the low-rider show put on by City College professor Ben Bac Sierra to raise money for a memorial to Alex Nieto. This lot, the lower Balboa Reservoir, is one of the largest tracts of undeveloped public land in land-starved San Francisco—and, for Save CCSF activists, it would become one more front in the fight.

The San Francisco Public Utilities Commission (SFPUC) completed the reservoir in 1957 and owns 60 percent of it but never used it to store water, instead leasing it to CCSF for parking. The rest of the parcel—"the upper reservoir"—belongs to CCSF. This is space for new construction, including the Multi-Use Building and the long-planned Performing Arts Education Center (PAEC), along with another parking lot that's packed to the gills on weekdays.

Dianne Feinstein, then mayor of San Francisco, initiated the first serious conversations about developing housing at the reservoir in 1983. Residents of the nearby Sunnyside and Westwood neighborhoods teamed up with City College faculty on four ballot initiatives that finally put that round of housing proposals to rest in 1991.[2]

Pressure on San Francisco's supply of housing, especially for low- and moderate-income residents, continued to build over the next twenty years. In 2014, the reservoir became the first site to be studied under San Francisco's Public Land for Housing Program, which aimed to ensure four thousand units of new housing by 2020, at least one-third of them defined as "affordable" by low- and middle-income San Franciscans.[3]

The reservoir had been on and off the SFPUC's list of "surplus property" since 2012.[4] Its appearance and disappearance pricked up Chris Hanson's ears. She was a lifelong learner at City College and an equine bodyworker by trade—she does massage and stretching for horses. She'd tangled with the SFPUC a few years back when the agency evicted her co-op stable from a plot of land in San Bruno. Though she and her colleagues settled with the SFPUC, she became deeply skeptical of the way it operates.

A November 2014 article in the *San Francisco Business Times* caught Hanson's attention. It quoted real estate developer and former San Francisco Planning Commissioner David Prowler: "Of the potential sites, Prowler described the Balboa Reservoir as being 'the best of the bunch.' Balboa Reservoir . . . is owned by the San Francisco Public Utilities Commission. It's currently home to a parking lot for a city college."[5]

In January 2015, as the fight for the Civic Center Campus erupted, the San Francisco Planning Department held the first public hearing on the new effort to build housing on the Balboa Reservoir. The meeting at a private high school across the street from Ocean Campus attracted about forty people. From the beginning, Hanson said, "It felt like a done deal, though we hadn't heard about it before." Participants were asked to prioritize the public benefits they would like the project to offer, not whether they thought it should be built at all. City College had no place in the conversation, even though the new development had big implications for the school. The project could take away parking that commuting students, faculty, and staff relied on, further clog traffic, and create another obstacle to completion of the PAEC.

Students Rekindle Their Organizing

Meanwhile, student activists were looking for ways to revitalize their organizing. Members of Socialist Organizer (SO) had stepped back, believing that they had made their contribution. "We saw the role a small group of organizers can play in mobilizing social movements," Eric Blanc said. But while SO's organizing skills furthered the fight, their insistence on bringing in a full anti-capitalist analysis disturbed some other students. "When we needed a solid plan, structure, people in SO had basic organizing tools," Martín Madrigal said. "I would listen to [SO's] ideas but wanted to explore at my pace. People were more united but not pushy. And when they were, it caused friction."

"You need to give people room to be themselves and have dialogue," said Deon Saunders, another student activist. He had to take a step back himself when life pressures caught up to him. Some issues had come up in his family; between that and school and the struggle, he had to let the organizing go. Several other people he'd worked closely with were housing-insecure. "Martín was living out of his car, and I was couch surfing. We'd put in our work, and it was time to let others take it up," he said.

Core student organizers who remained engaged turned their efforts toward groups mobilizing students of color. Lalo Gonzalez and Itzel Calvo had started a Movimiento Estudiantil Chicanx de Aztlán (MEChA) chapter at the end of 2013. After #BlackLivesMatter ignited in Summer 2014, Thea Matthews and two other students revived the Black Student Union (BSU) at CCSF. Win-Mon Kyi founded the Asian Student Union (ASU) in spring 2015, at the same time that Pilipinos for Education, Arts, Culture and Empowerment (PEACE) came together.

Gonzalez, Calvo, Kyi, and others proposed that these groups work together on a campaign to end the pay-up-front policy, which was kicking out thousands of students. This broader organizing would, the organizers hoped, engage the students most impacted by the various efforts to downsize the school. They targeted the payment policy as the most concrete example.

Building the alliance was not a simple or easy process. Some Black and Asian students had long-standing ties with Coleman Advocates from its powerful work in the San Francisco high schools, but members of the Coleman-sponsored group at City College, Students Making a Change (SMAC), clashed with Save CCSF over strategy. By spring 2015, though, a Solidarity Committee made up of MEChA, the BSU, PEACE, and the ASU came together and took its first actions—teach-ins and a demonstration at the board of trustees meeting that continued the student defense of Diversity Studies.

This organizing built toward a walkout on May 6 protesting class cuts, the special trustee, and the pay-up-front policy. Organizers pointed to the 1,400 students robo-dropped at the beginning of the semester and the 50 percent enrollment loss that Labor and Community Studies had suffered since the state takeover.

After walking out of classes at 12:30 p.m., participants marched around campus and then took over Conlan Hall. In solidarity with the occupation, Save CCSF quickly decided to move its general assembly to Conlan. For the first time at one of its public meetings, the coalition drew the connections between the gentrification of San Francisco and the downsizing of City College via land grabs and student pushout policies. The occupation ended peacefully when the students decided to leave that evening.

San Francisco Supervisors Grill Takeover Administration

The day after the walkout, the Neighborhood Services Committee of the board of supervisors, chaired by CCSF ally Eric Mar, held a hearing on the status of CCSF. The session had been calendared two months earlier, at the height of the uproar over the closure of the Civic Center Campus. Like the mass meetings organized by AFT 2121 and Save CCSF early on in the crisis, this hearing lifted up the meaning City College had for many in San Francisco. The hearing also showed a board of supervisors much more unified behind the college and definitely testy toward the takeover administration.

Supervisor David Campos asked why Special Trustee Guy Lease was not in attendance. His absence "illustrates the problem that we have a special trustee that is completely unaccountable, and when he is offered the opportunity to come and speak to the elected representatives of this city disrespects those constituents by not even showing up to a hearing in City Hall."

People lined up at the mic for public comment. Each wore a "We Are All City College" button with a big red heart. "ACCJC is a statewide problem," said AFT 2121 president Tim Killikelly. "It illegally meddles in labor negotiations. We are depressed, we are angry, we are frustrated, and we are ready to move. We are overworked and underpaid. How do you expect to maintain the quality of education at CCSF when the faculty salaries are currently 3.5 percent below 2007?" James Tracy from the newly formed Central City Coalition for Public Education (3CPE) had mobilized community support to save the endangered Civic Center campus. When he asked supporters to stand up, the first of many bursts of applause changed the tone of the hearing to a celebration of City College.

New Foes Come Swinging in on Ropes

Despite the students' renewed organizing and the growing support from the supervisors, "It was starting to feel like we were trapped in a kung fu movie where every time we defeat one opponent, three more come swinging in on ropes," Vicki Legion said. The land grabs were becoming more obvious, and the school remained under takeover—one Special Trustee with Extraordinary Powers had vanished only to be replaced by another. Restoration status kept the sanctions in place. Judge Karnow's final ruling in the City Attorney's suit proved to be a mixed bag.

In his February 17 injunction, the judge found that the ACCJC had broken four laws, which further eroded the agency's legitimacy. However, the judge stopped short of overturning the commission's ruling, saying that responsibility should fall to the Department of Education. Instead he ordered the same bad actor, the ACCJC, to provide the due process that it had denied before. The judge directed the commission to offer much more detail on CCSF's deficiencies and fairly consider the school's reply. The ACCJC did the bare minimum to comply, responding with a letter and report in April that reiterated the sanctions.

CFT president Joshua Pechthalt called on the CCSF trustees to contest this half-hearted effort by enlisting Dennis Herrera's office in a new round of litigation. "We are sure the SF City Attorney is willing to go back to Judge Karnow and request enforcement of the injunction so long as they are joined by City College as a Real Party in Interest," Pechthalt wrote to board president Rafael Mandelman. "Such a joinder should not require much in the expenditure of resources—the College just must file court papers saying that, as the Real Party in Interest, it joins in the City Attorney's motion. On behalf of the faculty, staff and students of CCSF we strongly encourage you to do so."

The trustees, who had regained some limited powers in March, heard public comment from two dozen people urging them to ask the city attorney to step in—and then voted 4–2 on June 8 not to challenge the ACCJC.[6] City College administrators submitted still more paperwork to the commission, while stating for the record: "the ACCJC has not complied with the Final Injunction and Order."

In July, the California Community Colleges Board of Governors (BOG) voted unanimously to restore the trustees' voting power, although the special trustee still held the power to veto all decisions.

In August 2015, the ACCJC once again affirmed its decision to terminate CCSF's accreditation, leaving "restoration" as the only option. But even as the commission held on, the BOG was moving to strip it of its authority. The board revised state regulations to revoke the ACCJC's status as the sole accreditor for California.[7] Chancellor Brice Harris had convened a Task Force on Accreditation, the third such work group set up by the chancellor's office in eight years.

"What was startling to me was how broadly there was agreement on what needed to happen," Los Angeles College Faculty Guild president Joanne Waddell told *Perspective*, the publication of CFT's Community College Council. Waddell, one of three faculty members on the task force, credited the legislative, judicial, and organizing work that had gone on in the past three years for shifting opinion. "The wave had crashed, and it was time."

The task force's report noted that the ACCJC had ignored all previous recommendations and "has made no significant effort to engage in meaningful or lasting reforms." It recommended that the BOG find a new accreditor and laid out a pathway to doing so. In response to the mounting pressure, the ACCJC held "listening sessions" across California. At a session in Sacramento, ACCJC vice president Steven Kinsella blamed the DOE for the commission's harsh stance. "The Department of Education told us twice that we had not been hard enough on City College," he said. Some heard this as a simple effort to deflect responsibility. But Vicki Legion remembered the DOE's 2006 Spellings Commission, which recommended that accreditation be used as a lever to restructure higher education. To her ears, Kinsella was acknowledging the agenda behind the ACCJC's sanctions—the same agenda revealed by the commission's support for the 2012 Student Success Act. No rogue agency this.

"Just So Tired": Breakups and Breakdowns

The long slog continued.

The all-volunteer enrollment outreach campaign launched in September 2013 by Leslie Simon, Susan Lopez, and Danny Halford kept up its efforts. Dozens of faculty members had joined in over the two years. They took course schedules, flyers, and posters to cafes, bookstores, senior centers, laundromats, and libraries all over town, set up card tables at busy intersections and transit stations, visited elementary schools with flyers for students to take home, and called on community organizations. "Susan Lopez supplied me with a list of all the CBOs [community-based organizations] in the Tenderloin, plus some nearby," Halford wrote. "It's difficult to overemphasize how effective this can be because of the ripple effect. CBO employees work hard every day to help the people who come to them, including giving them information about free and low-cost education. So one visit to a CBO can result in positive life-changes for who knows how many persons."

Halford also coordinated outreach efforts at "Sunday Streets," car-free Sunday festivals in various neighborhoods of the city. Volunteers at the 2015 event in Mission District tabled at the entrance of Mission Campus. They included former CCSF trustee Anita Grier, Latin American and Latino/a Studies Department chair Edgar Torres, Susan Lopez (who Halford referred to as the "BBOO, Brains Behind Our Operation"), and Biology Department chair Simon Hanson, on stilts, the better to direct passersby to the CCSF table.

AFT 2121 kept up its education campaign in its newsletter *Union Action*, publishing an updated timeline of "Our Epic Battle for Fair Accreditation" and the "Top Ten Lies of the ACCJC."[8] CFT continued to feature articles on City College in *Perspective*, keeping the crisis top of mind for members around the state. Activists from the union and Save CCSF rallied and testified at Board of Governors meetings in Sacramento, picketed the ACCJC in Oakland, and showed up at the monthly CCSF trustees meetings. They also trekked to the ACCJC's "listening sessions," where they gave public comment about the commission's agenda and tactics.

Chris Hanson, Wynd Kaufmyn, and Harry Bernstein drove three hundred miles for one of those sessions at Bakersfield Community College on October 30. "ACCJC was just like this thing you couldn't kill. . . . They just kept doubling down," Hanson said. "Prior to that, the guy who had been temporary chair of the commission, Raul Rodriguez, called CCSF's public process a 'witch hunt.'" To pass the time and lift their spirits on the dusty five-hour drive, Hanson read aloud from the transcript of the trial of the City Attorney's suit—offering a dramatic rendition of former vice chancellor of finance Peter Goldstein exposing the truth about CCSF's 2011 "deficit."

Nonetheless, the strain of three years of struggle was showing. People's health and relationships eroded, and there was personal and political drama in the student organizations. Civic Center ESL teacher Denise Selleck had just come back from a long-planned trip out of town when she heard about the campus being shut down. Two days later, her girlfriend (also an ESL teacher) broke up with her. Wynd Kaufmyn's husband of more than thirty years left her in the summer.

Other people felt the strain in their bodies. "From the first announcement in 2012, I was totally tense, my shoulders were up around my ears. Finally, I lost my voice for a long time," Legion said. "It started in March

2015 and persisted for more than a year. I had had a bumpy semester of teaching the fall before, and I remember croaking on the phone to my sister, who said, 'What's going on?'" She consulted a speech pathologist, who recommended Alexander vocal training, which a lot of singers and actors do. "Alexander teaches that tension leads to misuse of the vocal muscles, which can kind of spiral as you push to try to get the voice out," she said. Through the training, she realized that the shallow, high-in-the-chest breathing she'd been doing since the crisis started had choked off her voice.

December 2015: All the Work Still Matters

The fog of fatigue obscured the real gains made in this long year. The Board of Governors—one of the bodies that held actual power over the ACCJC—took the unusual step of exercising that power. It recommended that the Department of Education fire the agency and voted to amend California regulations so the state could change accreditors. "The current structure of the ACCJC, along with its lack of credibility as perceived by its peers and the public, no longer meets the current and anticipated needs of California community colleges," the board said in a November 2015 resolution. The board also pulled back the takeover and restored power to the locally elected trustees ahead of its original schedule.

After three and a half years of hard bargaining, the Department Chairperson Council beat back the administration's attempt to consolidate departments and virtually eliminate their positions. The department chairs kept their status as elected frontline managers, scoring a win for democratic governance. The Diversity Collaborative departments kept their autonomy. But the contract approved by the board of trustees in July 2015 reduced the budget for chairs by almost half, though the workload remained the same.

Students and Save CCSF supporters rebounded with a volley of activity in December. The Solidarity Committee called a walkout and packed the last trustees meeting of the year to protest the payment policy. Save CCSF held meetings with community organizations and the union to explore the possibility of working against the Balboa Reservoir development. The coalition organized a thirty-seven-person delegation to travel to Washington, DC, to testify again before the National Advisory Committee on Institutional Quality and Integrity (NACIQI), the federal advisory committee on accreditation.

Solidarity Committee members worked with the Save CCSF Research Committee, preparing and writing "An Open Letter to Guy Lease, Chancellor Lamb and the City College Board of Trustees: Stop Hemorrhaging Enrollment at City College: End the Racist Payment Policy." The letter, at once passionate and carefully documented, spelled out what the policy had cost the school and the students, and recommended new policies and procedures:

> Over only four semesters, 9,124 enrolled students have been robo-dropped from all their classes, with less than half (4,284, or 47 percent) ever managing to re-enroll, and 4,840 (53%) simply gone missing—in the middle of an enrollment crisis at the college! . . .
>
> Every time a full-time student is pushed out, the college loses up to $4,676 in state appropriations. Yet the average debt to City College is only $256, *so the college loses far more than it stands to collect.* The new policy only makes sense if the real goal is downsizing our public college, bringing in revenue for the for-profit colleges and student loan companies, and allowing asset stripping of College land by real estate developers. If the overarching goal is to rebuild enrollment, the policy is utterly counterproductive.
>
> Before thousands more enrolled students are dropped, the administration should put a moratorium on the current payment policy and overhaul it in line with the principles below.

These included improvements in financial aid advising, changes in the deadlines so payment would be due after financial aid arrived, clear and prominent explanations of the payment policy waiver for students with financial aid pending, collaboration with the city on a proposed fund to aid undocumented students, and termination of the contract with "predatory Nelnet Business Solutions."[9]

At the December 10, 2015, board of trustees meeting, Solidarity Committee members read the entire letter in public comment relay-style. Subdued, the trustees signaled that they agreed with the criticisms and asked Chancellor Lamb to follow up.

Community Organizations Weigh in on the Reservoir

Save CCSF joined forces with the Council of Community Housing Organizations and People Organizing to Demand Environmental Rights (PODER), which organizes with Latinx youth and families in the neighborhoods of Southeast San Francisco, to press their issues with the Balboa Reservoir site. Save CCSF picketed outside the December 14 meeting of the Balboa Reservoir Community Advisory Committee (BRCAC), demanding that the new project respect City College parking and the PAEC and include truly affordable housing.

During the meeting, ten PODER members stood up and unfurled a banner demanding 100 percent affordable housing on the site. Each of them made a statement. "We have to live crowded up," one woman said. "My kids ask me, 'Mami, when will we get a place of our own?' This is a chance to change that." Save CCSF successfully lobbied to put the Council of Community Housing Organizations on the agenda—but the affordable housing advocates got only a very small fraction of the presentation time given to supporters of the for-profit developers.

The members of the BRCAC were selected by the mayor and the supervisor who represented the district the reservoir was in. From the first meeting, they dismissed any mention of the PAEC, Chris Hanson said.

Staff from the SFPUC and two city departments with reputations as being pro-developer—the city's Office of Economic and Workforce Development and the Planning Department—worked directly with the committee and made lengthy presentations at every meeting. "The mayor brought his people out there to school us, show us what is what, and make a show of listening," said Monica Collins, who lived in the nearby Sunnyside neighborhood and had recently retired from CCSF's financial aid office.

City staff also worked closely—and secretly—with members of the City College administration, as PAEC supporter and CCSF music teacher Harry Bernstein learned via emails leaked to him beginning in late November. CCSF's special trustee, vice chancellors of finance and facilities, and sometimes the chancellor and general counsel had been meeting with city staff for eight months without informing the elected trustees, or even the trustee who sat on the BRCAC.

Another Trip to NACIQI

Save CCSF had mustered seven students and six teachers for the first trip to NACIQI in 2013, flying from California to Washington, DC, to give two-minute testimonies. In 2015, they arrived thirty-seven strong, with numerous allies to reinforce their message: Academic Senate leaders Karen Saginor and Lillian Marrujo-Duck; Disabled Students Programs and Services chair Muriel Parenteau; AFT 2121's Tim Killikelly and Alisa

Messer; CFT secretary-treasurer Jeff Freitas and president emeritus Marty Hittelman; CCSF trustee John Rizzo; Faculty Association of California Community Colleges executive director Jonathan Lightman; several teachers and trustees from community colleges around California.

In response to the 2013 CFT/AFT complaint, the DOE found ACCJC out of compliance with fifteen federal regulations. The ACCJC appealed on two items. NACIQI announced two weeks before the 2015 meeting that it wouldn't hear comments on the issues under appeal. "We had already been prepping, so that threw a monkey wrench into our work," said Wynd Kaufmyn, who once again coordinated the Save CCSF delegation. NACIQI also belatedly changed the date of the public comment, so everyone had to spend a lot of money to change their plane tickets.

Almost everyone involved with the proceedings was staying at the hotel in suburban Washington, DC, where the meeting was held. Chris Hanson remembers Lalo Gonzalez getting into a heated discussion with ACCJC vice president Steven Kinsella and following him into an elevator. Finally, Kinsella exploded with, "If the students can't get classes, they should just go get a job."

American Association of University Professors first vice president Hank Reichman also attended the meeting and praised the City College delegation in his blog. He lauded the faculty members "who spoke with both passion and reason. . . . But by far the most moving comments came from a group of CCSF students and recent alumni, whose eloquence, poise, and intelligence provided perhaps the most powerful testimony to the school's success." To follow up on the meeting, AFT legislative staff in DC coordinated a round of lobbying visits to educate Congress members on accreditation issues.

Just after the City College delegation returned home, Chancellor Art Tyler resigned; he left on December 21, five days before the *San Francisco Chronicle* published an article detailing his questionable use of funds. The *Chronicle* managed to cast Tyler's slippery ethics as yet another City College failing, even though he was handpicked by the special trustee and imposed on the college. "City College of San Francisco [i.e., the chancellor Art Tyler] has spent thousands of dollars on fancy restaurants and international and cross-country travel for two top administrators—often with no record of what the expenses were for—since the school's successful campaign in 2013 for a parcel tax to help save the college from bankruptcy, records show," reporter Michael Cabanatuan wrote in the lead.[10]

For college faculty, the Tyler revelations added an exclamation point to the sorry tale of the takeover's erosion of their working conditions and student learning conditions. Heading into 2016, AFT 2121 was gearing up for the first faculty strike in the school's eighty-year history.

CHAPTER FIFTEEN

Strike for the School Our City Deserves

Spring 2016

T he year started on an upswing: the CCSF board of trustees regained full power on January 1, 2016, ending the official state takeover. Following the Solidarity Committee's compelling presentation to the board of trustees in December, Chancellor Susan Lamb ended the pay-up-front policy. This was a major victory for two years of student organizing. "They won that campaign based on the strength of their organizing," Tarik Farrar said. "That was the first major victory in the struggle against the state takeover, and it was student-led." For the first time, a takeover policy had been rolled back.

This was the last year CCSF would get state stabilization funding, but the CFT and the AFT successfully lobbied for another type of funding support. "By 2016, there was 'City College fatigue' In Sacramento," said Alisa Messer. "There was resentment among other schools. To go back for more [stabilization funds] would have been too heavy a lift." But, working with state senator Mark Leno again, the unions got the "enrollment cap" lifted. Community colleges get funding based on the number of students enrolled, and the state normally will only increase the allotments for one or two percentage points of growth per year. Lifting the cap allowed CCSF to get paid for all the new students it could attract.

On March 18, the presidents and CEOs of the California Community Colleges voted to find an alternative to the ACCJC. The California Community Colleges Board of Governors did the same on March 21 and appointed two task forces. One was charged with recommending reforms to the ACCJC—again—this had happened several times already. The other set out to explore a longer-term alternative, replacing the ACCJC by aligning community college and four-year college accreditation.

Replacing the accreditor would take years, and, in the meantime, the disgraced commission still held City College in its jaws. Under restoration status, the school faced immediate closure if the ACCJC found it out of compliance with any standards. And although the state takeover had officially ended, the school's top administration was now staffed with agents of the takeover. "There is only one person in the senior administration who is not interim," Vicki Legion said. "They are all new, virtually all interim, 'serve at the pleasure,' and if they don't follow the script, they are out."

The new regime increased the burden of paperwork, administrative chores, and aggravation. "The 'work' that we are forced to do is not the work of education; it is the time-consuming work of compliance and form-filling, using complicated proprietary software," Legion said. "We made jokes throughout our department meeting, and everyone laughed, but it was gallows humor."

The push to standardize, quantify, and document their work wasn't just a bureaucratic burden for teachers; it ran counter to the way many saw their jobs. "I'm an old-fashioned guy who believes in the amazing things that happen between two human minds, the teacher's and the student's . . . opening students' minds to who they are," ESL Department chair Greg Keech said. "I know we do this, because students come back and say so."

"The faculty felt demoralized, not just disrespected but ground into the dirt," Alisa Messer said. The administration threw a nasty contract proposal full of take-backs into this toxic atmosphere. That move backfired big-time.

Union Gets Ready

In 2015, CCSF faculty members were earning less than they had in 2007, while the cost of living in San Francisco had shot up 21 percent from August 2007 to August 2015. Ongoing layoffs fell hardest on part-time faculty members. More than 170 had already lost their jobs. Many more had their loads cut, which put them at risk of losing health benefits if they worked less than half-time. The proposed 26 percent cut in classes by 2020 threatened another 350.

The union called for restoration of salaries to 2007 levels, a state cost of living adjustment (COLA), and a COLA to account for skyrocketing cost of living in San Francisco. The administration of the San Francisco Community College District offered the state COLA and restoration to 2007 levels for full-time faculty only. This divisive proposal would mark a big step backward. Ever since its first contract negotiations in 1979, the local had been working toward an equal pay rate for part-timers.[1] Beyond wages, the union aimed to reduce class cuts and "restore a role for faculty, students, and community in major District decisions."

Contract talks between AFT 2121 and the community college district began in February 2015. A year later, the two sides were still far apart. The district's hostile stance during the 2012–2013 bargaining—and the anti-union, teacher-blaming practice of the education reform movement in general—prepared the local for a fight. "Teachers unions have been buffeted by national reform headwinds for decades," Steven K. Ashby and Robert Bruno wrote in their comprehensive work on the 2012 Chicago teachers' strike.[2] "Both Republican and Democratic officials have largely adopted a narrative that public schools, and particularly public school teachers unions, are the source of the educational and economic malaise in the United States."

The ACCJC revealed its version of anti-union bias in a mass email Vice Chairman Steven Kinsella sent to community college CEOs in October 2013. Kinsella asked them to contact the Department of Education (DOE) in support of the commission, telling them, "You can't sit on the sidelines thinking someone else will take care of the faculty unions and their paid consultants in the Assembly and Senate. . . . This is nothing more than a fight for total control, void of all but legal constraints that enrich faculty with more entitlements every year. Once they control accreditation, they own you."[3]

AFT 2121 had begun organizing for this contract fight even before the fall 2013 vote on the previous agreement. At that point two things had become very clear: they needed to swallow the concession-laden two-year deal so they could focus on fighting the ACCJC, and they had some serious internal organizing to do.

Revising their precinct structure helped the union contact members more effectively and develop a new layer of leadership.[4] "We had very carefully mapped out a whole year ahead of time and the actions building up to peak power. We had teams in place, maps of each location, and leaders who had committed to being out on strike. We had even instituted a strike fund that people were contributing to out of their paychecks," AFT 2121 secretary Jessica Buchsbaum said.

The local also began talking through their situation and demands with community allies, in particular Jobs with Justice, Chinese Progressive Association, and Community Housing Partnership. "We were working toward the model of 'bargaining for the public good,'" said Malaika

Finkelstein, who had been recruited to work as a part-time grievance officer in spring 2014.

Over the 2015 summer break, the local started talking to as many members as possible to gauge their willingness to strike. Organizing community college faculty, especially part-timers, poses some particular challenges: they may work at multiple sites, their schedules vary widely, and they often live far apart. Then, in October, the administration proposed a 26 percent cut in classes by 2020. "Willingness to strike went up," AFT 2121 organizer Athena Waid said. "It became a strike to defend the college for our students."

Organizers ramped up their efforts in the winter. Mediation failed. More than 92 percent of the members who took part in a March 8 strike vote said they would walk. AFT 2121 members got support for their hard decision from community allies and their CFT colleagues around the state. The CFT held its annual convention in San Francisco and broke for lunch early on March 11, so delegates could attend a rally. Hundreds joined City College faculty and other San Francisco labor and community supporters in a noisy protest in front of the Financial District law office of the college's outside labor negotiator. Around twenty-five people were arrested for sitting in at the building entrance. CFT also helped AFT 2121 leadership with workshops on the nuts and bolts of running a strike, including member mobilization and media messaging.

The executive council of the Associated Students at City College passed a strike-support resolution by an 11–1 vote on March 15. Seven members of the San Francisco Board of Supervisors and representatives from two dozen community groups signed a letter calling on City College to negotiate with the teachers in good faith.

AFT 2121 took the final step in laying the groundwork for the strike when it filed an unfair labor practice charge with California's Public Employment Relations Board (PERB) on April 13.[5] It charged the community college district with violating the state's Educational Employment Relations Act, specifically the requirement to bargain in good faith. The union cited a letter from ACCJC associate vice president Norval Wellsfry to Chancellor Lamb in July 2015. Wellsfry informed Lamb that the commission was placing City College under "enhanced financial monitoring." Its criteria for doing so included the percentage of CCSF's budget that went to salary and benefits, and the college's contribution to retiree benefits— points the commission had been hammering on since it hit City with the show cause sanction in 2012. The union's charge concluded that the district's "unwillingness to engage in good-faith, give-and-take negotiations . . . and its fixation on securing increases in faculty OPEB [retiree health benefit] contributions beginning in 2020/21 are clearly driven by ACCJC's hidden or 'underground' criteria."

"No Justice, No Teach"

AFT 2121 called the first faculty strike in City College history for April 27, 2016. "We thought really hard about what date to do it," Buchsbaum said. "We tried to make sure it wouldn't be right at the beginning of the semester, where it would impact enrollment, or right at the end of the semester, where it would mess up students' exams. We called for a one-day strike only, because we wanted to be sure students didn't risk not having enough hours to meet the requirements of their program. If it didn't impact people it wouldn't be powerful, but the people you're impacting are your own students."

Chancellor Lamb ordered the college closed April 27, essentially turning the strike into a lockout—but neither that nor the driving rain discouraged early morning pickets throughout the city. CCSF students, along with members of other unions and people from the community, turned out in solidarity with AFT 2121 members' "Strike for the City College San Francisco Deserves." The slogan and message nodded to the 2012 walkout by the Chicago Teachers Union.

On the line at Ocean Campus, the strikers whooped and hollered, "Who are we? AFT!" and cheered a solidarity speech by Lita Blanc, president of United Educators of San Francisco, which represents the city's K–12 teachers. Some members of the classified staff joined the line. Win-Mon Kyi's parents delivered a tall stack of pizzas from their pocket-sized Mission District pizza shop.

Under the eyes of the "painted ladies"—colorful San Francisco Victorian homes—more than fifty people walked the line at John Adams Campus on the edge of the Haight-Ashbury neighborhood. "Faculty, students, community came out here in the rain and stood our ground," said AFT 2121 treasurer Alan D'Souza.

By midday, the rain gave way to blue sky and fitful sun shining on several hundred people gathered on the plaza next to Civic Center Campus. City College students and faculty took turns at the microphone with leaders of AFT 2121, the San Francisco Labor Council, other unions, and community groups. "If you go through any neighborhood, from Bayview to Fillmore to the Mission District where people are fighting for every square foot of this beautiful, beautiful city, making sure it remains our city, they talk about their anxieties, their fears, about not being able to live here one minute longer," said James Tracy of CHP, a key ally in the fight for Civic Center Campus. "They are worried, and they love City College, and they don't want City College to look like Heald College. They want it to look like this people's college we make it with our studies and our labor every single day."

Jessica Buchsbaum captained the strike line at Downtown Campus, in the shadow of looming office buildings and hotels where San Francisco's financial district butts up against its convention center. The campus offers ESL and classes in culinary arts and business, as well as foreign languages, real estate, and marketing.

At Mission Campus, the afternoon picket line turned into a street party, the mood buoyed by the sun (the Mission District has a reputation for the best weather in San Francisco) and lively music. Malaika Finkelstein recruited musician friends to come and play. Strikers and supporters sang along and danced. "It was high-energy, joyful, goofy, and strong," Finkelstein said.

By midafternoon at the Chinatown/North Beach Campus, three large sheets of butcher paper were covered with signatures—in bright colored marker—from folks who'd showed up to picket. The sign-in sheets taped to the side of the building above several empty boxes of coffee testified to a long and busy day.

The strike drew out many people who hadn't been publicly active before. "I hadn't been part of anything political for many years, but this time it seemed important.... [M]y participation is not only for myself, but I have to stand up and be part of this. It empowers me," said Peijue Chen, who'd taught in the child development program for fifteen years.

The walkout changed the chemistry within the union. "It showed us that our students and community supported us," Finkelstein said. "It changed the feeling about what we are doing, about what a union is.... It was a powerful experience."

Revived Lawsuit Tells ACCJC to Butt Out of Bargaining

The California Federation of Teachers and AFT 2121 had sued the ACCJC in September 2013, a month after San Francisco city attorney Dennis Herrera filed suit. The ACCJC lawyers ran through a repertoire of stall tactics, which included filing an anti-SLAPP motion that claimed the unions' lawsuit interfered with its right to free speech in evaluating colleges. The maneuver initially succeeded, but the California Appeals Court ruled in May 2016 that the unions' case could go forward.

The amended complaint filed days after the Appeals Court decision reflected the growing public awareness of the scope of damage the accreditor was inflicting on California community colleges. Three CFT locals and several individuals joined the state federation and AFT 2121 as plaintiffs. The complaint spoke directly to the unfair labor practice issue that was central to the AFT 2121 strike. It contended that the ACCJC violated state labor law by using sanctions and standards to dictate terms of faculty wages and working conditions. It also challenged the ACCJC's secretive practices, asserting that the commission should be covered by California open meeting laws.

Direct Action Gets the Goods

After the strike, AFT 2121 bargained for three more months before reaching a settlement that made substantial progress. The July 11, 2016, tentative agreement restored lost wages and provided raises for both full-time and part-time faculty. Members would get the biggest wage bump in the first year of the contract. All would see at least an 11.4 percent raise by the end of the three-year agreement.

"The goal of our contract campaign was to win a contract without concessions that supports the College that San Francisco deserves," AFT 2121 president Tim Killikelly said in his message to members. "This Tentative Agreement will support faculty in delivering quality and accessible public higher education. . . . We did not give into the District's tactics of trying to divide students from faculty and pit faculty against each other," he said. Still, he noted, "We were not able to unlock all of these moneys without agreeing to some conditions."[6]

After the contract expired in 2018, the pay increases would shrink if the Proposition A parcel tax was not renewed or if enrollment did not increase. AFT 2121 got the administration to drop a proposal that would have made it easier to cancel low-enrolled courses, but they were unable to push the minimum class size down.

Some members objected to the conditions attached to the wage increases and the union's willingness to accept restrictions on its ability to bargain over class cuts. The Educational Employment Relations Act separates the issues that management must bargain over from those it has the right to handle at will. Class cancellations fall under "management rights." Still, some members felt the union should have fought harder to expand the terrain. "Any discussion around the contract must include a discussion of what is the most critical issue: How can we successfully fight to stop the planned class cuts?" political science professor Rick Baum wrote in an online forum.[7]

After five weeks of discussion and voting, the union announced on August 24 that the tentative agreement had been approved by a vote of 574 to 16. With the new contract, AFT 2121 pushed back the attack on working conditions that was a central part of the makeover agenda. Even so, attempts to downsize the school gained momentum as real estate developers reshaped San Francisco. Families kept getting pushed out, and places they relied on went with them—bars and restaurants, theaters, and neighborhood stores.

CHAPTER SIXTEEN

Back to the Land
2016

B y 2016, the gentrification of San Francisco showed starkly in the neighborhood around City College's Mission Campus. Corner stores, Hunt's Donuts, El Mahahual Salvadoran/Colombian Restaurant, and the nearby drag bar Esta Noche had all shut down, replaced by trendy watering holes and pricey boutiques. As you headed toward the Ocean Avenue campus of City College on the no. 49 bus, the upscale retail gave way to neighborhood businesses—but Avalon's luxury apartment building had just gone up a few blocks from the campus, with a Whole Foods next door.

The changes in the physical space that come as people are displaced are part of breaking communities, Fernando Marti of the Council of Community Housing Organizations observed. Communities lose all kinds of resources—cultural spaces, nonprofits, stores. "The downsizing of City College fits that pattern," Marti said.

Several knotty development issues faced the City College trustees as soon as they regained their full power in January 2016. Discussions of development at the former Civic Center Campus site and at 33 Gough Street occupied a chunk of nearly every board agenda. The campus/community coalition that came together around the Civic Center closure kept pressing the board of trustees to rebuild classroom space rather than unaffordable housing at the beloved Eddy Street site. Save CCSF activists and allies urged the trustees to prioritize affordable housing development at 33 Gough and the Balboa Reservoir, rather than surrendering public land to private profit. They also called on the board to protect the site for the Performing Arts Education Center (PAEC) and make sure that parking and other transportation options were taken into account in the Reservoir development.

After several months of organizing, PAEC supporters won formal backing from the trustees for building the PAEC. San Francisco voters had twice approved the arts center, which offered the college a chance to add new courses and new revenues. Over the four years of crisis and downsizing, the elegant building had also come to stand for the message that "City College will rise again." The board passed a multipart resolution at its July 28, 2016, meeting that called for a stronger City College voice in the Reservoir development.

Advocacy at the Balboa Reservoir Community Advisory Committee (BRCAC) proved less fruitful. City planners kept paying lip service to protecting parking at the school, while relying on data that appeared to be purposely skewed,[1] putting forward a Transportation Demand Management (TDM) plan that minimized the need. TDM strategies explicitly aim to reduce car trips—a laudable goal, but one that depends on a highly functional transit system. In order not to compromise student access, transit would need to be frequent and reliable, and bus and rail lines within the city would have to connect smoothly with each other and with regional transit. This was not always the case, so mass transit often was not a viable option for City College students and teachers juggling school, family, and work.

"Our students' lives are fragile, packed. You have single parents, part-time workers, people who have to take a car if they want to go to City College. They don't have time to take one MUNI bus after another," said Monica Collins, who worked in the financial aid office for fifteen years. Faculty had a stake too: many of the growing numbers of part-time teachers were "freeway flyers" who traveled from college to college to piece together a living.

In June, yet another development issue zoomed into focus: the new Facilities Master Plan for the school. The plan called for tearing down and rebuilding so many of the aging buildings on the school's main campus that it seemed like an invitation to chaos and downsizing. "Now they are proposing the demolition of Cloud Hall, the main classroom building at Ocean, and literally almost all the other buildings," Vicki Legion noted. "Just the disruption from so much construction seems like it could have a major impact on shrinking the school."

A revived PAEC appeared in a later draft of the plan. Alongside the PAEC ran a sixty-foot-wide access road leading not into the campus, but into the planned reservoir housing development—despite the trustees' opposition to just such a road.

The trustees approved an agreement in October to develop housing at the 33 Gough Street site. The team of Equity Community Builders and Integral got a ground lease for seventy-five years, with an option to extend it another twenty-five years. They only promised 33 percent ostensibly "affordable" housing, the amount required by law.

Who Benefits?

From the beginning, Save CCSF saw privatization at work in the City College crisis and understood that the for-profit colleges and real estate developers stood to gain from City's losses. The first proposals to put the Gough Street administration building on the market suggested that real estate interests had their eyes on college land. The closure of the Civic Center Campus and the Reservoir development made this more obvious, and the Research Committee started digging deeper into the political interests at work and their connections to City College.

Bounded by water on three sides, San Francisco can't sprawl outward. This heightens the value of every square foot of its nearly forty-seven square miles—and the influence of its real estate industry. Developers (joined more recently by the tech industry) have been top political contributors. A 2016 investigative report in the *San Francisco Public Press* documented the flood of money unleashed by allies of Mayor Ed Lee to shape elections and public policy in the city.[2] "Last year spending on local elections was the highest on record, reaching nearly $28 million," wrote reporters Angela Woodall and Michael Stoll. "The outsized and increasing power of the tech and real estate sectors threatens to overwhelm any constituencies that might seek to challenge them."[3]

The Hearst family, which owns the *San Francisco Chronicle*, has been a real estate powerhouse since the late 1800s.[4] In 2015, the Hearst Corporation partnered with Forest City Realty on a four-acre megaproject to go up on land just a block from City College's Downtown Campus. From the first days of the accreditation crisis, the *Chronicle* had slammed City College and suggested it was just too big but could "recoup its academic standing" by shedding students and real estate.

"Developers are adept at catching waves," said Calvin Welch, who teaches postwar San Francisco history at San Francisco State University and was for years one of the city's key affordable housing activists. "If City College could be done in, it would make a lot of real estate available."

Enrollment Sabotage?

With development encroaching on its physical spaces, City College enrollment hit a low point of 36,453 for the fall 2016 semester, down 20 percent from the beginning of the crisis.

In January 2016, the administration had hired Susan Lopez as the Adult Enrollment Coordinator. An ESL teacher, Lopez had spent hundreds of hours of her "free" time helping to coordinate the all-volunteer enrollment outreach campaign. Now, for the first time, that campaign had institutional support, including money to hire assistants for the spring semester.

Funding for the vibrant faculty-led effort tremendously expanded the scope of the college's Office of Outreach, which up till then had only targeted high school seniors. Out of the office tucked away at Mission Campus, Lopez coordinated outreach for both noncredit and credit programs, as well as academic and career education programs and college services that promoted retention and success.

The short side hallway in front of the office became a staging area for outreach activities. Long tables held piles of the various outreach materials, "arranged in overlapping fashion like clay roof tiles. In all its multicolored, eye-catching glory, it reflected visually the broad college mission and the colorful variety of its classes and services. We aimed to maintain diversity at the college by creating translated materials and materials targeted to homeless, to LGBTQ, to African Americans, Asians, and Latinos, or neighborhoods rarely touched in the past by outreach," Lopez said. She developed a two-pronged strategy. "We combined what you might call 'bang for the buck outreach' to populations who already participated in significant numbers with thoughtful outreach to other populations who needed extra encouragement to enroll." Working full-time, she could recruit more volunteers who, with paid assistants, could do outreach at large community events like citywide citizenship fairs and the LGBT Pride Parade.

Funding also made it possible "to increase accountability by researching and quantifying both activities and effectiveness. As an experienced college researcher, I did a study of zip code penetration via outreach compared to increases in enrollment by zip code. Yes, we made a difference!!"

Lopez said. But funding for assistants was eliminated in fall 2016, hampering the outreach effort when it was most needed.

Course offerings plummeted even more steeply than enrollment, with noncredit getting hit twice as hard. The number of credit courses dropped by more than 22 percent, while the number of noncredit courses was nearly halved.[5]

A year earlier the administration announced its intention to cut 26 percent of classes by 2020. The seemingly irrational way class cuts got made led people to speculate about "enrollment sabotage."

"Classes are being closed before chairs can fully look at department offerings from spring 2016: We need to look at what worked, what didn't work and what needs to change," the Department Chairperson Council wrote in a September 2016 open letter published in CCSF's student newspaper, the *Guardsman*.

Even core vocational programs came under the knife. For years, City College had trained San Francisco's firefighters. A spurt of hiring by CalFire and local fire departments generated unprecedented enrollment, but the Fire Science Department couldn't offer enough prerequisite sections to meet students' needs. "Once a course is cut out of a program, we cannot offer that certificate, so we have had quite a few reductions over the last few years," said Business Department chair Ophelia Clark. She was among the dozens of students and faculty members who offered public comment protesting the cuts at the board of trustees meetings in October and November.

James Corsentino, a student at CCSF's Evans Campus and a recently separated Army veteran, showed up to both the November and December meetings to advocate for one of the specialized programs at City. "There are several veterans in the automotive, motorcycle, construction, and other technical programs at Evans Campus," Cosentino said. "If classes are cut, we're going to have to go to other schools, and there are no other schools in the Bay Area with a motorcycle program."

Older adults were hit hard by cuts in noncredit classes. Between spring 2015 and spring 2016, more than half of the noncredit students lost were older than fifty, and a majority were students of color, according to Susan Lopez. Most of the loss came from the school's decision to cut back health education classes at thirty-one sites around the city where seniors gathered for free hot lunch.

Substantial layoffs and retirement incentives shrank the faculty from 1,814 in fall 2011 to 1,426 in fall 2016. This too had an impact on course offerings. AFT 2121 reported that fifty-eight full-time faculty were retiring at the end of the 2016–2017 school year; nineteen of those were in ESL. The administration only planned to hire three full-time teachers as replacements. This would leave many sections unstaffed, five in Chinatown alone, cutting classes that were fully enrolled.[6] "In fall 2016, we were told to cut fifty hours from our schedule even though demand was high," Chinatown/North Beach ESL teacher Kate Frei said. Classes held anywhere from twenty to sixty-five students, the vast majority of them speakers of Mandarin or Cantonese, ranging in age from eighteen to eighty.

With all the stress and distress in the air, "You go in the classroom and see your students' faces, and that's what makes you want to fight and persist," Frei said.

Oh, Yes, ACCJC

Meanwhile, official efforts to reform and replace the ACCJC plodded on. Members of the Board of Governors and several CEOs of California community colleges cooperated all year in two work groups, one focused on reforming the ACCJC and the other on longer-range plans for changing accreditors.

Save CCSF raised funds for a third trip to the National Advisory Committee on Institutional Quality and Integrity (NACIQI), the DOE's advisory body on accreditation. A strongly worded letter to Education Secretary John King from House Minority Leader Nancy Pelosi and Representatives Jackie Speier and Anna Eshoo bolstered their case. The representatives urged the DOE to deny recognition to the ACCJC, because the agency "has inconsistently applied accreditation standards and ignored federal regulations; has lost support of California's chancellors, state officials, and unions; and has been the subject of multiple lawsuits. Simply put: neither the Department nor NACIQI can justify the continued recognition of ACCJC as a quality, fair or reliable accreditor."[7]

Fair or not, the ACCJC sent an evaluation team to City College in October 2016 before the make-or-break decision on the college's compliance. The two-year "restoration" period would expire in January 2017. If the commission determined that City College hadn't met the standards 100 percent, closure would be inevitable. The college was still on Death Row.

As AFT 2121, Save CCSF, and all their allies eroded the commission's legitimacy, they fought an ever-widening battle against downsizing the school. It looked like Pamila Fisher's prophecy might be coming true:

"You'll survive, but you won't recognize yourselves." Then a daring political jiujitsu move by the union changed the story: a proposal for a ballot measure that would make City College tuition-free again.

CHAPTER SEVENTEEN

Free City Flips the Script
2016

For four years, state officials, interim administrators, and local and national media had blistered CCSF for its broad interpretation of what a community college should do. The proposal to make City College tuition-free—Alisa Messer's inspiration—offered a practical way to bolster the college's battered enrollment, addressed the deepening inequality in San Francisco, and threw down a political challenge to the constricted vision of community college put out by the ACCJC and the corporate reformers.

"We're looking at competing visions, what we call a tale of two cities," said JJ Vivek Narayan, a member of the CCSF students' Solidarity Committee. "One vision is what we call McCity College, Inc., a downsized corporate model in which marginalized students are pushed out, and this mirrors the gentrification and eviction of diverse communities from San Francisco. It's a vision of the college and of San Francisco as a whole, because City College is the heart of San Francisco. Our vision is of community values being restored, enrollment being restored, community college being free again like it was before 1984, a college that supports the community and life-long learning."[1]

San Francisco Supervisor Jane Kim first announced Free City at an April 19 press conference on the City Hall steps, surrounded by a knot of union and community supporters holding the iconic yellow and red "Honk if you Love CCSF" banner. Board of Education president Matt Haney led the chant "No cuts! No fees! Education should be free!" Kim rolled out the proposal in more detail at the board of supervisors meeting May 24. She framed Free City as "a package of legislation that will help make another critical component in keeping our city's stability and growing our middle class. There is a pervasive sense that we are losing the city we once loved, along with the community, one person at a time. Friends, fellow parishioners, and neighborhood businesses to teachers, nurses, and artists, no one is immune to the wave of displacement that is sweeping our Bay Area."

Six more supervisors joined Kim in sponsoring the legislation, which would pay tuition for all students attending City College who lived in San Francisco, as well as those who worked for the city and county, the San Francisco Unified School District, and City College itself. Low-income students who already qualified for tuition assistance (about 70 percent of all students) would get $1,000 per year for books and school costs, including transportation.

Other states and cities had or were considering free college programs, and President Barack Obama had proposed America's College Promise. But these other efforts required students to follow a full-time transfer or certificate track and/or maintain a certain grade point average. Such conditions excluded most of the working students and community members for whom the community colleges were designed. San Francisco's Free City would be available to anyone who met the residency or work requirements, regardless of educational path, academic prowess, or immigration status. It affirmed the open-access vision at the heart of CCSF's fight to survive and put that vision to a vote.

Free City backers haunted City Hall at every step in the intricate process of turning a policy into a law. The first full board of supervisors vote on Free City, on July 12, brought out about 150 supporters for a rally and lobby day. After visiting each supervisor, the crowd filled the hall that led to the board's chambers, exhorting the lawmakers on their way in. When Jane Kim walked by in her trademark red suit, the crowd cheered and parted as if for royalty. The measure that passed that day by 10–1 committed the supervisors to supporting Free City by securing funding. The next week, they voted to put a revenue measure on the November ballot: a .25 percent tax on real estate transactions in San Francisco worth more than $5 million. The "mansion tax" measure became Proposition W. The supervisors opted to put it on the ballot as an unrestricted tax so it could pass with a simple majority.

The Free City campaign built on the successful defense of the Civic Center Campus. "At the end of that fight people were energized," said James Tracy of Community Housing Partnership. He noted that the community activists in 3CPE saw the AFT "treat them like actual people with analysis and talents," and the respectful relations paved the way for the Free City work. So did the working relationship 3CPE built with supervisor Jane Kim.

"There are so many organizations in the Tenderloin committed to keeping San Francisco vibrant and diverse, protecting vulnerable people, and that captures the core of how 2121 wants to engage," Athena Waid said. "3CPE led to Free City because of the relationship with Jane Kim and the power we built in the community." Several key organizations from 3CPE anchored the Free City coalition—AFT 2121, CHP, La Voz Latina, and Young Workers United—along with the San Francisco Labor Council and Jobs with Justice. As the campaign grew, it lined up twenty organizational endorsements. Members of the Solidarity Committee also put in many hours getting the word out and organizing mobilizations.

Shoe-leather efforts to pass Proposition W kicked up in earnest in the fall. James Tracy, who cochaired the campaign with Alisa Messer and SFLC executive director Tim Paulson, estimated the Free City team walked about one-third of San Francisco's six hundred precincts and made more than a thousand phone calls. AFT 2121 ran phone banks out of its small second-floor office Monday through Thursday for the final weeks of the campaign.

Playing in a High-Stakes Election

Proposition W shared the high-stakes 2016 ballot with twenty-two other local propositions, several important state initiatives, and pivotal elections for office holders from the White House to the school board. From the high-profile District 11 state senate race on down-ballot, the campaign reflected the battle between the city's progressives and more developer-friendly forces. Supervisor Jane Kim challenged fellow supervisor Scott Wiener for the state senate seat, with Free City central to her campaign. Wiener, along with three other supervisors, put Proposition Q on the ballot, which would have made it illegal to pitch tents on city sidewalks without a permit. Kim had beaten Wiener in the June primary, despite being outspent two to one, but neither won a clear majority, making a runoff necessary.

The progressives' one-vote majority on the board of supervisors hung in the balance, with three of their stalwarts termed out—Eric Mar, David Campos, and John Avalos—and heated races for six of the eleven seats on the board. Shanell Williams sought to translate her student activism for City College into a seat on the board of trustees.

The nearly two dozen San Francisco ballot measures included Proposition B, an extension and increase of the parcel tax passed in 2012 for City College teachers' salaries and instructional support. The statewide and local realtors' associations funded a pair of propositions that could have slowed the production of affordable housing and made it harder for low-income families to get into below-market-rate housing.

The polarized election set off an unprecedented flood of campaign contributions from outside the city. In the state senate race alone, outside committees donated $15 million to Scott Wiener by late October, five times as much as they gave to Jane Kim, according to the *San Francisco Chronicle*.[2]

At the state level, voters had the chance to approve two important education funding measures: Proposition 51, a bond issue to raise money for improving public school facilities; and Proposition 55, an extension of the 2012 "Millionaires Tax" to support public education, from kindergarten through community college.

The national presidential conventions had given way to the campaign, but the energy generated by Senator Bernie Sanders's run continued to animate activists. The Proposition W campaign benefited from his high-profile advocacy for free college, and Supervisor Jane Kim proudly carried his endorsement. Senator Sanders highlighted an October 15 GOTV rally organized by Kim's campaign to showcase the progressive candidates and issues. "Even I thought Free City College was a pipedream until Senator Sanders talked about it in his campaign. Then Alisa Messer and Mike Casey from the Labor Council came to my office, and here we are today," Kim said. She shared the stage with Shanell Williams and two other candidates for the board of trustees, gay activist Tom Temprano and board president Rafael Mandelman—along with three Board of Education candidates and one supervisorial hopeful. The crowd, packed shoulder to shoulder in Kim's Civic Center storefront office, shouted "Bernie, Bernie," and he answered the call.

"At the end of the day you make the revolution by mobilizing people to go door-to-door, make calls, and talk to their neighbors," Sanders reminded the crowd at the end of his stump speech, as much of a stem-winder as any he delivered that year. The real business of the day was a massive canvass of the one hundred most progressive precincts in the city.

Voters Affirm Free City

Footsore Free City campaigners saw the payoff for their hard work on November 8, when Proposition W passed with almost 62 percent of the vote. Proposition B, the college's parcel tax renewal, won with 83 percent, the biggest "yes" for anything on the ballot. Shanell Williams handily won her seat on the board of trustees. Voters gave the nod to Tom Temprano and Rafael Mandelman as well. State Propositions 51 and 55 also passed, promising to funnel more funding to schools.

The good news for City College proved the biggest bright spot in the election. San Francisco lost the progressive majority on the board of supervisors by four hundred votes, and the measures that would have reined in the mayor's power all went down to defeat. Jane Kim lost the state senate seat to Scott Wiener. Then there was the presidential election, delivered to Donald Trump by the Electoral College despite his loss of the popular vote. Massive protests and outbreaks of hate crimes followed.

"We didn't think things like this happened here," Venette Cook's ESL students told her. She and other teachers at Civic Center prepared handouts for the students on what to do if US Immigration and Customs Enforcement (ICE) came knocking. The board of trustees unanimously approved a resolution December 15 that declared, "City College of San Francisco joins the City and County of San Francisco in affirming its sanctuary status for all people of San Francisco." The city's sanctuary law made it a favorite Trump target, and Mayor Lee turned this hostility to his advantage; he refused to allocate Proposition W funds to Free City, saying that the city might have more pressing needs if the new president followed through on his threat to withhold federal funds from sanctuary cities. Now Free City, CCSF's newborn hope for boosting enrollment and bolstering open access, was threatened. But an even more serious threat loomed. ACCJC's two-year "restoration" period was to expire in January 2017. If the commission deemed CCSF had failed to meet any of its of its standards, accreditation would be pulled. Immediately. Game over. No appeal. There would be no CCSF to save.

CHAPTER EIGHTEEN

A Chance to Rebuild

January–February 2017

The ACCJC had accreditation decisions for thirty-four colleges on its January 13, 2017, agenda, including City College of San Francisco. It was a week before Trump's inauguration and the last day of winter break for CCSF. It was also the birthday of one of Alisa Messer's best friends, and Messer was driving to meet her for a movie matinee. "I had just parked and I was sitting in my car when the news came," Messer said. The ACCJC had announced that it was reaccrediting CCSF for the full seven years. "I just sat in the car and sobbed. Then I just started texting everyone I could think of. I was a little late meeting my friends. They looked at me and said, 'Oh my god, are you okay?' because I still had tears streaming down my face. I looked like the world had just ended, but I was crying tears of joy and relief."

Wynd Kaufmyn's phone beeped with the good news while she and Karen Saginor were heading east on Interstate 80 to attend the ACCJC meeting and make their umpteenth public comment. They decided to go to the meeting anyway. "It was so weird," Kaufmyn said. "Up until that time, every time that we went to these meetings, there were guards at the gate, security people escorting us out, a very tense, hostile, acrimonious situation. This time Karen and I walked in the room, and we were welcomed. We were hugged by a couple members of the commission. They were just so happy for us. 'Oh, you got your accreditation. Congratulations, you did such good work.' That was so hard to take. I thought, 'Really, you're just going to pretend that the destruction and trauma you put on us was our fault, and now we're good little children and got in line and everything's okay. And we're just going to be happy and forgive you?' It was a strange tension because the people who had been so mean to us were now being nice."

Even though it had been fired by the Board of Governors and put on notice by the Department of Education, the commission admitted no fault. It reaccredited the school but kept the "bad City College" spin going. Karen Saginor took exception. "When we spoke we said, 'This is great news. We're really happy to hear it. But there are issues you still need to deal with.'" Saginor said. "We felt like they didn't want to deal with these issues. They were basically saying to City College, 'Okay, we fixed your situation, now get off our backs. You got yours; sit down and shut up.' So, I think that one of the things we said was 'Thank you very much for City College, but there are structural issues you need to deal with, so you don't ever do this again.'"

For some, the impact of the announcement was muted by exhaustion and the whirl and worry of responding to the election. "Lalo [Gonzalez] kept saying we should have a party, but we were just too tired to plan it," Vicki Legion said. "But still, I felt like the ninth pyramid of Giza just slipped off my shoulders."

Other key actors in the accreditation fight joined a chorus of relief and celebration. "City College is part of the fabric of San Francisco. It provides hope, community, and opportunity to anyone who needs it. I'm happy we were able to do our part to help keep the school open, and I'm thrilled this vital institution will now be able to serve its students and our city for generations to come," City Attorney Dennis Herrera said in a press release. The national American Federation of Teachers, the California Federation of Teachers, and AFT 2121 all weighed in. "All of us at the college are so excited and relieved that the accreditation crisis is over," said AFT 2121 president Tim Killikelly, "but we mustn't forget that the accreditation crisis at CCSF should never have occurred. The quality of its education was never in doubt."

Recently elected City College trustee Shanell Williams had been a student at the school when the crisis began in 2012, and she spent the next four years organizing and advocating to keep it open. She said regaining the school's fully accredited status was "a dream come true," while acknowledging the difficult work ahead to rebuild enrollment. "Moving forward locally, we'll be able to regain thousands of students that we've lost over the years. We have to make sure that Free CCSF becomes a reality."

After almost five years of meetings, demonstrations, leaflets, and occupations, of staying up late and getting up early, of neglecting family and health and well-being, defenders of CCSF's mission and vision would barely have time to take a deep breath before the next battle.

Free City: Making the Mayor Deliver

Mayor Ed Lee used the election results as an excuse to refuse to fund Free City, defying the voters and the supervisors. His office cited the defeat of a local sales tax that would have funded transit improvements and services for homeless people and the fear that the city would lose federal dollars because it was a sanctuary city.[1]

Technically, Mayor Lee had the authority to shift budget priorities. San Francisco's city charter gives the mayor substantial power, including discretion over spending. Proposition W had been put on the ballot as an unrestricted tax so it would only need a simple majority to pass. (Taxes for restricted purposes, like the parcel tax, need a two-thirds vote.) But all the discussion of Proposition W linked it to Free City, as did the supervisors' votes, and posters all over town.

"A promise is a promise," Supervisor Aaron Peskin said at the December 15 board meeting. "Ten of eleven members of this board voted to prioritize City College with Proposition W, and it was all there in the campaign."

Free City backers rallied, determined to push the mayor to do the right thing. They lobbied some more, enlisted support from City College alum Danny Glover, and serenaded the supervisors with Free City carols. The supervisors took two more votes in favor of a $9 million appropriation for the project, but the fight dragged into the new year.

Supervisor Jane Kim and CCSF trustee Rafael Mandelman introduced a resolution in favor of full funding for Free City at the San Francisco Democratic County Central Committee meeting on January 25, 2017. Approval of the resolution by one of the most potent political forces in the city finally pushed Mayor Lee to stop blocking the program. "We hoped by building enough public pressure we could encourage Mayor Lee to avoid the embarrassment of going against the will of the voters who passed Prop W to fund Free City," said AFT 2121 organizer Athena Waid. On February 6, Supervisor Kim stood next to the mayor as they announced an agreement that the city would use $5.4 million of the mansion tax revenues to fund Free City. The news went viral, with Lee claiming his share of the credit for the project he tried to scuttle. "To California residents who are living in San Francisco, your community college is now free," Lee said at the news conference.

But Mayor Lee had drastically cut the funding for the program, singlehandedly halving the amount set aside for Free City by the board of supervisors.[2] The $5.4 million Lee decided to spend was only 12 percent of the $44 million the San Francisco Controller's Office estimated the tax would net in an average year. The funding cut meant that stipends for things like books and transportation would only run about $500 per year, instead of the $1,000 Proposition W backers originally hoped for.

Two-thirds of undocumented students, who pay hefty out-of-state tuition, were not eligible at all.[3] Had they been included in Free City, San Francisco would have had to cover the much pricier out-of-state tuition fees, $280 per unit, rather than the $46 per unit charged to California residents.[4] Students from the Solidarity Committee took the lead in protesting the exclusions at the board of trustees meeting on February 9. "There is no liberation for some of us unless there is liberation for all of us," said JJ Narayan. "If we are truly to be a sanctuary campus, we need to be committed to fighting to be sure this reaches all of our students."

The trustees responded with a resolution directing the college administration to secure funds for grants or scholarships to help the excluded students. Then they passed the Free City proposal amid much jubilation. Though it wasn't everything supporters had hoped for, it still stood as the most inclusive free college program in the United States. Following so closely on reaccreditation, the Free City agreement seemed to signal a new day. "Nothing could be better for City College than to turn the final pages of the accreditation crisis into a victory that looks like this," Alisa Messer said. "This is a victory for public education."

Rekindling the Vision: The Wins

It was a David and Goliath moment. City College was open, accredited—and free. The ACCJC was flat on its back. The campaign forced changes in the ACCJC's procedures and top leadership. Barbara Beno had already announced her plan to retire in June 2017, but the commission beat her to the punch and put her on administrative leave on December 15, 2016. The rest of her executive team resigned as well.

The holstering of reaccreditation as a weapon was a victory not just for CCSF but for all the other colleges in the region that had been subject to the arbitrary power of the ACCJC. Compton College in Los Angeles, a major educational asset for Latinx and Black communities, had its local board reinstated after a full decade of state takeover. The statewide sanction rate fell dramatically. At subsequent meetings, the commission affirmed accreditation for all the colleges under review.[5]

The settlement agreement in the CFT lawsuit, which would be reached later in the year, barred some of the most intrusive uses of accreditation sanctions. The ACCJC agreed not to meddle in collective bargaining, not to call for the use of Student Learning Outcomes in faculty evaluations, and not to tell colleges how to stabilize their finances.

Free City models an inclusive free college program, unlike the more common "free college lite" versions that apply only to first-time full-time students and may require them to fill out the onerous federal financial aid (FAFSA) paperwork. Not only does FAFSA call for extensive data that is difficult for many students to gather, but 70 percent of the proffered "aid" comes in the form of student loans.[6]

AFT 2121 built strength through the crisis. It knit broader and tighter relationships with community organizations and became more active and influential in the San Francisco labor movement and in city politics.

The campaign to keep an ESL campus open in the heavily immigrant Tenderloin was won by a powerful coalition of CCSF union organizers, immigrant rights groups, and advocates for the homeless. That victory improved the faculty union's relationship to these communities in San Francisco and kept a campus in a neighborhood near downtown that has successfully defeated developer land grabs for decades.

The consciousness of thousands of people would never be the same. After hundreds of meetings and scores of demonstrations, teachers who had previously lived in the small worlds of their home departments now knew people across the college's campuses and greeted members of allied community organizations with hugs. Generations of students had become committed organizers and activists and learned movement history and power analysis from faculty veterans. Hundreds of people had learned the basics of how to read an arcane budget.

Department chairs held off the attempt to make them serve at will. They retained their status as elected frontline leadership. The Diversity Collaborative (the Ethnic Studies and Social Justice Departments) mobilized their community allies and held on to the autonomy they needed to support students and help nurture their community ties.

A Chance to Rebuild

"People have more agency than they think they do," Karen Saginor observed, "and when people have a lot of power and tell you, 'You don't have any power; there's nothing you can do,' they're not telling you the truth. In fact, there's a lot people can do. The accreditation fight was such an uphill fight against an organization that seemed not to answer to anybody. Yet in the long run, because there were a lot of us, because we continued to resist, because we were smart about making the decisions about how we resisted and what we did, and all the different things people did to resist, eventually ACCJC lost."

People make struggle, and struggle makes people. And within the movement to save City College, a core of committed organizers, not just the OGs but younger faculty and students as well, gained a deeper understanding of the forces and issues involved. As Wynd Kaufmyn said, "What we won is the chance to rebuild."

One Struggle Sets the Table for the Next

Fall 2019

Alone among his colleagues at the Social Sciences Department meeting, Tarik Farrar did not clap and cheer at the news that City College had been reaccredited. "I was certainly glad that the threat of closing the school was over. But so much damage had already been done. . . . The agenda is set, and any chancellor that assumes power with the blessing of the state chancellor is going to push that agenda forward. And that's exactly what we see today."

City College was open, accredited, and free—but it bore deep battle scars. The five-year fight cost CCSF twenty-three thousand students, 42 percent of its enrollment, nearly one-quarter of its credit classes and more than 40 percent of its noncredit sections, mainly English as a Second Language and basic skills. The college lost a third of its full-time faculty, 12 percent of its part-time faculty, and 14 percent of its classified staff.

Downsizing also shrank the school's physical footprint. After leasing 33 Gough Street to a real estate developer, CCSF ended up spending $650,000 per year to rent back its own space for its business offices.[1] Plans to privatize the lower Balboa Reservoir for largely unaffordable housing were moving forward despite ongoing resistance.[2] The building that housed the Civic Center Campus had yet to be retrofit. In 2019, the administration contracted a real estate firm to study its sale and lease value, as well as that of the Downtown and Chinatown/North Beach Campuses.

In its first two semesters, the Free City program served 24,030 students of all ages, ethnicities, and San Francisco zip codes. AFT 2121 and the Free City coalition organized for more than a year to get ongoing funding. Finally, in September 2019, CCSF and the City and County of San Francisco signed a ten-year agreement on Free City for $15 million per year for ten years—but with no guarantee that the program will continue to be so inclusive. "Open access will still have to be defended," Alisa Messer said.[3]

Just before midnight on the day before spring 2020 registration opened, CCSF's top administrators slashed more than three hundred classes. The cuts decimated the Older Adults Program. Eighty-five classes that students needed to complete certificates and degrees were axed. The cuts took out 40 percent of the engineering classes, fifty-one art classes, forty-three physical education and dance classes, the last women's history class, and several Ethnic Studies courses. The cuts also cost more than one hundred part-time faculty members their jobs and/or health insurance.

CCSF chancellor Mark Rocha first presented the cuts as a budget-balancing measure. But then he rejected efforts to raise emergency funding, saying this was "part of a long-planned restructuring of the academic program to prioritize the graduation of students of color."[4] In fact, the Success Agenda was narrowing rather than widening opportunities. Over the five years of the accreditation crisis, that agenda—so wholeheartedly opposed by CCSF students, faculty, and administrators in 2012—had taken root in California.

"Student Success" Means Student Pushout Policies

Between 2008 and 2018, the California community colleges lost more than half a million students—a decline of 18 percent—while the state's population grew by 8 percent. Student Success Task Force measures and new regulations have become pushout policies.

- Financially needy students had been able to get free tuition at California community colleges since 1984 through the California Community Colleges Board of Governors fee waiver. The Academic Progress Rule restricts eligibility for the waiver to students who earn a grade point average of at least 2.0, complete at least 50 percent of their coursework, and do not miss two or more semesters in a row.
- The "repeatability rule" bars students from repeating a credit course if they have passed it, and from taking more than four skills-based classes in the same "family"—so no more than four in performing arts, visual arts, foreign languages, or physical education. This rule hits skills-based classes that require repeated practice and spelled major downsizing for physical education, arts, and music.

- The "unit cap" moves students with one hundred or more units to the back of the enrollment line, making it harder for them to get classes.

Tide of Corporate "Reform" Rises in California

New state chancellor Eloy Ortiz Oakley aggressively expanded the "student success" agenda. Soon after his appointment in 2016, he launched the "Vision for Success" strategic plan for the California Community Colleges, billed as the way to close the achievement gaps for students of color in ten years. "The success of California's broader system of higher education and workforce development stands or falls with the community colleges," the "Vision" declared. Its seven goals include: a 20 percent increase in associate degrees, certificates, credentials, "or specific skill sets that prepare them for an in-demand job"; a 35 percent increase in transfers to the California State University or University of California systems; a decrease in the average units students take before graduation from eighty-seven to seventy-nine.

The "Vision" also promotes full-time attendance and "on-time graduation," penalizes part-time students and lifelong learners, and moves control over curriculum and student services from the faculty and elected trustees of community college districts to the state chancellor's office. The document says nothing about the need to increase overall funding for the colleges to provide the supports students would need to meet these ambitious goals.

Speeding Students Through: Guided Pathways and Remediation Reform

The "Vision" relies on curriculum changes to speed up students' passage through school. Guided Pathways narrows much of the curriculum into six to ten meta-majors: full-time, highly prescribed, and standardized sequences. This sidelines offerings in the arts, humanities, and world languages, and the ethnic and social justice studies that previous generations of students fought for.

Former governor Jerry Brown loved Guided Pathways. In a speech to the California Chamber of Commerce, Brown likened education to the fast-food restaurant Chipotle. "What I like about Chipotle is the limited menu. You stand in the line, get either brown rice or white rice, black beans or pinto beans. You put a little cheese, a little this, a little that, and you're out of there. I think that's a model some of our universities need to follow. . . . [I]f universities would adopt a limited-menu concept, everyone would graduate on time."[5]

The "faster is better" trend also impacts assessment and support for students who arrived unprepared for college-level work. Students Making a Change (SMAC), which spurred the equity conversation at City, united with the Campaign for College Opportunity to lobby for state legislation that set up new rules for placement and remediation.[6] Now students can use their high school GPA to go directly into "transfer-level" English and math. While colleges can require "corequisite" courses, the legislation does not mandate extra tutoring or other supports.

"If you're a conventional learner, somewhat prepared, you'll do fine," CCSF English instructor Tehmina Khan said. But many students have experienced twelve years of profoundly unequal K–12 education, saddled with the least experienced teachers, the biggest class sizes, and crumbling facilities. If such students do not get sufficient extra help, the new approach could set them up to crash and burn. "If you learn differently and are less prepared, are more concerned about your own safety or your family, you may not do as well," Khan said. The jury is still out.

Free College Lite

In a frothy August 2019 press release, Governor Gavin Newsom announced that the state would be providing two years of free tuition "for the first time in decades" to an additional thirty-three thousand students. (California community colleges served nearly 2.4 million students in the 2018–2019 school year.)[7] First-time full-time students would be eligible, regardless of need. But the money, appropriated under the California Promise Program, comes with strings: colleges must implement Guided Pathways and participate in federal student loan programs. Most "free college" programs being proposed around the country either condition fee waivers on full-time attendance, as California Promise does, or only fill the gap left by other sources of assistance. But the push to go full-time can make free college expensive.

Guided Pathways, along with the attendance requirements in California Promise and the Academic Progress Rule, undermines the flexibility that has enabled students to avoid the debt trap by working while attending community college. CCSF Administration of Justice professor Fred Chavaria would ask his students how many were working, and three-quarters of them would raise their hands—mirroring the percent of part-time students in the state community college system.[8] Some of Chavaria's students had two or three jobs. It would be defeating to try to cram their education into two-and-a-half or three years. "Life happens, especially when you're supporting yourself," Chavaria said. He knew from experience: when he went to City on the GI Bill in the 1960s, it took him eight years to transfer to San Francisco State.

"Student Centered Funding Formula" Supports Success Agenda

Until 2018, state funding depended on the number of full-time equivalent students (FTES) enrolled in a community college district. This method supported the open-access mission. The new distribution—called the Student Centered Funding Formula, without a hint of irony—incorporates performance funding.

Ten percent of a district's appropriation is now based on the numbers of associate degrees, certificates, transfers, Career and Technical Education certificates, transfer-level math and English courses completed in the first year, and students earning a regional living wage in their first year out of school. Associate degrees for transfer bring the biggest incentive, followed by non-transfer associate degrees. Only full-time students are counted in these metrics.

The role of the mega-foundations in pushing the new wave of performance funding is no secret. The Lumina Foundation included the policy in its 2010 strategic plan and proclaims that it "has played a key role in the development of outcomes-based funding, and will continue to press for the implementation of next-generation approaches across the states."[9] In California, Lumina recruited former legislative analyst and Student Success Task Force executive director Amy Supinger to head its State Strategy Lab. Supinger cowrote the "Vision for Success," though her Lumina affiliation appears nowhere in the document.

Beyond Budgets: Collision of Visions at City College

Not a seat in the old-style lecture hall was empty when the City College board of trustees met December 12, 2019. People sat on the steps, stood two deep in the back, and hovered in the hall. In more than two hours of public comment—with speakers limited to a minute each—students, faculty, and supporters vented their anger and grief at the class cuts. Audience members responded to each testimony, cheering, clapping, and booing. The temperature in the room rose with the noise and fervor. Then

Brenda Garcia, an alumna of Project SURVIVE, stepped to the microphone, introduced herself—and choked, fighting back tears. The crowd fell silent. Board president Alex Randolph asked that the timer be paused while she collected herself. After a long quiet minute, a smattering of encouraging applause, and calls of "You've got this," Garcia regrouped. "I came to City College four years ago, after Heald College closed. I was twenty-six. I had left a domestic violence relationship. I heard about Project SURVIVE's classes. They helped me get a fresh start, helped me to restore myself to be the person I am now. City College was the only place I could be, because everything else was expensive. I work four jobs and still continue in school part-time. Project SURVIVE helped me and taught me a lot, and now I'm helping others in the community. This is why City College is important: because it's a community college. We help each other."

The trustees took no action on the class cuts.

The day before winter solstice, a new constellation of activists gathered to plan the next round of fightback, under the provisional name of Restore the Dream. As entrenched as the corporate reforms have become, the group can take heart from #RedForEd and community organizing in defense of K–12 public schools—and draw on lessons from the accreditation fight itself.

#RedForEd

When Chicago teachers struck in 2012, they took on a constellation of institutions, policies, and ideology three decades in the making. The teacher-blaming attack on public schools kicked off in the 1980s as part of the Reagan-era assault on the public sector. Charter schools, conceived as teacher-run experiments in the late 1980s, became big business over the 2000s and siphoned money from public schools. High-stakes testing previewed in Chicago after the city lost local control of its schools in 1995 and spread nationally after the 2001 passage of No Child Left Behind.

The Chicago Teachers Union organized with parents and community groups fighting school closures in Black and Latinx neighborhoods. "Fighting for the schools our children deserve," they not only made practical gains but began to change the conversation about education policy. In spring 2018, teachers struck in West Virginia, Arizona, and Oklahoma—red states where strikes were illegal. The next year saw teacher walkouts in Los Angeles, Denver, Chicago, and smaller cities in the growing #RedForEd movement. "The Spring 2018 movements radically shifted the national narrative about who is responsible for the education crisis," Eric Blanc wrote.[10]

One Struggle Sets the Table for the Next: Lessons from the CCSF Fight

Keeping City open and accredited "was a historic victory," CCSF Labor and Community Studies chair Bill Shields said. "That's hard to remember, because we're in another period of struggle now, but we're struggling on a higher plateau. We're in stronger shape because of the work we did then." Among the many lessons from that work:

Keep the Big Picture in Focus

In the fight to keep City College open, it was easy to lose sight of the agenda behind the education reform process. But the Save CCSF Research Committee persisted, identifying the tech billionaires and student loan companies, the foundations and their network of astroturf groups pushing the "student success" agenda.[11] Understanding the drivers of reform can make all the difference in organizing, as the K–12 organizing shows. As more information comes to light about charter school operators, the "greedy teacher" meme is eclipsed by calls like that in Oakland, California, to "Beat the Billionaires, No More Charter Schools."

All the Work Matters

To tackle the seemingly all-powerful and untouchable Accrediting Commission, organizers deployed strategies that reinforced each other. Real power to force the ACCJC to change lay with the Department of Education and the state Board of Governors. Elected officials had little direct impact, but AFT 2121 and CFT leveraged political relationships to move regulatory processes. Organizers found ways to engage skittish local, state, and federal elected officials with a combination of "street heat," careful research, and skillful lobbying. With state and local initiatives and support from legislators in the state capitol, organizers helped the college survive financially. The volunteer enrollment outreach campaign kept City College in the public eye and bolstered its student numbers.

Public outrage and off-the-record lobbying, plus the CFT/AFT complaint to the Department of Education, laid the basis for the City Attorney's lawsuit. The motion for an injunction to keep the college open bought valuable time. The suit educated the public and challenged the ACCJC's credibility, the trial exposed the agency, and Judge Karnow's ruling affirmed that City College had been treated unfairly. The settlement of the CFT/AFT suit forced reforms in the ACCJC's practices.

Build the Broadest Front Possible, and Start at Home

AFT 2121 had to shift its culture. It had relied on a small, committed (and sometimes radical) leadership to provide for members, but it had to systematically organize and activate its whole base in the many-sided fight to save the college. It changed its structures so members could more readily participate and visited faculty at home and at their offices. The local asked for and got vital support from its state and national union federations, the CFT and the AFT. It also worked with and alongside others who made their distinct contributions: the students, the Save CCSF coalition, and community groups like Jobs with Justice, Chinese for Affirmative Action, the Chinese Progressive Association, and all the Tenderloin neighborhood groups that came together to protest the closure of the Civic Center Campus. The Civic Center organizing fed into the campaign for Free City, which embodied the positive vision that powered the work.

Show People Something to Fight For

AFT 2121 and the Save CCSF Coalition won "the battle for the story." In a hostile media environment, they mobilized the love and support San Franciscans have for City College, embodied in the slogan "We Are All City College." They gave people something to fight for—first the Proposition A parcel tax, then Free City. In the end, this is a fight over who education is for and to what purpose.

The Journey for Justice Alliance is a national coalition of Black and Latinx–led community organizations that started in Chicago. Its vision for quality K–12 education encompasses "relevant, rigorous and engaging curriculum, supports for quality teaching and not punitive standardized tests, appropriate wrap-around supports for every child, student-centered school climate and transformative parent and community engagement, schools that serve as community hubs for parents, students, and neighborhood residents."[12]

How might we translate these ideas to serve our work in the community colleges? Positive vision is essential if we are to overturn reforms that dilute and diminish community college education and its power to transform students' lives. This isn't a prescription or a talking point; it's something that everyone in the fight will build together out of our lived stories and our dreams.

Afterword

As we were turning in the manuscript for *Free City!* the COVID-19 pandemic was upending life on the planet, and the United States rapidly became the epicenter.

Education at all levels was forced online; what had been one option was suddenly the only game in town. CCSF faculty and students scrambled to cobble together the remainder of the school year. Teachers suddenly had to adapt classes for online learning, using a specific for-profit software. The switch to distance learning was hardest on faculty and students who lacked home access to broadband internet, quiet workspace, and experience with online courses.

Like any deep crisis, the pandemic provided an opportunity to tighten austerity and privatize public services. (Think of the conversion of New Orleans public schools to charters after Hurricane Katrina.) The City College administration ordered more classes slashed, on top of the fall 2019 cuts. More than 250 faculty lost their jobs, including 60 part-time ESL teachers. Noncredit classes, especially ESL, bore the brunt of the cuts. Wraparound support programs that helped marginalized students stay in school continued to blink out one by one.

Faculty, staff, and students faced a fight to keep the cuts, the move online, and other crisis-created changes from becoming permanent—and they had some unexpected wind in their sails. Not two months after the pandemic hit the US, exposing so many social fault lines, the murder of George Floyd sparked a breathtakingly broad and deep movement against police violence and the systemic racism that creates it. The public health crisis magnified the challenges facing City College, community colleges, and public education in general, but the anti-racist uprising offered the prospect of meaningful change. Organizers linked defunding the police with investing in education and other people-serving programs, challenging austerity budgeting with concrete demands to reallocate resources and plans for how to do so. Millions of people were taking stock of our history, asking, "What are we for? What do we want to build?" Education for all can help answer those questions; it offers a powerful tool for expanding democracy, repairing the damages of inequality, and embodying a vision of a just, peaceful, and creative world.

August 2020

Acknowledgments

By November 2015, Vicki Legion was beside herself. A longtime faculty member in CCSF's Health Education Department, Legion was deeply involved with the Save CCSF Coalition and was a founder of its Research Committee. She and other members of the coalition had been bird-dogging journalists for a couple of years, trying to get in-depth coverage of the accreditation crisis at City. Almost everyone said it was just too complicated. Then a colleague introduced her to Marcy Rein, an experienced labor and community journalist and a contributing editor for *Race, Poverty and the Environment* (RP&E). They wrote and edited a package of articles in *RP&E* 21, no. 1. It was published in mid-2016, but there was still a lot more to learn and to say about the struggle to save City College. So Legion and Rein called in Mickey Ellinger, a Bay Area author and activist with an academic history and publishing experience, and *Free City!* was born, a book with its ending as yet unknown.

Necessary Disclaimers

When the crisis started, City College had the population of a medium-sized city, with more than ninety thousand students, and campuses and community sites all over San Francisco. People's experiences of the school and the turbulent years of the accreditation crisis varied depending on where they worked or studied. The crisis hit students, staff, and faculty in different ways. We are looking through a particular lens, that of the activists in and around Save CCSF and the faculty union, AFT 2121.

This story really belongs to the students, faculty, staff, union activists, and community members who waged and won the fight. There are so many characters. Some people were consistent visible leadership in the student movement, the union, and the Save CCSF Coalition. Other people did some wonderful thing, and then disappeared. We met a lot of people, and we know we left out people who were important to the story—just as there were scores of rallies, press conferences, and significant meetings we couldn't even mention.

Housekeeping

Direct quotes in the text were drawn from our own interviews, unless we note otherwise, and weren't footnoted. A list of interviews can be found on pages 187–189 below, followed by a list of other resources. Some of the endnotes refer to materials we found on the internet. Such items are always at risk of disappearing, so we captured many of them as PDFs and posted them to our website, www.freecitythebook.org. They are cited that way in the notes.

Two topics—Student Learning Outcomes (SLOs) and the corporate "reform" power network—needed more detailed presentations but didn't belong in the text or a note. These appear in the appendices, along with a chronology of the struggle.

Gratitude

More than eighty people gave interviews for this book, and many more waged the campaign to save City College. We are profoundly grateful to them all.

Special thanks to Alisa Messer, Wynd Kaufmyn, Tarik Farrar, Karen Saginor, Madeline Mueller, Chris Hanzo, Everardo "Lalo" Gonzalez, Allan Fisher, Leslie Simon, Joe Berry, Helena Worthen, Chris Hanson, Athena Waid, Fred Glass, Susan Lopez, Danny Halford, and Sarah Thompson. You talked with us for hours and answered swarms of questions, shared your special expertise, and tracked down answers to questions, or did all of that. Many of you also read drafts of the book and took pains to point out our errors and omissions. Thanks also to our other readers, Jody Sokolower, Barbara Frost, and Kim Starr-Reid, and to Harry Bernstein who copyedited as he read.

Many thanks also to our editor Terry Bisson for helping us wrangle the story and to our friends at PM Press. Special gratitude to Clif Ross and Scott Braley, who shared their kitchen tables with this project, and bore with spells of intense preoccupation from Marcy and Mickey.

We wrote this book not just for union activists and people in the education justice movement but for everyone who cares about public services and the common good. We wrote it for everyone who believes that education is a human right and learning offers a path to liberation. We wrote it because we believe in honoring and celebrating our movement victories— even though we know they are way stations on a long road.

Acronym Key

3CPE	Central City Coalition for Public Education
ACCJC	Accrediting Commission for Community and Junior Colleges
AFT	American Federation of Teachers
ALEC	American Legislative Exchange Council
BOG	Board of Governors
BRCAC	Balboa Reservoir Community Advisory Committee
CAA	Chinese for Affirmative Action
CCCI	California Community College Independents
CCSF	City College of San Francisco
CFT	California Federation of Teachers
CHP	Community Housing Partnership
COLA	cost of living adjustment
CPA	Chinese Progressive Association
CTA	California Teachers Association
CTU	Chicago Teachers Union
DCC	Department Chairperson Council
DOE	Department of Education (federal)
DSPS	Disabled Students Programs and Services
ESL	English as a Second Language
FACCC	Faculty Association of California Community Colleges
FCMAT	Fiscal Crisis and Management Assistance Team
FTES	full-time equivalent students
GASB	Governmental Accounting Standards Board
GED	graduate equivalency degree (high school graduation)
JWJ	Jobs with Justice
MEChA	Movimiento Estudiantil Chicanx de Aztlán

NACIQI	National Advisory Committee on Institutional Quality and Integrity
NPR	National Public Radio
PAEC	Performing Arts Education Center
SEIU	Service Employees International Union
SFLC	San Francisco Labor Council
SFPUC	San Francisco Public Utilities Commission
SFUSD	San Francisco Unified School District
SLAPP	strategic lawsuit against public participation
SLO	student learning outcome
SMAC	Students Making a Change
STWEP	Special Trustee with Extraordinary Powers
UESF	United Educators of San Francisco
VIDA	Voices of Immigrants Demonstrating Achievement

Interviews

John Avalos, interviewed by Marcy Rein, October 3, 2019.
Jeanette Bemis, interviewed by Marcy Rein, April 12, 2017; April 25, 2017.
Joe Berry, interviewed by Marcy Rein, July 27, 2017.
Bob Bezemek, interviewed by Marcy Rein, October 16, 2019.
Eric Blanc, interviewed by Marcy Rein, November 25, 2017.
Jessica Buchsbaum, interviewed by Marcy Rein, January 17, 2018; January 26, 2018.
Kathe Burick, interviewed by Marcy Rein, December 28, 2017; January 31, 2018.
Peter Byrne, interviewed by Vicki Legion and Marcy Rein, May 25, 2018.
Lena Carew, interviewed by Marcy Rein, June 13, 2018.
Fred Chavaria, interviewed by Marcy Rein, October 15, 2019.
Peijue Chen, interviewed by Marcy Rein, April 27, 2016.
Monica Collins, interviewed by Marcy Rein, December 10, 2016; January 9, 2019.
Venette Cook, interviewed by Marcy Rein, September 25, 2018.
Kevin Cross, interviewed by Marcy Rein, September 18, 2018.
Phil Day, interviewed by Mickey Ellinger, January 8, 2018.
Sara Eisenberg, interviewed by Marcy Rein, February 12, 2018.
Beth Ericson, interviewed by Marcy Rein, September 28, 2018.
Tarik Farrar, interviewed by Marcy Rein, January 6, 2016; July 21, 2017; August 2, 2017.
Malaika Finkelstein, interviewed by Marcy Rein, January 18, 2019.
Allan Fisher, interviewed by Marcy Rein, May 25, 2017; by Vicki Legion, October 28, 2019.
Conny Ford, interviewed by Marcy Rein, February 12, 2020.
Kate Frei, interviewed by Marcy Rein, April 26, 2017.
Fred Glass, interviewed by Marcy Rein, May 7, 2019; email correspondence, January 8, 2020, January 14, 2020.
Lalo Gonzalez, interviewed by Marcy Rein, January 8, 2016; March 29, 2018; by Mickey Ellinger, December 18, 2018.
Kelly Guajardo, interviewed by Marcy Rein, February 23, 2016.
Danny Halford, interviewed by Vicki Legion (email responses), January 11, 2020; January 16, 2020; January 21, 2020.
Terry Hall, interviewed by Vicki Legion, May 9, 2018.

Jenny Hammer, interviewed by Marcy Rein, October 17, 2018.

Rich Hansen, interviewed by Marcy Rein and Mickey Ellinger, March 5, 2019.

Chris Hanson, interviewed by Marcy Rein, December 9, 2016; December 23, 2016; September 17, 2018; March 13, 2019.

Simon Hanson, interviewed by Marcy Rein, February 17, 2016.

Chris Hanzo, interviewed by Marcy Rein, December 27, 2017; by Mickey Ellinger, January 10, 2020.

Evan Hawkins, interviewed by Marcy Rein, December 19, 2019.

Dennis Herrera, interviewed by Marcy Rein, March 1, 2018.

Thomas Hetherington, interviewed by Marcy Rein, April 25, 2019.

Martin Hittelman, interviewed by Marcy Rein and Mickey Ellinger, June 21, 2019.

Vivian Ikeda, interviewed by Marcy Rein, September 17, 2018; October 9, 2018; email correspondence, January 4, 2020.

Rick Kappra, interviewed by Marcy Rein, September 13, 2018.

Wynd Kaufmyn, interviewed by Marcy Rein, November 12, 2016; July 24, 2017; August 7, 2017.

Greg Keech, interviewed by Marcy Rein, October 10, 2018.

Tehmina Khan, interviewed by Marcy Rein, October 21, 2019.

Tim Killikelly, interviewed by Marcy Rein, March 2, 2018.

Tim Killikelly and Alyssa Picard, interviewed by Marcy Rein, May 15, 2018.

Kimberley King, interviewed by Vicki Legion and Mickey Ellinger, July 13, 2018.

Win-Mon Kyi, interviewed by Marcy Rein, February 24, 2016; by Mickey Ellinger and Marcy Rein, January 3, 2019.

Peter Lauterborn, interviewed by Marcy Rein, April 19, 2018.

Emily Ja-Ming Lee, interviewed by Marcy Rein, 2016 (n.d.); February 17, 2020.

Jonathan Lightman, interviewed by Mickey Ellinger, February 15, 2019.

Susan Lopez, interviewed by Marcy Rein and Vicki Legion, February 24, 2019; email correspondence, March 19, 2020.

Micheál Madden, interviewed by Marcy Rein, August 1, 2017.

Martin Madrigal, interviewed by Marcy Rein, November 18, 2017.

Jim Mahler, interviewed by Marcy Rein, October 8, 2019.

Pecolia Manigo, interviewed by Marcy Rein, July 11, 2018; November 8, 2019.

Eric Mar, interviewed by Marcy Rein and Vicki Legion, January 8, 2018.

Danyelle Marshall, interviewed by Marcy Rein, February 24, 2019.

Thea Matthews, interviewed by Marcy Rein, November 7, 2017.

John McDowell, interviewed by Marcy Rein, October 12, 2019; December 3, 2019.

Carole Meagher, interviewed by Marcy Rein, July 31, 2018.

Alisa Messer, interviewed by Marcy Rein, February 24, 2016; July 6, 2017; February 14, 2019; February 22, 2019; February 15, 2020.

Laura Mezirka, interviewed by Marcy Rein, January 17, 2019.

Madeline Mueller, interviewed by Marcy Rein, December 15, 2016; July 19, 2018.

Madeline Mueller and Monica Collins, interviewed by Marcy Rein, January 9, 2019.

Khin Thiri Nandar Soe, interviewed by Marcy Rein, October 17, 2017.

Vivek "JJ" Narayan, interviewed by Marcy Rein, August 8, 2017.

Sunny Ngo, interviewed by Marcy Rein, October 15, 2018.

Vincent Pan, interviewed by Marcy Rein, October 4, 2019.

Alyssa Picard and Tim Killikelly, interviewed by Marcy Rein, May 15, 2018.

Alyssa Picard, interviewed by Marcy Rein, June 12, 2018.

Otto Pippenger, interviewed by Marcy Rein, April 13, 2017.

Ron Rapp, interviewed by Marcy Rein, October 2, 2019.

Jules Retzlaff and Deon Saunders, interviewed by Marcy Rein, May 2, 2019.

John Rizzo, interviewed by Marcy Rein, February 23, 2016.

James Rogers, interviewed by Marcy Rein, April 30, 2019.

Karen Saginor, interviewed by Marcy Rein, July 17, 2018; July 24, 2018; email correspondence, October 19, 2019; November 18, 2019; January 17, 2020.

Deon Saunders and Jules Retzlaff, interviewed by Marcy Rein, May 2, 2019.

Rodger Scott, interviewed by Marcy Rein, October 2, 2019.

Denise Selleck, interviewed by Marcy Rein, September 18, 2018.

Bill Shields, interviewed by Marcy Rein, October 22, 2019.

Leslie Simon, interviewed by Marcy Rein, January 8, 2016; October 8, 2019.

Leslie Smith, interviewed by Mickey Ellinger, September 27, 2017; November 1, 2017.

Juanita Tamayo, interviewed by Mickey Ellinger, March 7, 2018.

Sarah Thompson, interviewed by Vicki Legion (email responses), January 20, 2020; January 23, 2020; January 25, 2020.

Edgar Torres, interviewed by Marcy Rein, January 19, 2016; August 21, 2017; January 18, 2019.

Rosario Villasana, interviewed by Vicki Legion, September 29, 2019.

Athena Waid, interviewed by Marcy Rein, February 13, 2018; October 2, 2018.

Diane Wallis, interviewed by Marcy Rein, September 20, 2018.

Calvin Welch, interviewed by Marcy Rein and Vicki Legion, January 12, 2018.

Shanell Williams, interviewed by Marcy Rein, August 11, 2017.

Windsong, interviewed by Marcy Rein, November 20, 2017.

Sally Winn, interviewed by Marcy Rein, September 18, 2018.

Helena Worthen, interviewed by Marcy Rein, July 27, 2017.

Resources

These are books, documents, and websites that helped us understand the context for *Free City!* Our website www.freecitythebook.org includes documents cited in the book and a frequently updated version of this resource list.

Ashby, Steven K., and Robert Bruno. *A Fight for the Soul of Public Education.* Ithaca, NY: Cornell University Press, 2016. About the Chicago Teachers Union strike of 2012.

Au, Wayne. *A Marxist Education.* Chicago: Haymarket Books, 2018.

Biondi, Martha. *The Black Revolution on Campus.* Berkeley: University of California Press, 2014.

Blanc, Eric. *Red State Revolt: The Teachers' Strike Wave and Working-Class Politics.* London: Verso Books, 2019.

Brint, Steven, and Jerome Karabel. *The Diverted Dream: Community Colleges and the Promise of Educational Opportunity in America, 1900–1985.* New York: Oxford University Press, 1991.

Byrne, Peter. *Going Postal: US Senator Dianne Feinstein's Husband Sells Post Offices to His Friends, Cheap.* Byrne Ink, 2013.

Coles, Gerald. *Miseducating for the Global Economy: How Corporate Power Damages Education and Subverts Students' Futures.* New York: Monthly Review Press, 2018. A deconstruction of the myth of meritocracy through education.

Dougherty, Kevin J., Sosanya M. Jones, Hana Lahr, Rebecca S. Natow, Lara Pheatt, and Vikash Reddy. *Performance Funding for Higher Education.* Baltimore: Johns Hopkins University Press, 2016.

Fabricant, Michael, and Stephen Brier. *Austerity Blues.* Baltimore: Johns Hopkins University Press, 2016. Focuses on the City University of New York and California's state universities.

Federici, Silvia, George Caffentzis, and Ousseina Alidou, eds. *A Thousand Flowers: Social Struggles against Structural Adjustment in African Universities.* Trenton, NJ: Africa World Press, 2000.

Folbre, Nancy. *Saving State U.* New York: New Press, 2010.

Gilmore, Ruth. *Golden Gulag: Prisons, Surplus, Crisis and Opposition in a Globalizing California*. Berkeley: University of California Press, 2007.

Giroux, Henry. *Neoliberalism's War on Higher Education*. Chicago: Haymarket Press, 2013.

Glass, Fred. *From Mission to Microchip: A History of the California Labor Movement*. Berkeley: University of California Press, 2016.

Journey for Justice Alliance. *Death by 1000 Cuts: Racism, School Closures and Public School Sabotage*. www.freecitythebook.org/J4Jdeath1000cuts.pdf.

Klein, Naomi. *The Shock Doctrine: The Rise of Disaster Capitalism*. Toronto: Alfred A. Knopf Canada, 2007.

Lipman, Pauline. *The New Political Economy of Urban Education: Neoliberalism, Race and the Right to the City*. New York: Routledge, 2011. A uniquely insightful analysis by a scholar-activist of the connection between school reform and gentrification; formative in our work.

Marsh, John. *Class Dismissed: Why We Can't Teach or Learn Our Way Out of Inequality*. New York: Monthly Review Press, 2011.

Mettler, Suzanne. *Degrees of Inequality: How the Politics of Higher Education Sabotaged the American Dream*. New York: Basic Books, 2014. A long history of for-profit college lobbying.

Morel, Domingo. *Takeover: Race, Education, and American Democracy*. New York: Oxford University Press, 2018.

Newfield, Chris. *Unmaking of the Public University: The Forty-Year Assault on the Middle Class*. Cambridge, MA: Harvard University Press, 2011.

Pastor, Manuel. *State of Resistance: What California's Dizzying Descent and Remarkable Resurgence Mean for America's Future*. New York: New Press, 2019.

Ravitch, Diane. dianeravitch.net. A blog addressing education, excellent compilation of multi-blogs, recently reviewed as "most influential in education history."

Rhoades, Gary. *Closing the Door, Increasing the Gap: Who's Not Going to (Community) College?* Center for the Future of Higher Education Policy Report no. 1, April 2012. Accessed July 30, 2020. https://www.insidehighered.com/sites/default/server_files/files/ClosingTheDoor_Embargoed.pdf.

Robinson, William. "Global Capitalism and the Restructuring of Education," *Social Justice* 43, no. 3 (2016): 1–24. Accessed July 30, 2020. https://www.academia.edu/36133681/GLOBAL_CAPITALISM_AND_THE_RESTRUCTURING_OF_EDUCATION.

Ryan, Howard. *Educational Justice: Teaching and Organizing against the Corporate Juggernaut*. New York: Monthly Review Press, 2016. Combines strong analysis with narratives on organizing.

Samuels, Robert. *Why Public Higher Education Should Be Free: How to Decrease Cost and Increase Quality at American Universities*. New Brunswick, NJ: Rutgers University Press, 2013.

Shapiro, Peter, and William Barlow. *An End to Silence, the San Francisco State Student Movement in the '60s*. New York: Pegasus Books, 1971.

Soederberg, Susanne. *Debtfare States and the Poverty Industry*. New York: Routledge, 2014.

Sunkara, Bhaskar, ed. *Class Action: An Activist Teacher's Handbook.* Brooklyn: Jacobin Magazine, 2014. A collection of articles that includes a section on the Chicago Teachers Union (CTU).

Trinational Coalition to Defend Public Education. Accessed July 30, 2020. http://www.trinationalcoalition.org. An important international coalition of education organizers formed in 1995, bringing together people from Mexico, Canada, the US, and the colony of Puerto Rico.

UCLA Civil Rights Project. Accessed July 30, 2020. https://www.civilrightsproject.ucla.edu. "We generate and synthesize research on key civil rights and equal opportunity policies that have been neglected or overlooked"; e.g.: Gándara, Patricia, Elizabeth Alvarado, Anne Driscoll, and Gary Orfield. "Building Pathways to Transfer: Community Colleges That Break the Chain of Failure for Students of Color." Civil Rights Project, February 14, 2012. Accessed July 30, 2020. https://civilrightsproject.ucla.edu/research/college-access/diversity/building-pathways-to-transfer-community-colleges-that-break-the-chain-of-failure-for-students-of-color.

Uetricht, Micah. *Strike for America: Chicago Teachers against Austerity.* New York: Verso/Jacobin, 2014. About the Chicago Teachers Union strike of 2012.

Walker, Richard. *Pictures of a Gone City: Tech and the Dark Side of Prosperity in the San Francisco Bay Area.* Oakland: PM Press, 2018.

Zemsky, Robert. *Making Reform Work: The Case for Transforming American Higher Education.* New Brunswick, NJ: Rutgers University Press, 2009. Tell-all report on the Spellings Commission by disgruntled (mainstream) commissioner.

APPENDICES

Chronology of the Crisis

2012

January 9	The California Community Colleges Board of Governors (BOG) approves the Student Success Task Force recommendations over vociferous opposition of City College of San Francisco (CCSF) students and faculty.
April	CCSF chancellor Don Q. Griffin retires after brain tumor diagnosis.
April 29	The CCSF board of trustees hires Pamila Fisher for six months as interim chancellor.
July 2	The Accrediting Commission for Community and Junior Colleges (ACCJC) report places City College on show cause, requiring the college to justify why it should not be disaccredited and closed down.
July	Congress cuts Pell grants from eighteen semesters to twelve.
August 23	The board of trustees approves a shrunken mission statement, hears a report from the Fiscal Crisis and Management Assistance Team (FCMAT) that outlines an austerity program for City College, and recommends that CCSF request a special trustee.
August 30	The Student Success Act passes both houses of California legislature; the governor signs it on September 27, 2012.
September 11	Students disrupt the CCSF board of trustees meeting to protest the appointment of a special trustee.
September 21	The ceremonial opening of the Chinatown/North Beach Campus takes place.

October 25	Interim Chancellor Pamila Fisher's last board of trustees meeting. The board votes to table the preconstruction contract for the Performing Arts Education Center (PAEC), close and cut back childcare centers, and approve the pay-up-front policy.
November 6	Almost seventy-three percent of San Francisco voters approve Proposition A, the parcel tax for City College funding.[1]
November 12	The first meeting of Save CCSF Coalition, a student/faculty/staff/community group.

2013

January 10	San Francisco community organization Coleman Advocates calls for unity and for complying with the ACCJC.
January 11	Flex Day: faculty boycott the interim chancellor's speech.
January 24	The board of trustees votes to hire mega–real estate firm CBRE for advice on a number of matters, including "disposition" of a college administration building at 33 Gough Street.
April	The ACCJC visiting team praises work on Student Learning Outcomes (SLOs).
April 25	Pauline Lipman speaks in San Francisco, linking education reform and gentrification.
April 30	California Federation of Teachers (CFT) and American Federation of Teachers (AFT) Local 2121 file complaint against the ACCJC with the Department of Education (DOE).
July 3	The ACCJC announces termination of CCSF's accreditation in one year.
July 8	Changing their rules to do so, the California Community Colleges BOG imposes the takeover of CCSF and appoints Robert Agrella as Special Trustee with Extraordinary Powers (STWEP).
July 9	Thousands march in San Francisco to protest the ACCJC's decision and the takeover.
August 13	The DOE upholds major sections of CFT/AFT complaint against the ACCJC and gives the accreditor a year to fix the problems.
August 20	CCSF students sit in at City Hall, asking "Where's Ed Lee?"

August 21   The California Joint Legislative Audit Committee orders an audit of the ACCJC.

August 22   San Francisco City Attorney Dennis Herrera files a suit against the ACCJC.

September 6   STWEP Robert Agrella cancels construction of the PAEC.

September 16   The San Francisco Budget and Legislative Analyst details the economic cost to San Francisco of CCSF closure (about $300 million/year).

September 23   CFT and AFT 2121 file a suit against the ACCJC.

October   CCSF announces it will begin enforcing a pay-up-front policy that will require students to pay all their fees at registration, even if their financial aid hasn't arrived, and automatically drop them from classes if they owe money.

November 13   AFT 2121 organizes a forum on accreditation. US Representatives Jackie Speier and Anna Eshoo participate and insist that the event be held at Ocean Campus.

December 7   Voting closes on a new AFT 2121 contract. With record turnout, members approve a disappointing deal, so they can focus on fighting to keep the school open.

December 12   Fifteen people organized by the Save CCSF coalition give public comment to the National Advisory Committee on Institutional Quality and Integrity (NACIQI), the panel that advises the DOE accreditation division.

December 26 and 30   Hearings are held on San Francisco City Attorney's motion for an injunction to keep City College open.

2014

January 3   Judge Curtis Karnow grants a preliminary injunction keeping CCSF open until the City Attorney's lawsuit is decided.

January 6   Nancy Pelosi speaks at the Chinatown/North Beach campus and promises to help CCSF.

January   Under the pay-up-front policy, 2,259 students are automatically dropped from classes. Close to half do not reenroll.

February 10   State senator Mark Leno introduces a proposal for "stabilization funding" for City College.

March 13   San Francisco police use force against student demonstrators at Conlan Hall. Some students occupy the building overnight, while others keep vigil outside.

March 21	CCSF student Alex Nieto is shot dead by San Francisco police on Bernal Hill.
June 6	CFT organizes a statewide demonstration in Sacramento to demand that the ACCJC grant City College's appeal of the termination decision.
June 11	The ACCJC offers CCSF new "restoration" status, which is opposed as a trap by AFT 2121 and reluctantly accepted by CCSF administration.
June 13	The ACCJC denies CCSF's appeal of termination.
June 26	The California state auditor issues a report blasting the ACCJC.
October 27–31	The trial of the City Attorney's lawsuit exposes the ACCJC's unfair practices.

2015

January 9	Chancellor Tyler announces the closure of the Civic Center campus one workday before classes start.
January 16	Judge Karnow decides for CCSF, ruling that the ACCJC must offer the college due process.
January 21	The first public hearing on development at Balboa Reservoir takes place.
January 31	STWEP Agrella leaves abruptly and is replaced by Guy Lease.
March 5	Six hundred people march to City Hall protesting the closure of the Civic Center campus.
May 5	The CCSF administration announces it will rent space at 1170 Market Street for Civic Center classes.
June 5	STWEP Lease demotes Chancellor Art Tyler to vice chancellor of facilities. Susan Lamb becomes interim chancellor.
June 8	CCSF trustees vote not to contest the ACCJC's half-hearted compliance with Judge Karnow's ruling.
June 8	The California Court of Appeals rejects the ACCJC's anti-SLAPP motion against the CFT/AFT 2121 lawsuit.
August 20	The Board of Governors votes to restore power to the CCSF board of trustees, but STWEP Lease retains veto power.
August 28	The task force appointed by the state chancellor's office recommends that the ACCJC be replaced, and the BOG accepts the report and orders that it be sent to NACIQI.

December 10	Students protest the pay-up-front policy at the board of trustees meeting.
December 16	Save CCSF brings thirty-seven people to give public comment at NACIQI, with substantial participation by AFT and CFT.
December 21	Art Tyler resigns as vice chancellor of facilities just before the *San Francisco Chronicle* exposes his misuse of funds.

2016

January 1	The board of trustees regains full powers.
January 26	Interim Chancellor Susan Lamb cancels the pay-up-front policy.
January 28	The board of trustees gets its first presentation on development at the Balboa Reservoir.
March 18	Presidents and CEOs of California Community Colleges vote to find an alternative to the ACCJC, and the BOG does the same three days later.
April 19	Supervisor Jane Kim and AFT 2121 announce the Free City campaign.
April 27	A one-day faculty strike takes place, the first in CCSF history.
July 12	The San Francisco Board of Supervisors takes its first vote in support of Free City.
July 13	AFT 2121 and CCSF reach a tentative agreement on a new contract.
October	ACCJC "listening sessions" are held around the state, including one on October 30 in Bakersfield.
October 13	The board of trustees approves a seventy-five-year ground lease of 33 Gough Street by Equity Community Builders and Integral.
November 8, Election Day	The Free City campaign wins on the same day that Donald Trump garners an electoral vote majority, which will give him the US presidency although he lost the popular vote.
December	The ACCJC puts its president Barbara Beno on administrative leave, and she resigns.

2017

January 13, 2017	ACCJC announces full seven-year reaccreditation of City College, bringing the crisis to a close.

The Policy Network That Drives Community College Education "Reform"

Who Are the Players? Who Stands to Gain?

A corporate policy network is downsizing and reshaping the California community colleges. Its prescriptions generate profits via student loans, outsourcing, and online offerings. The retooling prioritizes workforce-oriented education at public expense and at the expense of rich community-centered education. This resembles the restructuring in K–12 education, where charter schools and online offerings have proliferated, standardized testing has narrowed the curriculum, and teachers have lost autonomy and job security. The new policies are generated by national players and moved forward at the state level.

The national "reform" agenda pushed in all fifty states equates "student success" with the rapid completion of transfer, degrees, and certificates of workforce value. The push for full-time attendance squeezes out students who cannot go full-time, students who are not necessarily headed toward the corporate workforce, and those who need and want education for other reasons, such as lifelong learners.

This cluster of new policies erodes courses and programs that develop critical thinking and a radical imagination, such as ethnic studies and women's and gender studies—curricula that movements fought for in the 1960s. The "reform" policies also undermine community-serving programs such as English as a Second Language, citizenship classes, and world languages, music, dance, art, and exercise classes available at low or no cost to everyone, including people with disabilities and seniors.

The Department of Education (DOE) implements federal policy and sets the tone for the national education conversation. Its officials cycle through the revolving door between government and business. As the City College crisis was starting, the Save CCSF Research Committee quickly found examples:

- *Vickie Schray* played a leading role in shaping accreditation rules for the DOE for thirteen years. In January 2012, she left to become the vice president responsible for regulatory affairs for the second biggest for-profit career college.
- *Sally Stroup* began as a lobbyist for the University of Phoenix, then became the assistant secretary of postsecondary education under George W. Bush (overseeing accreditation and student loans). She then became vice president of Scantron and vice president of the main lobbying group for the for-profit career college industry, the Association of Private Sector Colleges and Universities.
- *Arthur Rothkopf*, the vice chair of the National Advisory Committee on Institutional Quality and Integrity (NACIQI), the panel that advises DOE's accreditation division, was a longtime industry lobbyist and vice president of the Chamber of Commerce, the lead lobbying arm of the Fortune 500. He joined the board of the Education Testing Service, a major standardized testing company that stands to profit from the Degree Qualifications Profile funded by the Lumina Foundation and piloted at some fifteen California community colleges, again with funding from Lumina. President Barack Obama's Education Secretary Arne Duncan hired top officers from the Gates Foundation and the NewSchools Venture Fund (a major Gates grantee) as his undersecretary of education and director of the Race to the Top competition.[1]

Philanthrocapitalist mega-foundations shape the network. These foundations bankroll the incubators of corporate philosophy and ideology.

- The Lumina Foundation, founded in 2001, is the largest foundation focused on US postsecondary education. Their strategic goals: Guided Pathways; standardized credentials based on student learning outcomes; funding based on outcomes measures. They run "state strategy labs" as resource centers for policy makers and influencers that provide research, data, peer advice, and technical support. Lumina was entirely funded by the behemoth Student Loan Marketing Corporation (Sallie Mae). It funded California's Student Success Task Force and the ACCJC.

- The Gates Foundation, reported to be the largest private foundation in the world, is a chief architect of the Common Core and high-stakes standardized testing in K–12 education and promotes online modalities that create demand for Microsoft hardware and software.

The *Chronicle of Higher Education* described foundation influence as the "Gates Effect": the Gates Foundation doesn't jump on the band-wagon, "it has worked to build that bandwagon in ways that are not always obvious. . . . The effect is an echo chamber of like-minded ideas, arising from research commissioned by Gates and advocated by staff members who move between the government and the foundation world."[2]

Think tanks and nonprofits design the reform and advocate for it. They develop frames and talking points repeated so often that they become common sense.

- The *Community College Research Center* (CCRC) at Columbia University is the major academic center for community college reform. Their 2015 book *Redesigning the Community Colleges* is considered the definitive work. They advocate Guided Pathways that funnel students into a narrow range of full-time studies and emphasize completion and performance funding based on completion. CCRC got twelve major grants on performance funding from 2009 to 2013 and issued twelve reports.
- Google, Gates, and Lumina are major funders of the *New America Foundation*, whose higher education director and *New York Times* columnist Kevin Carey advocates the disruption of in-person education and the triumph of online education. (Carey wrote a *New York Times* column disparaging California community colleges, City College of San Francisco in particular.)[3]
- *Complete College America* (CCA), a national nonprofit, is a prime mover in promoting performance funding and the speedy completion of a college career. Performance funding conditions college funding on metrics such as number of degrees and certificates. From 2006 to 2011, CCA was funded by some $9 million from Gates and $1.2 million from Lumina.
- In California, the *Campaign for College Opportunity* (CCO) reports on equity issues and plays a major role in gaining public

endorsement for the "student success" agenda. They organized press conferences and endorsements supporting the passage of the Student Success Act of 2012. CCO was cofounded by the California Business Roundtable, whose president Bill Hauck chaired CCO's board of directors for seven years.

Professional associations both legitimate and lobby for the policies, while receiving substantial infusions of foundation cash.

- The *National Governors Association* website includes the following: "Workforce development and postsecondary education are at the center of governors' economic development agenda." From 2009 to 2011, the association received $2.3 million from the Gates Foundation and $1.5 million from Lumina.[4]
- The *American Association of Community Colleges* (AACC) advocates at the national level. The Lumina and Gates Foundations poured more than $15 million into the AACC between 2004 and 2012.[5]
- The *Association of Private Sector Colleges and Universities* lobbies in Washington, DC, on behalf of for-profit colleges.

The *American Legislative Exchange Council* (ALEC) was formed in 1973 by Charles and David Koch to write and push pro-corporate model state legislation.[6] ALEC has about two thousand Republican state lawmakers as members and many corporate affiliates who pay to participate in its task forces that propose the model legislation.[7] ALEC has a model resolution supporting for-profit colleges and a bill promoting full-time associate degrees for transfer. Lumina was a major funder of the 2011 ALEC national meeting.[8]

Both political parties support the student success agenda.

- The *Democratic National Committee* affirms that "Democrats are committed to increasing the college-completion rate as well as the share of students who are prepared for budding industries with specific job-related skills."[9]
- *Republicans*, for their part, "believe that expanding community college programs, technical institutions, private training schools, online universities, life-long learning, and work-based learning in the private sector, to create competition for four-year schools, is a

good way to not only make worthwhile education more accessible now, but to motivate four-year schools to match these alternatives' costs and levels of job-preparedness."[10]

Corporate media echo the goals and talking points of the reformers. The reaccreditation crisis at CCSF attracted attention from the *New York Times*, the *Wall Street Journal*, and the *Washington Monthly*; the *San Francisco Chronicle* supported the attacks on CCSF until many false charges were exposed in the City Attorney's lawsuit.

Who Stands to Gain?

EdTech

The sale of educational technology is a huge and growing market. EdSurge reports "a record year for venture capital in the US education technology sector in 2019. . . . [I]nvestment in edtech companies reached at least $1.66 billion across 105 deals in 2019, a five-year high in value."[11] Microsoft and Apple have pocketed billions selling hardware and software, as well as postsecondary education, to K–12 schools. Commercial software is increasingly being used for administrative functions like enrollment. Homegrown IT departments are being replaced with commercial software that institutions must buy, for example, the Ellucian contract at CCSF discussed in Chapter 10.

Online courses have expanded at community colleges, making up more than 10 percent of total classes offered at CCSF in spring 2020. California's newest community college is entirely online. Online education is managed by businesses called "online program managers," who not only take a cut of enrollment revenue (typically between 50 and 60 percent) but often develop the course and even provide instruction.[12]

The third largest source of advertising revenue for Google is for-profit colleges.[13]

For-profit colleges compete with community colleges for the same pool of students. These operations cost seventeen times as much as parallel programs at City College,[14] prey on students of color,[15] and drive students to take on predatory loans: 96 percent of students at the for-profits take out loans, in contrast to 13 percent at community colleges. In the Bay Area, less than 4 percent of two-year students attend for-profit schools. If the for-profit schools are to grow, the public community colleges must shrink.

A two-year investigation of for-profit colleges led by Senator Tom Harkin found "overwhelming documentation of exorbitant tuition, aggressive recruiting practices, abysmal student outcomes, taxpayer dollars spent on marketing and pocketed as profit, and regulatory evasion and manipulation. These practices are not the exception—they are the norm. They are systemic throughout the industry."[16]

Loan Sharks: Sallie Mae and the Big Banks

Students, their families, and the economy are burdened by $1.5 trillion in student debt. Debt payments, interest and principal, further the profits of the big banks. Two of the five big banks dominate the market in high-interest private student loans: *JP Morgan Chase* (whose board member Charles Miller chaired the DOE's Commission on the Future of Higher Education, the 2006 Spellings Commission), and *Wells Fargo Bank*, which owned 25 percent of the stock in the fraudulent Corinthian/Heald for-profit college.

Understanding this bigger picture helps activists make sense of new policies as they emerge.

Student Learning Outcomes: SLO Torture

Student Learning Outcomes (SLOs) mimic an industrial management technique called "management by objectives"; managers and experts define rigorous measurable standards that individuals must meet. This is only a short step away from rewards and punishments.

Education researcher Boyce Brown lists the beliefs underlying this process:

> that people are lazy by nature and need specific direction, close management, and material incentives to work most efficiently; that teachers are just like other workers; that schools are just like any other plant or work place that needs to be organized for maximum efficiency; that administrators should be separate from, and superior in authority to, teachers; and that the outcomes of school can be measured, and the measures could be used to compare schools and teachers. The achievement products could thus be related in straightforward ways to costs, and therefore to efficiency.[1]

Advocates of SLOs in education say they improve accountability by using empirical data to refine courses and programs and improve student learning. In practice, this means that instructors list three or four learning outcomes at the top of the syllabus that specify what the student will know or be able to do at the end of the course. "Doing SLOs" means that the instructor focuses on one of the learning outcomes, identifies a fact or bit of knowledge aligned with that outcome, and finds a way to test students on it. The instructor then makes some (usually minor) change in the course to try to raise the percentage, and tests again to see if the targeted percentage went up. "Full SLO compliance" means that instructors enter data on every student in every course every semester (at City College of San Francisco into a proprietary database owned by the CurricUNET corporation).

Critics see SLOs as a metric promoted as a way to pretend to quantify educational results, "running education like a business," with students as the raw material and SLOs as the product. An exhaustive 2014 study by Laura Chapman reviews four federally funded reports that portray the uses of SLOs. These reports point out the absence of evidence to support any use of SLOs other than securing teacher compliance with administrative mandates.[2]

In a January 2018 commentary, history professor Erik Gilbert reviews the literature from assessment professionals, finding that "the whole assessment process would fall apart if we had to test for reliability and validity and carefully model interactions before making conclusions about cause and effect." However, not doing so, and then applying "common sense" analysis to the dubious data "is akin to a Rorschach test."

Gilbert continues:

Because it's fairly obvious that assessment has not caused (and probably will not cause) positive changes in student learning, and because it's clear that this has been an open secret for a while, one wonders why academic administrators have been so acquiescent about assessment for so long.

Here's why: It's no accident that the rise of learning-outcomes assessment has coincided with a significant expansion in the use of adjunct faculty, the growth of dual enrollment, and the spread of online education. Each of these allows administrators to deliver educational product to their customers with little or no involvement from the traditional faculty. If they are challenged on the quality of these programs, they can always point out that assessment results indicate that the customers are learning just as much as the students in traditional courses.[3]

Notes

Chapter One

1   City College of San Francisco served 90,352 students in the 2011–2012 school year; see California Community Colleges Chancellor's Office, "Management Information Systems Data Mart;" accessed July 31, 2020, https://datamart. cccco.edu/Students/Student_Term_Annual_Count.aspx. Enrollment figures in this book are what the chancellor's office calls "headcount," the number of individuals who take classes. The other measurement is "FTES," Full-Time Equivalent Students," a composite number that doesn't reflect the number of people whose lives are touched by the school.

2   City College of San Francisco has eleven sites called "campuses" or "centers" and also offers classes at community centers and libraries throughout San Francisco. Ocean Campus is the oldest.

3   The Diversity Collaborative brings together ten departments: African American Studies, Asian American Studies, Asian Studies, Disabled Students Programs and Services, Interdisciplinary Studies, Labor and Community Studies, Latin American and Latino/a Studies, LGBT Studies, Philippine Studies, and Women's Studies. In late 2019, the Collaborative was renamed "Ethnic Studies and Social Justice."

4   FY 2002–2003 Annual Report, Chapter 2—Who We Serve, accessed July 22, 2020, https://www.sfdph.org/dph/files/reports/PolicyProcOfc/2002-03AnnlRpt/2002-03AnnlRptChapt02.pdf.

5   Austin White, *History of City College of San Francisco* (San Francisco: Arcadia Publishers, 2010), 7.

6   For more on the development of the Master Plan, see "the History and Future of the California Master Plan for Higher Education," accessed July 22, 2020, https://www.lib.berkeley.edu/uchistory/archives_exhibits/masterplan/1960.html. The architects of the Master Plan devised the community college system as a moat to protect the University of California system from political pressure to open its doors more widely. University of California chancellor Clark Kerr: "When I was guiding the development of the Master Plan for Higher Education in California in 1959 and 1960, I considered the vast expansion of the community colleges to be the first line of defense for

the University of California as an institution of academic renown"; Clark Kerr, "Higher Education: Paradise Lost?" *Higher Education* 7, no. 3 (August 1978): 267.

7   "The Master Plan dramatically reduced the percentage of those admitted to state colleges, from the top 70 percent of high school graduates to the top 33 percent. Compared to other state colleges, San Francisco State had an unusually large number of Black students before the Master Plan and before the introduction of standardized entrance tests in 1965. In just four years, Black student presence plunged from 10 to 4 percent of the student body, fueling what became the longest student strike in US history: the Third World Strike"; Martha Biondi, *The Black Revolution on Campus* (Berkeley: University of California Press, 2012), 51.

8   Jeffrey Kahn, "Ronald Reagan Launched Political Career Using UC Berkeley as a Target," UC Berkeley News, June 8, 2004, accessed July 22, 2020, https://www.berkeley.edu/news/media/releases/2004/06/08_reagan.shtml.

9   Robert O. Self, *American Babylon: Race and the Struggle for Postwar Oakland* (Princeton, NJ: Princeton University Press, 2003), 316–27.

10   Robert Kuttner, *Revolt of the Haves* (New York: Simon and Schuster, 1980), 85.

11   Proposition 98 guaranteed about 11 percent of state revenue to the community colleges and is one way the community colleges avoided drastic tuition hikes.

12   "Historical Tuition Rates," California State University, accessed July 22, 2020, https://tinyurl.com/y6g8ohmb.

13   Marty Hittelman, "A Report on the Commission on Innovation Report," October 29, 1993, accessed August 21, 2020, http://www.mlhittel.com/?p=489; archived at https://www.freecitythebook.org/chapter-notes/chapter-1/commission-on-innovation-1993-choosing-the-future; cited in John Chandler, "Instructors Decry Report on Colleges," *Los Angeles Times*, November 28, 1993, accessed July 22, 2020, https://www.latimes.com/archives/la-xpm-1993-11-28-me-61960-story.html; also cited in Community College League of California, *"Toward a State of Learning: Community College Governance,"* February 1998, accessed July 22, 2020, https://www.ccleague.org/sites/default/files/pdf/TowardStateLrng.pdf.

14   "'Missing' Students on Display in S.F.," *SFGate*, August 21, 2004, accessed July 22, 2020, https://www.sfgate.com/bayarea/article/Missing-students-on-display-in-S-F-2732006.php.

15   Jonathan Lightman, "Reflections and Transitions," accessed November 2, 2019, unavailable July 22, 2020, http://www.faccc.org/wp-content/uploads/2018/11/Reflections-and-Transitions.pdf, archived at https://www.freecitythebook.org/chapter-notes/chapter-1/jonathan-lightman-transitions-and-reflections.

16   Beth Frerking, "For Achievers, a New Destination," *New York Times Magazine*, April 22, 2007, accessed July 22, 2020, https://www.nytimes.com/2007/04/22/education/edlife/bestccs.html.

17   "State Government Revenue and Expenditure in California from Fiscal Year 2000 to 2020," Statista, accessed July 22, 2020, https://www.statista.com/statistics/313176/california-state-government-revenue-and-expenditure.

18 Sarah Bohn, Belinda Reyes, and Hans Johnson, *The Impact of Budget Cuts on California's Community Colleges*, Public Policy Institute of California, March 2013, accessed July 22, 2020, https://www.ppic.org/content/pubs/report/R_313SBR.pdf.

19 *The Real Cost of College*, Campaign for College Opportunity, July 2014, accessed July 22, 2020, collegecampaign.org/wp-content/uploads/2014/07/Real_Cost_of_College_Full_Report_CCC-1.pdf.

20 City College Finances 2006–06—2013–14, California Community Colleges Annual Financial and Budget Report (CCSF 311), Federal State and Local. This report on official "311" report filings has been twice reviewed and verified by the California Community Colleges chancellor's office and Board of Governors.

21 David P. Gardner et al., *A Nation at Risk, ERIC* (Washington, DC: Department of Education, 1983), accessed October 3, 2020, https://files.eric.ed.gov/fulltext/ED226006.pdf.

22 Kathy Emery, "Corporate Control of Public School Goals," *Teacher Education Quarterly* (Spring 2007), accessed July 22, 2020, https://files.eric.ed.gov/fulltext/EJ795152.pdf.

23 Alexandra Tinsley, "Subtracting Schools from Communities," Urban Institute, March 23, 2017, accessed July 22, 2020, https://www.urban.org/features/subtracting-schools-communities.

24 Columbia University Community College Research Center has led the "redesign" effort; see Thomas Bailey, Shanna Smith Jaggars, and Davis Jenkins, *Redesigning America's Community Colleges* (Cambridge, MA: Harvard University Press, 2015).

25 California Student Success Initiative, "Implementation of Student Success Task Force Recommendations," July 28, 2014; archived at https://www.freecitythebook.org/chapter-notes/chapter-1/student-success-task-force-recommendations. For the full report, see California Community Colleges Student Success Task Force, "Advancing Student Success in the California Community Colleges," January 17, 2012; archived at https://www.freecitythebook.org/chapter-notes/chapter-1/student-success-task-force-final-report.

26 The California Community College Independents (CCCI) links the thirteen faculty associations that aren't affiliated with either the California Federation of Teachers or the California Teachers Association.

27 The Faculty Association of California Community Colleges (FACCC) advocates at the state and federal levels for all the colleges, regardless of union affiliation.

28 Lightman, "Reflections and Transitions."

29 California Community Colleges Chancellor's Office, "Management Information Systems Data Mart," accessed July 22, 2020, https://datamart.cccco.edu/students/Unit_Load_Status.aspx. 25.

30 Accrediting Commission for Community and Junior Colleges and Western Association of Schools and Colleges, March 2012, unavailable July 31, 2020, http://www.ccsf.edu/Offices/Research_Planning/pdf/2006-06_

WASC_Report.pdf; archived at https://www.freecitythebook.org/chapter-notes/chapter-1/accreditation-report-2006.

31 Thomas Figg-Hoblyn, "Chancellor Don Q. Griffin Retires," *Guardsman*, May 2, 2012, accessed July 22, 2020, https://issuu.com/theguardsmanonline/docs/vol153_issue7.

32 "Grants Database," Lumina Foundation, accessed July 22, 2020, https://tinyurl.com/y6yfd25u.

33 Department chairs function as frontline supervisors. They "hire, orient, schedule, supervise and evaluate" substitute faculty, emergency faculty hires, classified staff, student workers, contract workers, and volunteers. They develop and recommend class schedules and budgets for their departments, function as a bridge between higher levels of administration and the faculty and handle numerous other responsibilities; from the 2014–2018 Department Chairperson Council contract.

34 The California legislature passed AB 1725 in 1988. The legislation included provisions that strengthened key features of City College's institutional culture. It established the right of faculty, staff, and students to meaningful participation in college and district governance; this right was exercised in CCSF's College Advisory Council. AB 1725 also obligated trustees and administrators to consult the Academic Senate on academic and professional matters. Its section on faculty standards set a goal of having 75 percent of classes taught by full-time instructors. Academic Senate for California Community Colleges and Community College League of California, *Participating Effectively in District and College Governance*, 1998 (revised 2012 and 2018), accessed July 22, 2020, https://asccc.org/sites/default/files/publications/FinalGuidelines_0.pdf.

35 FCMAT describes its mission as "to help California's local educational agencies fulfill their financial and management responsibilities by providing fiscal advice, management assistance, training and other related school business services. . . . FCMAT also provides management studies for school districts, county offices of education, charter schools and community colleges that request them. FCMAT coordinates statewide professional development efforts for school business officials"; "Fiscal Crisis and Management Assistance Team (FCMAT)," Inglewood Unified School District, accessed July 22, 2020, https://tinyurl.com/y4lrdbaz.

Chapter Two

1 Jobs with Justice is a long-term strategic alliance that brings unions and other workers' organizations together with student, faith-based, and community groups. Some of its campaigns are national, and some are carried out by local groups in twenty-four states. Jobs with Justice San Francisco was formed in 2010 and includes AFT 2121, SEIU 1021, Coleman Advocates, the Chinese Progressive Association, Causa Justa :: Just Cause, and Community Housing Partnership among its thirty-two member organizations and is a key part of many grassroots mobilizations in the city. See Jobs with Justice San Francisco, accessed July 22, 2020, www.jwjsf.org.

2   "ACCJC to CCSF, July 2, 2012"; see https://www.freecitythebook.org/chapter-notes/chapter-2/accjc-letter-july-2-2012.

3   Nanette Asimov, "City College of San Francisco on brink of closure," *San Francisco Chronicle*, July 3, 2012, accessed July 22, 2020, https://www.sfgate.com/education/article/City-College-of-San-Francisco-on-brink-of-closure-3682955.php.

4   Lee Romney, "Report Finds City College of San Francisco riddled with problems," *Los Angeles Times*, Monday, July 15, 2012, accessed July 22, 2020, https://www.latimes.com/local/la-xpm-2012-jul-15-la-me-sf-city-college-20120716-story.html.

5   When Beno served as president of Vista Community College in Berkeley from 1998 to 2000, the faculty union filed thirteen grievances against her in two years and won all of them (email from Fred Glass to Marcy Rein, January 8, 2020). Beno also shut down an innovative and effective program for working adults and tried to pull Vista out of the Peralta Community College District. That effort only failed after CFT filed suit claiming that the secession would have a racially discriminatory impact.

Chapter 3

1   For more discussion of SLOs, see appendix titled "Student Learning Outcomes: SLO Torture," 205–6, this volume.

2   The categorical programs are for "protected groups," for example, disabled students and students from low-income families: Educational Opportunity Programs (EOPs), etc.

3   "Let me outline how the model used at Lassen CCD and Solano CCD allowed the local board to retain its authority while a Special Trustee performed the following functions: (1) Provide advice and counsel, and make recommendations on all matters relating to the operation of the district, including governance and administration; finances, accounting and other economic issues; collegiality and college community relationships; title 5 compliance; education and accreditation standards; and any other matters that may arise regarding the operation of the district. (2) Review, provide advice, and make recommendations regarding recent ACCJC reports, appropriate audit reports, State title 5 compliance and federal compliance reports, and reports submitted by the State Chancellor's Office. (3) As necessary, stay and/or rescind board actions where such actions are inconsistent with the developed recovery plan, accreditation standards, and the fiscal health of the district." Note that "stay and/or rescind" is a euphemism for "veto." California Community Colleges chancellor Jack Scott, letter to board of trustees president John Rizzo and Interim Chancellor Pamila Fisher, included with the agenda packet for the board of trustees special meeting on September 11, 2012, accessed July 23, 2020, https://www.ccsf.edu/en/about-city-college/board-of-trustees/bot_meetings1/bot_meetings_2012.html; archived at https://www.freecitythebook.org/chapter-notes/chapter-3-notes/jack-scott-to-ccsf-trustees-sept-13-2012.

4   Joel D. Montero, *California Community Colleges Chancellor's Office City College of San Francisco: Fiscal Review*, FCMAT, September 14, 2012, accessed July 23, 2020, https://www.fcmat.org/PublicationsReports/SFCityCollegefinalreport9142.pdf.

5   Before AFT 2121 made "equal pay for equal work" a priority, part-time faculty got paid on a lower scale than full-timers teaching the same classes. Over almost three decades, the local organized and bargained to put all faculty on the same scale, with part-time pay set at a percentage of full-time—"prorated," so it is called "pro rata" pay. Full-timers have some nonteaching duties that part-timers do not, hence the higher pay—but all faculty who worked more than half-time got health benefits. Part-timers retained recall rights for four semesters; if they were laid off, i.e., they got no assignment, they got the first offer if assignments became available, rather than prospective new employees. And they had the first shot at new full-time positions: the administration would have to prove that an outside candidate was more qualified than any part-time faculty member already employed at the college. Carl Friedlander's comments come from his statement to the California Community Colleges Board of Governors Special Meeting on City College of San Francisco, October 4, 2012; see "Statement of Carl Friedlander President of The California Federation of Teachers Community College Council," California Federation of Teachers, October 5, 2012, accessed July 23, 2020, https://www.cft.org/sites/main/files/file-attachments/release_carl_friedlander_statement_10.4.pdf.

6   Nanette Asimov, "S.F. City College can't afford all of its campuses," *San Francisco Chronicle*, June 1, 2012, accessed July 23, 2020, https://www.sfgate.com/education/article/S-F-City-College-can-t-afford-all-its-campuses-3601067.php.

7   "City College of San Francisco Special Report," September 21, 2012, 47; see https://www.freecitythebook.org/chapter-notes/chapter-3-notes/special-report-draft.

8   Nanette Asimov, " City College dismantles faculty leadership," October 26, 2012, https://www.sfchronicle.com/education/article/City-College-dismantles-faculty-leadership-3984671.php.

9   Naomi Klein, *The Shock Doctrine: The Rise of Disaster Capitalism* (Toronto: Alfred A. Knopf Canada, 2007).

10   "City Currents at CCSF," Facebook, October 31, 2012, accessed July 23, https://www.facebook.com/citycurrents/photos/a.20268100650579 9/322831621157403/?type=1&theater.

11   Email from John Rizzo to Alisa Messer, July 6, 2012. In that email Fisher also noted, "I held an Open Forum this afternoon. [Trustees] Anita [Grier] and Milton [Marks] attended and there were more than 200 people with standing room only and others outside the room. There were a number of questions and comments. One of the more outlandish ones (which I have heard elsewhere and is being promoted by some) is that the Commission decision is a part of some right-wing conspiracy. I refuted that as strongly as I could and received a lot of applause for my comments"; see https://www.freecitythebook.org/chapter-notes/chapter-3-notes/email-john-rizzo-to-alisa-messer.

12   "Statement of Carl Friedlander President of The California Federation of Teachers Community College Council," California Federation of Teachers, October 5, 2012, accessed August 1, 2020, https://www.cft.org/sites/main/files/file-attachments/release_carl_friedlander_statement_10.4.pdf.

Chapter Four

1   Richard Walker, "The Boom and Bust Bombshell: The New Economy Bubble and the San Francisco Bay Area," in Giovanna Vertova, ed., *The Changing Economic Geography of Globalization* (London: Routledge, 2005) 121–47.

2   Examiner Staff, "San Francisco Mayor Ed Lee downplays Willie Brown connection," *San Francisco Examiner*, August 10, 2011, accessed July 23, 2020, https://www.sfexaminer.com/news/san-francisco-mayor-ed-lee-downplays-willie-brown-connection.

3   This was embedded in Proposition C, a November 2012 ballot initiative originated by Mayor Ed Lee's office that created an affordable housing trust fund.

4   Calvin Welch, "Ed Lee's development legacy and the end of 'balanced growth,'" 48hills, January 7, 2018, accessed July 23, 2020, http://48hills.org/2018/01/ed-lees-record.

5   Richard Walker, *Pictures of a Gone City* (Oakland: PM Press, 2018), 196.

6   Other notable fights against displacement included the decade-long battle to save the International Hotel in Manilatown, the Mission Coalition Organization's work to keep redevelopment out of the largely Latinx Mission District, organizing in the Tenderloin to preserve affordable housing, and the fight over public housing; see James Tracy, *Dispatches against Displacement* (Oakland: AK Press, 2014).

7   "CalChamber Opposes 'Virtually Permanent' Prop 30 Tax," California Policy Center, May 23, 2016, accessed August 1, 2020, https://californiapolicycenter.org/tag/california-business-roundtable-cbrt.

8   "Special Report Draft Master," 13; see https://www.freecitythebook.org/chapter-notes/chapter-4-notes/special-report-sept-21-2012.

9   AFT 2121, *Union Action*, October 2012, accessed July 23, 2020, http://aft2121.org/PDF/October_2012.pdf.

Chapter Five

1   Folsom Lake College is in the Los Rios Community College District. Just days after Scott-Skillman took over as interim chancellor at CCSF, former Los Rios chancellor Brice Harris took office as chancellor of the California community college system.

2   Athena Stef and several other SEIU 1021 City College chapter leaders declined to be interviewed for this book.

3   AFT 2121, *Union Action*, April 2013, accessed July 24, 2020, https://aft2121.org/PDF/April_2013-special.pdf.

4   Nanette Asimov, "Reeling CCSF announces layoffs, pay cuts," *San Francisco Chronicle*, December 19, 2012. https://www.sfchronicle.com/education/article/Reeling-CCSF-announces-layoffs-pay-cuts-4129701.php.

5   Robert Agrella would later confirm his $1,000 per day compensation. He had retired as president of Santa Rosa Junior College a year and a half before becoming the special trustee; Kerry Benefield, "Retired SRJC President Robert Agrella tapped to save City College of San Francisco," *Press Democrat*, July 10, 2013, accessed July 24, 2020, https://www.pressdemocrat.com/news/2209185-181/former-srjc-president-robert-agrella.

6   Martin Hittelman, *ACCJC Gone Wild*, Los Rios College Federation of Teachers Local 2279, March 1, 2013, 12, accessed August 1, 2020, http://lrcft.org/wp-content/uploads/2013/03/ACCJC-Gone-Wild-3-1-2013.pdf.

7   Ibid., 37–38.

8   Will Kenton, "Regulatory Capture," *Investopedia*, October 23, 2019, accessed July 24, 2020, https://www.investopedia.com/terms/r/regulatory-capture.asp.

9   See appendix titled "The Policy Network That Drives Community College Education 'Reform,'" 199–204, this volume.

10   President George W. Bush's secretary of education Margaret Spellings appointed Texas investment banker Charles Miller to lead a blue-ribbon commission to reenvision postsecondary education. Miller was a board member of JPMorgan Chase, one of the top purveyors of private student loans in the US. Miller ran a heavily staff-directed commission; one of his three key staffers was Dr. Robert C. Dickeson, who had been a senior vice president of the Lumina Foundation; see Robert Zemsky, *Making Reform Work: The Case for Transforming American Higher Education* (New Brunswick, NJ: Rutgers University Press, 2009).

11   Doug Lederman, "When Is Student Learning 'Good Enough'?" *Inside Higher Education*, February 23, 2007, accessed July 24, 2020, https://www.insidehighered.com/news/2007/02/23/when-student-learning-good-enough.

12   Department of Education, *A Test of Leadership*, 2006, 25, accessed July 24, 2020, https://www2.ed.gov/about/bdscomm/list/hiedfuture/reports/final-report.pdf.

13   Chris Kirkham, "For-Profit Colleges Mount Unprecedented Battle for Influence in Washington," Huffington Post, April 25, 2011, accessed July 24, 2020, https://www.huffpost.com/entry/for-profit-colleges_n_853363. The US Senate Committee on Health, Education, Labor, and Pensions conducted a two-year investigation of the for-profits, publishing their results as *For-Profit Higher Education: The Failure to Safeguard the Federal Investment and Ensure Student Success* (Washington, DC: US Government Printing Office, 2012), accessed July 24, 2020, https://www.help.senate.gov/imo/media/for_profit_report/PartI-PartIII-SelectedAppendixes.pdf.

14   Save CCSF/Fight Back, "What is the ACCJC: Facts and Analysis," accessed July 24, 2020, https://www.facebook.com/CitizensForEducationRestoration/posts/419181931498925; archived at https://www.freecitythebook.org/chapter-notes/chapter-5-notes/accjc-facts-and-analysis.

15   Students Making a Change (SMAC), "Our Demands for Sustaining City College," accessed October 6, 2020, https://tinyurl.com/yxrwgzoj.

Chapter 6

1   Carol Caref, Sarah Hainds, Kurt Hilgendorf, Pavlyn Jankov, and Kevin Russell, *The Black and White of Education in Chicago's Public Schools: Class, Charters & Chaos* (Chicago: Chicago Teachers Union, 2012), accessed July 24, 2020, http://www.ctunet.com/root/text/CTU-black-and-white-of-chicago-education.pdf.

2   Pauline Lipman, *High Stakes Education: Inequality, Globalization and Urban School Reform* (London: RoutledgeFalmer, 2004), 7–8.

3   Ibid.

4   San Francisco is both a city and a county. The San Francisco Community College District is geographically identical—but each has its distinct governing body. The City and County of San Francisco has the board of supervisors, and the community college district has the board of trustees. The board of supervisors has no formal power over City College's operations and policies. Neither does the mayor.

5   Robert Bezemek worked for the National Labor Relations Board in the early 1970s. He was also one of the first four lawyers hired for California's Agricultural Labor Relations Board and helped litigate early cases that bolstered farmworkers' right to organize. He was involved with cases that won bargaining rights for employees of K–12 and community college districts in California, as well as *Cervisi v. California Unemployment Insurance Appeals Board* (1989), which won laid off part-time faculty the right to unemployment compensation.

6   California Federation of Teachers, AFT, AFL-CIO, AFT Local 2121, et al., *Third Party Complaint and Comment to the US Department of Education in the Matter of the Accrediting Commission for Community and Junior Colleges and City College of San Francisco*, April 30, 2013, 193; archived at https://tinyurl.com/y5k2tsqq.

7   Ibid.

8   Ibid., 108.

9   Leslie Simon, "OPEB Made Simple," November 1, 2014; archived at https://www.freecitythebook.org/chapter-notes/chapter-6-notes/opeb-made-simple.

10   GASB is a private organization that sets accounting standards for governments and public agencies; see GASB, accessed July 25, 2020, www.gasb.org.

11   In late 2006, Congress passed the "Postal Accountability and Enhancement Act," which required the Postal Service "to prepay 75 years of retiree health care benefits totaling $55 billion over ten years. . . . And *presto!* a $5.5 billion annual deficit was born"; Peter Byrne, *Going Postal: US Senator Dianne Feinstein's Husband Sells Post Offices to His Friends*, Cheap (Byrne Ink, 2013) 16.

12   California Federation of Teachers et al., *Third Party Complaint and Comment to the US Department of Education in the Matter of the Accrediting Commission for Community and Junior Colleges and City College of San Francisco*, 99.

13   AFT 2121, "What Does the Accreditation Report Say?"; archived at https://www.freecitythebook.org/chapter-notes/chapter-6-notes/what-does-the-accreditation-report-say.

14   "Our Administration has focused attention on human resources and initiated many changes. It is unclear to me how well some of the changes align

with the standards and eligibility requirements. The commission expressed concern with the stability of our administrative leadership and directed us to fully integrate human resource planning with the planning and budgeting process. Changes currently underway at CCSF have not been integrated with the cycle of planning that starts with program review and some seem more likely to decrease, rather than increase, stability in leadership. The administration will be hiring for all the administrative positions in Academic Affairs (to start with) with no guarantees that the experienced incumbents will be rehired. The short-term uncertainties and the potential for major losses in continuity will challenge, rather than strengthen, administrative oversight and leadership"; Karen Saginor, "How Do We Measure Up?" January 3, 2013; archived at https://www.freecitythebook.org/chapter-notes/chapter-6-notes/how-do-we-measure-up.

15   Karen Saginor, "How Was the Visit? An Informal Composite Summary Culled from Informal Faculty Notes About the Accreditation Visit April 4–5"; archived at https://www.freecitythebook.org/chapter-notes/chapter-6-notes/how-was-the-visit.

Chapter Seven

1   ACCJC Decision to Terminate, July 3, 2013; archived at https://www.freecitythebook.org/chapter-notes/chapter-7/accjc-decision-to-terminate.

2   Barbara Beno email to Brice Harris; archived at https://www.freecitythebook.org/chapter-notes/chapter-7/beno-to-brice.

3   Brice W. Harris and Ed Lee, "A strong hand needed now at CCSF," *San Francisco Chronicle,* July 7, 2013, accessed October 8, 2020, https://www.sfgate.com/opinion/openforum/article/A-strong-hand-needed-now-at-CCSF-4649474.php.

4   Kim Philips-Fein, *Fear City: New York's Fiscal Crisis and the Rise of Austerity Politics* (New York: Metropolitan Books, 2017).

5   Chris Savage, "With Detroit Under an Emergency Manager, Half of Michigan Blacks Will Have No Elected Local Government" (blog), eclectablog, February 20, 2013, accessed July 25, 2020, https://tinyurl.com/y2tcowu7.

6   Domingo Morel, *Takeover: Race, Education, and American Democracy* (New York: Oxford University Press, 2018); Morel studied one hundred school districts that had been taken over by state governments.

7   Robert Gammon, "Phone Logs Link 'Politics' to School Takeover: Records show FCMAT officials made repeated calls to city's leaders before Chaconas' ouster," *Oakland Tribune,* August 18, 2003, accessed July 25, 2020, http://www.safero.org/perata/news/phonelogs.html.

Chapter Eight

1   Labor Video Project, "Thousands of CCSF Students, Faculty and Supporters March & Rally against Attack on Public Education" (video), YouTube, July 10, 2013, accessed July 25, 2020, https://www.youtube.com/watch?v=gY1j3JnMYhE.

2   Project SURVIVE is City College's sexual violence prevention program. Housed in the Women's and Gender Studies Department, it trains students as peer educators and creates a community of current and former peer educators and mentors; Project SURVIVE, City College of San Francisco, accessed July 30, 2020, https://tinyurl.com/yc5voapl.

3   "Barbara Beno Is Arrogant Condescending & Dismissive to Senators" (video), YouTube, August 23, 2013, accessed July 25, 2020, https://www.youtube.com/watch?v=lmMwEMrTh6w&t=103s.

4   "Herrera sues to block accreditors from shuttering City College of San Francisco," City Attorney of San Francisco, August 22, 2013, accessed July 25, 2020, https://tinyurl.com/y4yzgjpl.

5   "Off Target" (editorial), *San Francisco Chronicle*, August 23, 2013.

Chapter Nine

1   A commercial research organization, Interact, did a phone survey followed by focus groups that found that, on the one hand, people valued CCSF, and, on the other, did not understand its status and prospects because of the accreditation sanctions; Pamela Cox-Otto and Mark Mastej, City College of San Francisco Image Research, Interact, December 18, 2013, accessed July 26, 2020, https://tinyurl.com/y4j76xgk; archived at https://www.freecitythebook.org/chapter-notes/chapter-9/image-research-report-2013.

2   Megan Messerly, "City College's accreditation loss stuns students," *San Francisco Chronicle*, July 3, 2013, accessed July 26, 2020, https://www.sfchronicle.com/education/article/City-College-s-accreditation-loss-stuns-students-4646404.php; Nanette Asimov, "CCSF students race to finish classes—or withdraw," *San Francisco Chronicle*, July 9, 2013, accessed July 26, 2020, https://www.sfchronicle.com/bayarea/article/City-College-of-SF-students-tying-up-loose-ends-4655769.php; Kathleen Pender, "S.F. City College bonds downgraded amid woes," *San Francisco Chronicle*, August 14, 2013, accessed July 26, 2020, https://www.sfgate.com/business/networth/article/S-F-City-College-bonds-downgraded-amid-woes-4677036.php.

3   Hayley Sweetland Edwards, "America's Worst Community Colleges," *Washington Monthly*, September–October 2013, accessed July 26, 2020, https://washingtonmonthly.com/magazine/septoct-2013/americas-worst-community-colleges; Edwards would go on to write *Time* magazine's influential "rotten apples" cover story trashing teacher tenure, which appeared in the November 23, 2014 issue; Hayley Sweetland Edwards, "The War on Teacher Tenure," October 30, 2014, accessed July 26, 2020, https://time.com/3533556/the-war-on-teacher-tenure.

4   Karen Saginor, "Ongoing Concerns About the Staying Open Plan (aka the Road Map, aka the Accreditation Action Plans)," Academic Senate, October 28, 2013, accessed July 26, 2020, unavailable October 6, 2020, http://www.ccsf.edu/Organizations/Academic_Senate/RoadMapConcerns20131028.pdf; archived at https://www.freecitythebook.org/chapter-notes/chapter-9/road-map-concerns.

5   Arthur Q. Tyler's bio, Parras, Grande & Associates LLC, accessed July 26, 2020. http://www.parrasgrande.com/our-team.html.

6   Letter from California Community Colleges Chancellor Brice Harris to San Francisco City Attorney Dennis Herrera, January 2, 2014; archived at https://www.freecitythebook.org/chapter-notes/chapter-9/brice-harris-letter-to-herrera-1-2-2014.

7   Nelnet had bilked the DOE of $278 million between 2003 and 2005 by overbilling for student loan servicing. The company settled with the DOE in 2007 and agreed to stop the practice—but got to keep the money. In 2010, it paid $55 million to settle a civil suit over the same practice. Danielle Douglas-Gabriel, "The Student Loan Scandal That Just Won't Die," *Washington Post*, October 21, 2015, accessed July 26, 2020, https://www.washingtonpost.com/news/grade-point/wp/2015/10/21/the-student-loan-scandal-that-just-wont-die; also see Alan Michael Collinge, *The Student Loan Scam* (Boston: Beacon Press, 2009), 70.

8   *Guardsman,* November 22, 2013.

9   Nanette Asimov, "CCSF seeks millions in unpaid registration fees," *San Francisco Chronicle*, October 25, 2013, accessed July 26, 2020, https://www.sfgate.com/education/article/CCSF-seeks-millions-in-unpaid-registration-fees-4927254.php.

10   Students are eligible for California resident tuition under AB 540 if: they either attended high school in California for three years or had the equivalent of three years of high school coursework and had three or more years at California elementary and secondary schools; they graduated from a California high school or passed a high school equivalency exam; they enrolled in a California college or university; they legalized their status as soon as that was an option; they did not hold another nonimmigrant visa; see "California Dream Act Application," California Student Aid Commission, accessed July 26, 2020, https://www.csac.ca.gov/california-dream-act.

11   *AFT 2121 on Behalf of Itself and Its Members, California Federation of Teachers, et al. v. Accrediting Commission for Community and Junior Colleges*, Complaint filed in California Superior Court, San Francisco, September 23, 2013, 152, 157; archived at https://www.freecitythebook.org/chapter-notes/chapter-9/aft-cft-complaint-2013.

12   Andrea Koskey, "Cry for help unheeded at CCSF," *San Francisco Examiner*, September 15, 2013, accessed July 26, 2020, http://www.sfexaminer.com/cry-for-help-unheeded-at-ccsf.

13   City and County of San Francisco, Board of Supervisors Budget and Legislative Analyst, "Evaluation of the Impact of the Potential Closure of City College," September 16, 2013, accessed July 26, 2020, https://sfbos.org/sites/default/files/FileCenter/Documents/46531-BLA.CityCollege.FINAL%20091613.pdf; archived at https://www.freecitythebook.org/chapter-notes/chapter-9/sf-budget-analyst-cost-of-ccsf-closure.

14   CCSF Forum on Accreditation" (video), CFT Videos, November 8, 2013, accessed July 26, 2020, https://www.youtube.com/watch?v=2ENeqZytcNQ.

15   "Deputy City Attorney on CCSF Accreditation" (video), TheGuardsmanOnline, January 27, accessed July 26, 2020, https://www.youtube.com/watch? v=bLQFMO-_HUw, 8:30–8:40.s

Chapter Ten

1   Typically, corporations use SLAPP suits—strategic lawsuits against public participation—against social movements, as Energy Transfer Partners did when it sued Greenpeace and other groups that participated in the indigenous-led resistance to the Dakota Access Pipeline; see Valerie Volcovici, "Energy Transfer Sues Greenpeace Over Dakota Pipeline," Reuters, August 22, 2017, accessed July 26, 2020, https://tinyurl.com/yxh3q3vo.

2   "City College Wins Reprieve, as Court Enjoins ACCJC from Terminating Accreditation," City Attorney Dennis Herrera News Release, January 2, 2014, accessed July 26, 2020, https://tinyurl.com/y3f64qvj; archived at https://www. freecitythebook.org/chapter-notes/chapter-10/preliminary-injunction.

3   "Deputy City Attorney on CCSF Accreditation" (video), TheGuardsmanOnline, January 27, 2014, accessed July 26, 2020, https://www.youtube.com/ watch?v=bLQFMO-_HUw.

4   Alisa Messer, "President's Message: A Good Start to 2014," January 4, 2014, accessed July 26, 2020, http://www.aft2121.org/2014/01/presidents-message-a-good-start-to-2014.

5   Brice Harris Letter to Herrera, January 2, 2014; archived at https://www. freecitythebook.org/chapter-notes/chapter-10/brice-harris-to-dennis-herrera.

6   Peter Byrne documented via public records that CBRE had sold postal properties—public assets—to developers for far less than market value and received commissions as high as 6 percent for representing both seller and buyer in these transactions. Richard Blum served as chair of CBRE when this happened. Blum's investment firm, Blum Capital Partners, owned 6.9 percent of CBRE's stock in 2013. Board members and associates of Blum Capital also invested heavily in CBRE. Altogether they owned a total of 22 percent of CBRE's stock. See Peter Byrne, *Going Postal: US Senator Dianne Feinstein's Husband Sells Post Offices to His Friends, Cheap* (Byrne Ink, 2013), 26.

7   "Regular Meeting of the Board of Trustees San Francisco Community College District City College of San Francisco, City College of San Francisco"; see comments by Vice Chancellor of Student Development Samuel Santos, October 22, 2015, accessed July 26, 2020, http://ccsf.granicus.com/MediaPlayer.php?view_id=2&clip_id=557, 3:24:00.

8   The Save CCSF Research Committee recorded the figures Vice Chancellor Samuel Santos presented to the board of trustees at its October 22, 2015 meeting:

Semester and date of the robo-drop	Number of students dropped	Number that re-enrolled	Number pushed out
Spring 2014 12/20/13 Nelnet approved by BOT…	2,259	1,202	1,057
Fall 2014 8/12/14	2,917	1,300	1,617
Spring 2015 1/6/15	1,292	609	683
Fall 2015 8/5/15	2,656	1,173	1,483
Totals:	**9,124**	**4,284 (47%)**	**4,840 (53%)**

Calculations of money lost are based on a 2013–2014 state apportionment to City College of San Francisco of $4,704 per student, making the total for 1,057 students $4,972,128. CCSF recouped $270,592, an average of $256 per student. The difference between what the school recouped and what it would have gotten from the state was $4,701,536. The apportionment figure comes from the California Community Colleges chancellor's office budget workshop 2013–2014, unavailable September 21, 2020, http://extranet.cccco.edu/Divisions/FinanceFacilities/FiscalServicesUnit/BudgetWorkshopDocuments.aspx.

9   Alisa Messer, "President's Message," *Union Action*, March 2014. https://www.aft2121.org/2014/03/priorities-fact-or-science-fiction.

10   "Memorialize previously approved salaries of Vice Chancellor of Academic Affairs, Vice Chancellor of Finance and Administration, Vice Chancellor of Student Services, and General Counsel (Resolution No. 140227-III-B-55)," February 27, 2014, accessed July 26, 2020, http://www.ccsf.edu/BOT/2014/February/55.pdf; " Appointment- Non-Educational Administrator Chief Information Technology Officer (Resolution No. 140123-II-C-18), January 23, 2014, accessed July 26, 2020, unavailable October 7, 2020, https://www.ccsf.edu/en/about-city-college/board-of-trustees/bot_meetings2014/January.html; also see Chris Hanzo, "Upside Down Priorities at CCSF Continue," *Union Action*, March 2014, accessed October 7, 2020, https://issuu.com/aft2121/docs/march-2014, 4.

11   Resolution allocating money to enter into a contract with Ellucian at "trustees" meeting December 19, 2013.

12   Ary Spatig-Amerikaner, *Unequal Education: Federal Loophole Enables Lower Spending on Students of Color*, Center for American Progress, August 2012, accessed July 26, 2020, https://cdn.americanprogress.org/wp-content/uploads/2012/08/UnequalEduation.pdf.

13   Hans Johnson, "Evaluating Student Success at CCSF," Public Policy Institute of California, March 3, 2014, accessed July 26, 2020, https://www.ppic.org/blog/evaluating-student-success-at-the-city-college-of-san-francisco.

14   Joe Fitzgerald Rodriguez, "Democracy for None," *San Francisco Bay Guardian*, accessed July 26, 2020, http://www.scrollkit.com/s/o1NsnxX.

15   The CPA, founded in 1972, organizes low-wage and working-class Chinese immigrants in San Francisco. The Tenant Worker Center educates workers on their rights and helps them organize against wage theft and other abuses. It also collaborates on a hospitality and vocational training program with City College. CPA works on civic engagement as well. It was a founding member of the San Francisco Rising electoral alliance and runs the Political Empowerment Campaign to build leadership skills and knowledge of political issues in the Chinese immigrant community. CPA youth members have initiated various campaigns, including the City College work and Our Healing in Our Hands, which aimed to improve access to and competency of mental health services for Asian American youth; see Chinese Progressive Association, accessed October 7, 2020, www.cpasf.org.

16   *San Francisco Bay Guardian* 48, no. 26, April 2, 2013.

17   The "Twitter tax break," also called the "Mid-Market Tax Break," or, formally, the Central Market/Tenderloin Payroll Tax Exclusion, passed in 2011, exempting businesses from San Francisco's 1.5 percent payroll tax if they agree to relocate to the Mid-Market area. For a breakdown of the lost tax revenue for 2013, see "San Francisco's Mid-Market Tax Break by the Numbers," June 24, 2014, accessed July 27, 2020, https://sfist.com/2014/06/24/san_franciscos_mid-market_tax_break.

18   Richard Walker, "Why Is There a Housing Crisis?" *East Bay Express*, March 23, 2016, accessed July 27, 2020, http://www.eastbayexpress.com/oakland/why-is-there-a-housing-crisis/Content?oid=4722242.

19   *San Francisco's Widening Income Inequality*, San Francisco Human Services Agency, May 2014, accessed July 27, 2020, https://tinyurl.com/y6zuetpe.

Chapter Eleven

1   "Transcript of Pelosi Remarks at City College of San Francisco," January 7, 2014, accessed July 27, 2020, https://www.speaker.gov/newsroom/transcript-pelosi-remarks-city-college-san-francisco.

2   DOE Letter to ACCJC, January 28, 2014; archived at https://www.freecitythebook.org/chapter-notes/chapter-11/doe-letter.

3   "Two Year Rule—Karen Saginor," May 29, 2014; archived at https://www.freecitythebook.org/chapter-notes/chapter-11/two-year-rule.

4   Nanette Asimov, "CCSF accrediting group can extend deadline, feds tell Pelosi," *San Francisco Chronicle*, May 20, 2014, accessed September 21, 2020, https://www.sfchronicle.com/education/article/CCSF-accrediting-group-can-extend-deadline-feds-5492222.php; archived at https://www.freecitythebook.org/chapter-notes/chapter-11/doe-to-pelosi.

5   Nanette Asimov, "State auditor slams accrediting group that sanctioned CCSF," *San Francisco Chronicle*, June 26, 2014, accessed July 27, 2020, https://

www.sfgate.com/education/article/State-auditor-slams-accrediting-group-that-5582725.php.

6   Restoration status is published as part of the commission policies, but we have been unable to find correspondence with CCSF suggesting they apply for it.

7   "Restoration Status and Union Analysis," AFT 2121, June 26, 2014, accessed August 6, 2020, https://www.aft2121.org/2014/06/restoration-status-union-analysis-and-comment.

8   Alvin Ja. RestorationNoGoodAlvinPerfect100%, email communication; see https://www.freecitythebook.org/chapter-notes/chapter-11/alvin-ja-restoration-no-good.

9   Nanette Asimov, "CCSF's Last Option to Avoid Closure Is Full of Uncertainty," *San Francisco Chronicle*, July 30, 2014, accessed July 27, 2020, https://www.sfchronicle.com/education/article/CCSF-s-last-option-to-avoid-closure-is-full-of-5658386.php.

10   "ACCJC Press Release: Commission's Decision on Remand Review," accessed July 27, 2020; archived at https://www.freecitythebook.org/chapter-notes/chapter-11/accjc-remand-review-july-21-2014.

11   Harris-Beno Exchange, June 2014; archived at https://www.freecitythebook.org/chapter-notes/chapter-11/harris-beno-exchange.

12   Ibid.

Chapter Twelve

1   *People of the State of California v. Accrediting Commission for Community and Junior Colleges*, (transcript), October 27, 2014, 7.

2   Ibid., 67.

3   Ibid., 99.

4   Ibid., 156.

5   Tim Killikelly, "'This Case Is About Fairness'—Day One of 'The People vs. ACCJC,'" AFT 2121, October 27, 2014, accessed July 27, 2020, https://www.aft2121.org/2014/10/this-case-is-about-fairness-day-one-of-the-people-vs-accjc.

6   Tim Redmond, "ACCJC Prez Admits City College Got Unfair Treatment," 48hills, October 28, 2014, accessed July 27, 2020, https://48hills.org/2014/10/accjc-prez-admits-city-college-got-unfair-treatment.

7   Nanette Asimov, "Dramatic testimony shakes up City College of San Francisco trial," *San Francisco Chronicle*, October 28, 2014, accessed October 7, 2020, https://www.sfchronicle.com/bayarea/article/Dramatic-testimony-shakes-up-City-College-of-San-5854492.php.

8   *People of the State of California v. Accrediting Commission for Community and Junior Colleges* (transcript), October 31, 2014, 950.

9   "'The People vs. ACCJC'—A day-by-day Report, October 27–31," California Federation of Teachers; archived at https://www.freecitythebook.org/chapter-notes/chapter-12/trial-report-day-by-day.

Chapter Thirteen

1   Figures from a presentation to the CCSF board of trustees on October 22, 2015, by vice chancellor of Student Development Samuel Santos, item XI. A. The policy enforced by STWEP Agrella required students to pay all their fees at the time of enrollment, before their financial aid had arrived. Those who couldn't pay were automatically dropped (robo-dropped) from their classes; see chapter 10 notes 7 and 8.

Chapter Fourteen

1   City College's upper and lower parking areas have a combined total of 2,100 spaces, which turn over a number of times during the day as students rush in and out. When City College was at an enrollment high point in 2008, both lots would be full during prime times, Monday through Thursday.

2   For a detailed account of the "Reservoir Wars," see Amy O'Hair, "Ballot Battles and Campus Claims: The History of the Balboa Reservoir 1983–1991," Sunnyside History Project, April 8, 2018, accessed July 28, 2020, https://tinyurl.com/y58t633z.

3   Affordable for whom? San Francisco's dramatic income inequality means that median income is a misleading measure. While San Francisco median income looks high, more than $70,000 for a single person, when we look at the federal definition of affordable housing as no more than 30 percent of income, a different picture emerges. According to recent San Francisco estimates, clerks make $48,568 per year; 30 percent is $1,200 per month. A teacher with three years of experience makes $59,197 per year; 30 percent is $1,480 per month. Ninety-four percent of available rentals in San Francisco cost more than $2,000 a month.

4   In 2012, the annual Golden Shovel Competition run by the Bay Area Chapter of the NAIOP Commercial Real Estate Development Association focused on the Balboa Reservoir—even though the property wasn't officially slated for development and had not been declared surplus. The competition challenges teams of graduate students to design a development proposal for the chosen site; see NAIOP Commercial Real Estate Development Association San Francisco Bay Area Chapter, accessed July 28, 2020, https://naiopsfba.org/about/history.

5   Mary Ann Azevedo, "Public Land Sites Could Hold Thousands of Units of Housing in S.F.," November 17, 2014, accessed July 28, 2020, https://tinyurl.com/y4a6bpvh.

6   "Newly Appointed City College of San Francisco Special Trustee to Guide Return of Control to Locally Elected Board of Trustees" (press release), California Community Colleges Chancellor's Office, February 23, 2015. This press release, issued to announce Guy Lease's arrival at CCSF notes, "The Board of Trustees is already participating in meetings, receiving trainings and briefings on the college's finances, academics and operations. Under an updated transition plan, it will assume authority for student services and academic programs in March and by July will have responsibility for all

functions, including finance"; archived at https://www.freecitythebook.org/chapter-notes/chapter-14/stwep-and-trustee-resumption-of-power.

7 The California Education Code requires the Board of Governors to define accreditation conditions for colleges to receive state funding. Each college must be accredited by an accreditor recognized by the US secretary of education, recommended by the state chancellor, and approved by the Board of Governors. For a complete history of the California Community Colleges Chancellor's Office and task forces on accreditation, see "California Community Colleges Chief Executive Officers Accreditation Reform Timeline 2009–2017," accessed July 28, 2020, https://tinyurl.com/y2fogk5m.

8 "The Epic Battle for Fair Accreditation: CCSF, Community & Leaders Stand Up for Fair Accreditation," accessed August 7, 2020, https://www.aft2121.org/wp-content/uploads/Epic-Battle.pdf; archived at https://www.freecitythebook.org/chapter-notes/chapter-14/timeline-epic-battle-for-fair-accreditation.; "Top Ten Lies of the ACCJC," AFT 2121, April 27, 2015, accessed August 7, 2020, https://www.aft2121.org/2015/04/top-accjc-lies.

9 "Open Letter on Payment Policy," December 2015"; archived at https://www.freecitythebook.org/chapter-notes/chapter-14/open-letter-on-payment-policy.

10 Michael Cabanatuan, "City College of S.F. exec Art Tyler resigns amid controversy," *San Francisco Chronicle*, January 7, 2016, accessed September 26, 2020, https://tinyurl.com/y2beevhf.

Chapter Fifteen

1 Laurie Fried-Lee, "Some History: Former AFT 2121 President Recounts the Trials of Bargaining for Our First Contract," AFT 2121, accessed July 28, 2020, https://www.aft2121.org/some-history.

2 Steven K. Ashby and Robert Bruno, *A Fight for the Soul of Public Education: The Story of the Chicago Teachers Strike* (Ithaca, NY: Cornell University Press, 2016).

3 ACCJC Vice Chair Steven Kinsella's Exchange with San Mateo Community College Chancellor Ron Galatolo; archived at https://www.freecitythebook.org/wp-content/uploads/2020/04/3-Kinsella-Galatolo-exchange-October-2013.pdf.

4 Before AFT 2121's delegate assembly voted in 2014 to revise the structure, "We had some precincts that were ninety-five people with one rep, and it was completely unmanageable, so we either added reps, or we split precincts . . . to try to reduce the number of people each person was responsible for and make the groupings more reflective of existing relationships," AFT 2121 secretary Jessica Buchsbaum said in an interview. "It was all about making it easier for the union to reach members and members to connect to each other. Some of the precincts were just natural, like English at Ocean Campus . . . and we had some others that were [not], for example, 'Mission-other,' any faculty member who taught at Mission Campus that were not in ESL. You can imagine that was a precinct that was completely impossible to organize. They didn't know each other, never saw each other, had no existing awareness

of each other. We couldn't get a rep for that, could never contact people, no idea what they were doing, where they were, who they were. So one of the things we did in the revision of the precincts was return those people to their departments, because the departments are a more natural connection. Someone who taught an evening class at Mission didn't think of themselves as a Mission person, they were a math instructor at City College, so a Math Department rep had a better chance of being able to get information to them."

5   Workers who strike over violations of labor law—"unfair labor practices"—can't legally be fired for striking. If they walk out for other reasons, such as low pay, they can be permanently replaced.

6   "CCSF faculty Reach Tentative Contract Agreement with CCSF District Administration," AFT 2121, July 29, 2016, accessed July 28, 2020, https://www.aft2121.org/2016/07.

7   Rick Baum, "Lack of Democracy Weakens Organized Labor: The Example of City College of San Francisco During Its Accreditation Crisis," United Public Workers for Action, August 20, 2016, accessed July 28, 2020, https://www.upwa.info/documents/8-20-16%20Rick%20Baum%20CCSF%20accreditation%20crisis.htm.

Chapter Sixteen

1   Chris Hanson and Alvin "A.J." Ja dug into the data and methods the planners relied on. The parking survey that informed the TDM was taken by the Nelson/Nygaard company during the week before final exams, commonly referred to as "dead week," because the campus is so quiet. It showed the Lower Reservoir lot less than 10 percent full, based on an average occupancy that included the hours between 10:00 a.m. and 4:00 p.m. and those between 10:30 pm and 12:00 a.m.; the latter time slot is long after evening classes let out. Hanson and Ja concluded that the parking report had been skewed to show a low need for parking. Another survey commissioned the school and done by the Sandis firm during the first week of school during the fall 2016 semester showed the lot filling to almost 50 percent of capacity during the school day—and this in the semester where enrollment hit its lowest point since the crisis began.

2   Angela Woodall and Michael Stoll, "In Bid for Dominance, Mayor's Allies Flood S.F. Politics with Corporate Cash," *San Francisco Public Press,* August 17, 2016, accessed July 29, 2020, https://tinyurl.com/y5w5z8s8.

3   Among the many examples cited was that of Alex Tourk, a lobbyist and former aide and campaign manager to Gavin Newsom who bundled campaign contributions for Lee. As they were collecting cash, Tourk and other fundraisers "were actively asking for favors from City Hall," Woodall and Stoll noted. Tourk lobbied on behalf of Lyft and a real estate company seeking a good deal on a South of Market Project. He had twenty-six meetings with supervisors and city officials in the planning and housing departments between February and mid-November—including one with an official "to find underutilized properties for potential development"; ibid.

4   Gray Brechin, *Imperial San Francisco* (Berkeley: University of California Press, 1999).

5   "Final Damage Count to City College of San Francisco from the Five-Year Accreditation Crisis," Research Committee Serving the Struggle to Save City College, unpublished paper, 2018; archived at https://www.freecitythebook. org/chapter-notes/chapter-16/final-damage-count.

6   "Administration's Policy of Cutting Full Time Faculty Positions Undermines Enrollment," AFT 2121, March 15, 2017, accessed September 25, 2020, https:// tinyurl.com/y457f7dl.

7   "Pelosi, Spier, and Eshoo Urge DOE to Delist ACCJC"; archived at https://www. freecitythebook.org/chapter-notes/chapter-16/pelosi-speier-eshoo-to-doe.

Chapter Seventeen

1   JJ Narayan at Save CCSF media briefing, October 5, 2016, CCSF Mission Campus.

2   Joaquin Palomino and Emily Green, "Powerful Interest Groups Funding Wiener-Kim State Senate Race," *San Francisco Chronicle*, October 23, 2016, accessed August 7, 2020, https://tinyurl.com/yxwcxh38.

Chapter Eighteen

1   Emily Green, "Trump's sanctuary city threat, shortfalls lead SF to revise budget," *San Francisco Chronicle*, November 28, 2016, accessed July 29, 2020, https://www.sfchronicle.com/politics/article/Trump-s-sanctuary-city-threat-shortfalls-lead-10638974.php.

2   Then director of JWJ Gordon Mar pointed out that the mayor spent more of the funds on street trees than on the "Free City" program that headlined the campaign for the new tax.

3   In 2018–2019, City College had only 218 of these AB 540/California Dream Act undocumented students who had graduated with three or more years of high school in California; estimates are that there are twice as many undocumented students who do not meet these criteria.

4   There has also been discussion of getting the program to apply to anyone who works in San Francisco, given the large numbers of community people who have been gentrified over to the East Bay.

5   At its January and June 2018 meetings, ACCJC reaffirmed accreditation for all the colleges under review; Marty Hittelman, accessed November 3, 2019, unavailable October 7, 2020, www.accreditationwatch.org/intro.

6   "Two years after the BAPCPA [cancellation of bankruptcy protection for students] was enacted, federal loans accounted for 70 percent of the educational funding provided to students"; Susanne Soederberg, *Debtfare States and the Poverty Industry: Money, Discipline and the Surplus Population* (Milton Park, UK: Routledge, 2014), 124; also see William Zumeta, David W. Breneman, Patrick M, Callan, and Joi E. Finney, *Financing American Higher Education in the Era of Globalization* (Cambridge, MA: Harvard Education Press, 2012), 77.

Epilogue

1   According to then vice chancellor of facilities Reuben Smith, City College was paying $55,000 per month to lease back its office space at 33 Gough Street; Vicki Legion, "Notes from City College Facilities Committee Meeting," April 23, 2018.

2   The project's website says that 50 percent of the 1,100 housing units will be affordable. The breakdown tells a different story: 18 percent low-income units, 17 percent moderate income, and 17 percent subsidized by the city; see Balboa Reserve, accessed July 29, 2020, www.balboareservoir.com. The Mayor's Office of Housing and Community Development defines low-income as 55 percent of the area median income (AMI), $60,950 for a family of three; moderate income is 120 percent AMI, $133,000 for a family of three. Some of the city-subsidized units will be rentals affordable at 55 percent AMI and 120 percent AMI, and some will be for sale affordable at 105 percent AMI. There's no specification on what the mix will be; see "2019 AMI—SF Income Limits Chart," accessed July 29, 2020, https://sfmohcd.org/file/62258.

3   "About Us: Free City College," accessed October 7, 2020, https://www.dcyf.org/ccfaf.

4   Sam Lew, "Supes approve City College money: Will mayor veto?" 48hills, January 29, 2020, accessed October 7, 2020, https://48hills.org/2020/01/supes-approve-city-college-money-will-mayor-veto.

5   Alexei Koseff, "Be more like Chipotle, Jerry Brown tells California Universities," *Sacramento Bee*, May 24, 2018, accessed September 21, 2020, https://www.sacbee.com/news/politics-government/capitol-alert/article211828544.html.

6   The Sacramento-based CCO was cofounded by the California Business Roundtable, the state's most powerful corporate lobby group, composed of the CEOs of California's two dozen largest transnational corporations; the president of the Roundtable was the founding chairman of the CCO board and served for seven years. The Lumina and Gates Foundations have been consistent funders of CCO. The organization has anchored advocacy for the completion agenda, organizing press conferences and collecting endorsements for the Student Success Act and other measures. It is also a main source of data about the issue of equity for students of color in postsecondary education.

7   Governor's Press Office, "As California Students Return to School, Governor Newsom Highlights New State Investments to Make Two Years of Community College Tuition Free," August 27, 2019, accessed July 29, 2020, https://tinyurl.com/y4d7ygt2.

8   In fall 2019, only 26.78 percent of California community college students took a full-time load of twelve units or more, while 73.22 percent attended part-time; see California Community Colleges Chancellor's Office, "Management Information Systems Data Mart," ca.gov, accessed September 20, 2020, https://datamart.cccco.edu/students/Unit_Load_Status.aspx.

California Community Colleges Chancellor's Office
Student Enrollment Status Summary Report

	Fall 2019	Fall 2019
	Student Count	Student Count (%)
State of California Total	1,568,655	100.00 %
0 Units	56	0.00 %
0.1–2.9	80,040	5.10 %
3.0–5.9	392,851	25.04 %
6.0–8.9	267,282	17.04 %
9.0–11.9	224,798	14.33 %
12.0–14.9	313,947	20.01 %
15+	146,881	9.36 %
Non-Credit	142,800	9.10 %

Report Run Date As Of: 9/20/2020 3:47:47 PM

9   *Lumina Foundation Strategic Plan for 2017 to 2020*, accessed July 29, 2020, https://www.luminafoundation.org/files/resources/strategic-plan-2017-to-2020-apr17.pdf.
10   Eric Blanc, *Red State Revolt* (New York: Verso, 2019), 209.
11   See appendix titled "The Policy Network that Drives Community College Education 'Reform,'" 199–204, this volume.
12   "25,000 Community Schools by 2025," Journey for Justice Alliance, accessed July 30, 2020, https://j4jalliance.com/project-details-3.

Chronology of the Crisis
1   "City College of San Francisco parcel tax, Proposition A (November 2012)," accessed October 6, 2020, https://ballotpedia.org/City_College_of_San_Francisco_parcel_tax,_Proposition_A_(November_2012).

The Policy Network That Drives Community College Education "Reform"
1   Megan Tompkins-Stange, *Policy Patrons* (Cambridge, MA: Harvard Education Press, 2016), 82; Diane Ravitch, "*Wall Street Journal*: Obama Staffers Flee to Broken For-Profit College Sector" (blog), February17, 2016, accessed July 30, 2020, https://dianeravitch.net/2016/02/17/wall-street-journal-obama-staffers-flee-to-broken-for-profit-college-sector.
2   Quoted in Boyce Brown, *A Policy History of Standards-Based Education in America* (Bern, CH: International Academic Publishers, 2015), 35.
3   Kevin Carey, "A Tale of Too Big to Fail in Higher Education," *New York Times*, July 14, 2014, accessed July 30, 2020, https://www.nytimes.com/2014/07/15/upshot/city-college-of-san-francisco-survives.html.
4   Juliet Scherer and Mirra Anson, *Community Colleges and the Access Effect* (London: Palgrave Macmillan, 2014), 32.

5   "Grants Database," Lumina Foundation, accessed July 31, 2020, https://www.luminafoundation.org/resources/grants/grant-database.

6   According to the Center for Media and Democracy, "ALEC is a corporate bill mill. It is not just a lobby or a front group; it is much more powerful than that. Through ALEC, corporations hand state legislators their wish lists to benefit their bottom line. Corporations fund almost all of ALEC's operations. They pay for a seat on ALEC task forces where corporate lobbyists and special interest reps vote with elected officials to approve 'model bills'"; see "ALEC Exposed," accessed July 31, 2020, https://www.alecexposed.org/wiki/ALEC_Exposed. As early as August 2009, ALEC's board of directors approved the "Resolution Calling for Greater Productivity in American Higher Education." This model legislation prefigured the language of California's Student Success Task Force: "The [state] Legislature recognizes the need to increase and reward college completion rates while promoting efficiency and cost-effectiveness at colleges and universities and recognizing alternative, innovative forms of postsecondary education, including community colleges and the lessons of for-profit models."

7   Peter Temin, *The Vanishing Middle Class: Prejudice and Power in a Dual Economy* (Boston: MIT Press, 2017), 19.

8   Zaid Jilani, "EXPOSED: The Corporations Funding The Annual Meeting of the Powerful Right-Wing Front Group ALEC," ThinkProgress, August 5, 2011, accessed October 7, 2020, https://tinyurl.com/y29cq4lu.

9   Democratic National Committee, "Where we stand: Education," accessed September 25, 2020, https://democrats.org/where-we-stand/the-issues/education.

10   "Republican Views on Education," Republican Views on the Issues, April 3, 2014, accessed July 31, 2020, https://www.republicanviews.org/republican-views-on-education.

11   Tony Wand and Tyler Millward, "US Edtech Closes Decade with Record $1.7 Billion Raised in 2019," EdSurge, January 15, 2020, accessed July 31, 2020, https://www.edsurge.com/news/2020-01-15-us-edtech-closes-decade-with-record-1-7-billion-raised-in-2019.

12   Stephanie Hall, "TCF Analysis of 70+ University-OPM Contracts Reveals Increasing Risks to Students, Public Education," Century Foundation, September 12, 2019, accessed July 31, 2020, https://tinyurl.com/y47zw3bt.

13   Natasha Singer and Daisuke Wakabayashi, "New Mexico Sues Google, Charging It Spied on Children," *New York Times*, February 21, 2020, accessed July 31, 2020, https://www.nytimes.com/2020/02/20/technology/new-mexico-google-lawsuit.html.

14   San Francisco Board of Supervisors Budget and Legislative Analyst, "Evaluation of the Potential Impact of the Closure of San Francisco City College," September 16, 2013, accessed July 31, 2020, http://www.sfbos.org/Modules/ShowDocument.aspx?documentid=46531.

15   Jorge Rivas, "For-Profit Colleges' Mostly Black and Latino Students Face Higher Debt and Unemployment," ColorLines, January 4, 2012, accessed July 31, 2020, https://tinyurl.com/y47thdoa.

16 US Senate Committee on Health, Education, Labor, and Pensions, "For-Profit Higher Education: The Failure to Safeguard the Federal Investment and Ensure Student Success," Washington, DC: US Government Printing Office, July 30, 2012; "Executive Summary," accessed July 31, 2020, http://www.help.senate.gov/imo/media/for_profit_report/ExecutiveSummary.pdf.

Student Learning Outcomes: SLO Torture

1 Mary Lee Smith, Linda Miller-Kahn, Walter Heinecke, and Patricia Jarvis, *Political Spectacle and the Fate of American Schools* (New York: RoutledgeFalmer, 2004), 195; quoted in Boyce Brown, *A Policy History of Standards-Based Education in America* (New York: Peter Lang Publishing, 2015), 47.

2 Laura Chapman, "The Marketing of Student Learning Objectives (SLOs): 1999–2014" (prepublication draft); archived at https://www.freecitythebook.org/chapter-notes/slo-torture-2.

3 Erik Gilbert, "An Insider's Take on Assessment: It May Be Worse Than You Thought," *Chronicle of Higher Education*, January 12, 2018, accessed July 31, 2020, https://www.chronicle.com/article/an-insiders-take-on-assessment-it-may-be-worse-than-you-thought.

Index

"Passim" (literally "scattered") indicates intermittent discussion of a topic over a cluster of pages.

About the Authors

Marcy Rein is a writer, editor, and organizer who worked for the International Longshore and Warehouse Union for almost twelve years, writing for its newspaper and serving as the communications specialist for its organizing department. Her articles have appeared in women's, queer, labor, and left publications from *Off Our Backs* to *Race, Poverty & the Environment*. With her husband, Clifton Ross, she edited *Until the Rulers Obey: Voices from Latin American Social Movements* (PM Press, 2014).

Mickey Ellinger writes regularly for *News from Native California* and other California-based publications. She is the author of *Allensworth, the Freedom Colony: A California African American Township* (Heyday Books, 2007). She has served as treasurer of the Bay Area chapter of the National Writers Union and is a member of the board of the Making Contact social justice radio project.

Vicki Legion has been on the faculty at City College of San Francisco since 1994 and is part of the long-standing network of social justice organizers in public education. She was a core activist of the Save City College Coalition, convening its Research Committee and uncovering the role of lobbyists in the manufacture of the City College accreditation crisis. She has presented to several national audiences, among them the American Association of University Professors and the Campaign for the Future of Higher Education.

Pauline Lipman is a professor in the Educational Policy Studies Department at the College of Education, University of Illinois at Chicago and the author of *The New Political Economy of Urban Education: Neoliberalism, Race, and the Right to the City* (Routledge, 2011).

ABOUT PM PRESS

PM Press is an independent, radical publisher of books and media to educate, entertain, and inspire. Founded in 2007 by a small group of people with decades of publishing, media, and organizing experience, PM Press amplifies the voices of radical authors, artists, and activists. Our aim is to deliver bold political ideas and vital stories to all walks of life and arm the dreamers to demand the impossible. We have sold millions of copies of our books, most often one at a time, face to face. We're old enough to know what we're doing and young enough to know what's at stake. Join us to create a better world.

PM Press
PO Box 23912
Oakland, CA 94623
www.pmpress.org

PM Press in Europe
europe@pmpress.org
www.pmpress.org.uk

FRIENDS OF PM PRESS

These are indisputably momentous times—the financial system is melting down globally and the Empire is stumbling. Now more than ever there is a vital need for radical ideas.

In the years since its founding—and on a mere shoestring—PM Press has risen to the formidable challenge of publishing and distributing knowledge and entertainment for the struggles ahead. With over 450 releases to date, we have published an impressive and stimulating array of literature, art, music, politics, and culture. Using every available medium, we've succeeded in connecting those hungry for ideas and information to those putting them into practice.

Friends of PM allows you to directly help impact, amplify, and revitalize the discourse and actions of radical writers, filmmakers, and artists. It provides us with a stable foundation from which we can build upon our early successes and provides a much-needed subsidy for the materials that can't necessarily pay their own way. You can help make that happen—and receive every new title automatically delivered to your door once a month—by joining as a Friend of PM Press. And, we'll throw in a free T-shirt when you sign up.

Here are your options:

- **$30 a month** Get all books and pamphlets plus 50% discount on all webstore purchases

- **$40 a month** Get all PM Press releases (including CDs and DVDs) plus 50% discount on all webstore purchases

- **$100 a month** Superstar—Everything plus PM merchandise, free downloads, and 50% discount on all webstore purchases

For those who can't afford $30 or more a month, we have **Sustainer Rates** at $15, $10, and $5. Sustainers get a free PM Press T-shirt and a 50% discount on all purchases from our website.

Your Visa or Mastercard will be billed once a month, until you tell us to stop. Or until our efforts succeed in bringing the revolution around. Or the financial meltdown of Capital makes plastic redundant. Whichever comes first.

Teaching Resistance: Radicals, Revolutionaries, and Cultural Subversives in the Classroom

Edited by John Mink

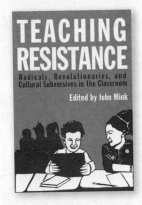

ISBN: 978-1-62963-709-9
$24.95   416 pages

Teaching Resistance is a collection of the voices of activist educators from around the world who engage inside and outside the classroom from pre-kindergarten to university and emphasize teaching radical practice from the field. Written in accessible language, this book is for anyone who wants to explore new ways to subvert educational systems and institutions, collectively transform educational spaces, and empower students and other teachers to fight for genuine change. Topics include community self-defense, Black Lives Matter and critical race theory, intersections between punk/DIY subculture and teaching, ESL, anarchist education, Palestinian resistance, trauma, working-class education, prison teaching, the resurgence of (and resistance to) the Far Right, special education, antifascist pedagogies, and more.

Edited by social studies teacher, author, and punk musician John Mink, the book features expanded entries from the monthly column in the politically insurgent punk magazine *Maximum Rocknroll*, plus new works and extensive interviews with subversive educators. Contributing teachers include Michelle Cruz Gonzales, Dwayne Dixon, Martín Sorrondeguy, Alice Bag, Miriam Klein Stahl, Ron Scapp, Kadijah Means, Mimi Nguyen, Murad Tamini, Yvette Felarca, Jessica Mills, and others, all of whom are unified against oppression and readily use their classrooms to fight for human liberation, social justice, systemic change, and true equality.

Royalties will be donated to Teachers 4 Social Justice: t4sj.org

"Teaching Resistance *brings us the voices of activist educators who are fighting back inside and outside of the classroom. The punk rock spirit of this collection of concise, hard-hitting essays is bound to stir up trouble.*"
—Mark Bray, historian, author of *Antifa: The Anti-Fascist Handbook* and coeditor of *Anarchist Education and the Modern School: A Francisco Ferrer Reader*

"*Where was* Teaching Resistance *when I was in school? This essay collection both makes a compelling case for why radical classrooms are necessary and lays out how they can be put into practice. A perfect guide for educators and anyone working with young people, this book vitally also speaks to the student's experience. Even for the kid-adverse activists among us,* Teaching Resistance *reminds us that kids can be our comrades if we meet them halfway. The younger generations deserve more from us— this is the primer for how to start providing it.*"
—Shawna Potter, singer for War on Women, author of *Making Spaces Safer*

Anarchism and Education: A Philosophical Perspective

Judith Suissa

ISBN: 978-1-60486-114-3
$19.95   184 pages

While there have been historical accounts of the anarchist school movement, there has been no systematic work on the philosophical underpinnings of anarchist educational ideas—until now.

Anarchism and Education offers a philosophical account of the neglected tradition of anarchist thought on education. Although few anarchist thinkers wrote systematically on education, this analysis is based largely on a reconstruction of the educational thought of anarchist thinkers gleaned from their various ethical, philosophical, and popular writings. Primarily drawing on the work of the nineteenth-century anarchist theorists such as Bakunin, Kropotkin, and Proudhon, the book also covers twentieth-century anarchist thinkers such as Noam Chomsky, Paul Goodman, Daniel Guérin, and Colin Ward.

This original work will interest philosophers of education and educationalist thinkers as well as those with a general interest in anarchism.

"This is an excellent book that deals with important issues through the lens of anarchist theories and practices of education . . . The book tackles a number of issues that are relevant to anybody who is trying to come to terms with the philosophy of education."
—*Higher Education Review*

The People's Republic of Neverland: The Child versus the State

Robb Johnson

ISBN: 978-1-62963-795-2
$20.00   288 pages

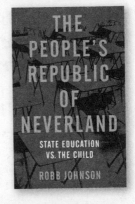

There once was a time when teachers and communities were able to exercise democratic control over their schools. Now that power has been taken away, both centralised and privatised, under the guise of "reform." There is a forgotten history of the time before reform, and within it a bright horizon is visible, reachable only if educators and society at large can learn the lessons of the past.

Robb Johnson entered the classroom as a new teacher in the 1980s and has spent a lifetime alongside his pupils encouraging both creativity and a healthy distrust of authority. This book is both memoir and polemic, a celebration of children's innate desire to learn, share, cooperate, and play, as well as a critique of bureaucratic interference. Johnson details how we ended up with the contemporary mass education systems and why they continually fail to give children what they need. Combining practical experience as a teacher with detailed pedagogical knowledge, and a characteristic playful style, Johnson is both court chronicler and jester, imparting information and creatively admonishing the self-important figureheads of the reform agenda.

This book considers how schools and education relate to the wider society in which they are located and how they relate to the particular needs and abilities of the people who experience them. It shows that schools and education are contested spaces that need to be reclaimed from the state, and turned into places where people can grow, not up, not old, but as individuals. It offers alternative ways of running classrooms, schools, and perhaps even society.

"I have rarely seen a book that is so embedded in what education is for and that then directs the reader to how to pursue the goals, in practice and at all levels of school infrastructure so that the way schools are structured adds to the goodness of society."
—Marcelo Staricoff, author of *Start Thinking*, fellow of the Chartered College of Teaching, and former headteacher

"The People's Republic of Neverland: The Child versus the State by Robb Johnson shows the stark reality of the current situation for education. Education is at a crossroads, and this book comes at an important time raising awareness and exposing the flaws in our current system. Read this, and then join the campaign to fight for a fairer, fully funded, comprehensive education system!"
—Louise Regan, ex-president of National Education Union (UK)

Anarchist Pedagogies: Collective Actions, Theories, and Critical Reflections on Education

Edited by Robert H. Haworth
with an afterword by Allan Antliff

ISBN: 978-1-60486-484-7
$24.95   352 pages

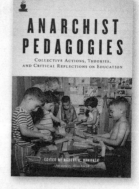

Education is a challenging subject for anarchists.
Many are critical about working within a state-run
education system that is embedded in hierarchical, standardized, and authoritarian
structures. Numerous individuals and collectives envision the creation of
counterpublics or alternative educational sites as possible forms of resistance,
while other anarchists see themselves as "saboteurs" within the public arena—
believing that there is a need to contest dominant forms of power and educational
practices from multiple fronts. Of course, if anarchists agree that there are no
blueprints for education, the question remains, in what dynamic and creative
ways can we construct nonhierarchical, anti-authoritarian, mutual, and voluntary
educational spaces?

Contributors to this edited volume engage readers in important and challenging
issues in the area of anarchism and education. From Francisco Ferrer's modern
schools in Spain and the Work People's College in the United States, to
contemporary actions in developing "free skools" in the U.K. and Canada, to
direct-action education such as learning to work as a "street medic" in the
protests against neoliberalism, the contributors illustrate the importance of
developing complex connections between educational theories and collective
actions. Anarchists, activists, and critical educators should take these educational
experiences seriously as they offer invaluable examples for potential teaching and
learning environments outside of authoritarian and capitalist structures. Major
themes in the volume include: learning from historical anarchist experiments
in education, ways that contemporary anarchists create dynamic and situated
learning spaces, and finally, critically reflecting on theoretical frameworks and
educational practices. Contributors include: David Gabbard, Jeffery Shantz,
Isabelle Fremeaux & John Jordan, Abraham P. DeLeon, Elsa Noterman, Andre
Pusey, Matthew Weinstein, Alex Khasnabish, and many others.

*"Pedagogy is a central concern in anarchist writing and the free skool has played
a central part in movement activism. By bringing together an important group of
writers with specialist knowledge and experience, Robert Haworth's volume makes an
invaluable contribution to the discussion of these topics. His exciting collection provides
a guide to historical experiences and current experiments and also reflects on anarchist
theory, extending our understanding and appreciation of pedagogy in anarchist
practice."*
—Dr. Ruth Kinna, Senior Lecturer in Politics, Loughborough University, author of
Anarchism: A Beginners Guide and coeditor of *Anarchism and Utopianism*

Out of the Ruins: The Emergence of Radical Informal Learning Spaces

Edited by Robert H. Haworth and
John M. Elmore

ISBN: 978-1-62963-239-1
$24.95   288 pages

OUT OF THE RUINS
*The Emergence of
Radical Informal Learning Spaces*
Edited by Robert H. Haworth & John M. Elmore

Contemporary educational practices and policies
across the world are heeding the calls of Wall Street for
more corporate control, privatization, and standardized accountability. There are
definite shifts and movements towards more capitalist interventions of efficiency
and an adherence to market fundamentalist values within the sphere of public
education. In many cases, educational policies are created to uphold and serve
particular social, political, and economic ends. Schools, in a sense, have been tools
to reproduce hierarchical, authoritarian, and hyper-individualistic models of social
order. From the industrial era to our recent expansion of the knowledge economy,
education has been at the forefront of manufacturing and exploiting particular
populations within our society.

The important news is that emancipatory educational practices are emerging.
Many are emanating outside the constraints of our dominant institutions and
are influenced by more participatory and collective actions. In many cases, these
alternatives have been undervalued or even excluded within the educational
research. From an international perspective, some of these radical informal
learning spaces are seen as a threat by many failed states and corporate entities.

Out of the Ruins sets out to explore and discuss the emergence of alternative
learning spaces that directly challenge the pairing of public education with
particular dominant capitalist and statist structures. The authors construct
philosophical, political, economic and social arguments that focus on radical
informal learning as a way to contest efforts to commodify and privatize our
everyday educational experiences. The major themes include the politics of
learning in our formal settings, constructing new theories on our informal practices,
collective examples of how radical informal learning practices and experiences
operate, and how individuals and collectives struggle to share these narratives
within and outside of institutions.

Contributors include David Gabbard, Rhiannon Firth, Andrew Robinson, Farhang
Rouhani, Petar Jandrić, Ana Kuzmanić, Sarah Amsler, Dana Williams, Andre Pusey,
Jeff Shantz, Sandra Jeppesen, Joanna Adamiak, Erin Dyke, Eli Meyerhoff, David I.
Backer, Matthew Bissen, Jacques Laroche, Aleksandra Perisic, and Jason Wozniak.

Until the Rulers Obey: Voices from Latin American Social Movements

Edited by Clifton Ross and Marcy Rein
with a Foreword by Raúl Zibechi

ISBN: 978-1-60486-794-7
$29.95   528 pages

Until the Rulers Obey brings together voices from the movements behind the wave of change that swept Latin America at the turn of the twenty-first century. These movements have galvanized long-silent—or silenced—sectors of society: indigenous people, campesinos, students, the LGBT community, the unemployed, and all those left out of the promised utopia of a globalized economy. They have deployed a wide range of strategies and actions, sometimes building schools or clinics, sometimes occupying factories or fields, sometimes building and occupying political parties to take the reins of the state, and sometimes resisting government policies in order to protect their newfound power in community. This unique collection of interviews features five dozen leaders and grassroots activists from fifteen countries presenting their work and debating pressing questions of power, organizational forms, and relations with the state. They have mobilized on a wide range of issues: fighting against mines and agribusiness and for living space, rural and urban; for social space won through recognition of language, culture, and equal participation; for community and environmental survival. The book is organized in chapters by country with each chapter introduced by a solidarity activist, writer, or academic with deep knowledge of the place. This indispensable compilation of primary source material gives participants, students, and observers of social movements a chance to learn from their experience.

Contributors include ACOGUATE, Luis Ballesteros, Marc Becker, Margi Clarke, Benjamin Dangl, Mar Daza, Mickey Ellinger, Michael Fox, J. Heyward, Raphael Hoetmer, Hilary Klein, Diego Benegas Loyo, Courtney Martinez, Chuck Morse, Mario A. Murillo, Phil Neff, Fabíola Ortiz dos Santos, Hernán Ouviña, Margot Pepper, Adrienne Pine, Marcy Rein, Christy Rodgers, Clifton Ross, Susan Spronk, Marie Trigona, Jeffery R. Webber, and Raúl Zibechi.

"This is the book we've been waiting for. Anyone interested in the explosion of social movements in Latin America—and the complex interplay between those forces and the 'Pink Tide' governments—should inhale this book immediately. Until the Rulers Obey gives us country-specific context from a superb team of 'introducers,' who then step aside so we can hear a chorus of voices from some of the most inspiring grassroots organizations on the continent. This is a people's history in real time, bubbling up from below."
—Avram David "Avi" Lewis, documentary filmmaker and former host of Al Jazeera English show *Fault Lines* and Naomi Klein, author of *No Logo* and *Shock Doctrine: The Rise of Disaster Capitalism*

Pictures of a Gone City: Tech and the Dark Side of Prosperity in the San Francisco Bay Area

Richard A. Walker

ISBN: 978-1-62963-510-1
$26.95   480 pages

The San Francisco Bay Area is currently the jewel in the crown of capitalism—the tech capital of the world and a gusher of wealth from the Silicon Gold Rush. It has been generating jobs, spawning new innovation, and spreading ideas that are changing lives everywhere. It boasts of being the Left Coast, the Greenest City, and the best place for workers in the USA. So what could be wrong? It may seem that the Bay Area has the best of it in Trump's America, but there is a dark side of success: overheated bubbles and spectacular crashes; exploding inequality and millions of underpaid workers; a boiling housing crisis, mass displacement, and severe environmental damage; a delusional tech elite and complicity with the worst in American politics.

This sweeping account of the Bay Area in the age of the tech boom covers many bases. It begins with the phenomenal concentration of IT in Greater Silicon Valley, the fabulous economic growth of the bay region and the unbelievable wealth piling up for the 1% and high incomes of Upper Classes—in contrast to the fate of the working class and people of color earning poverty wages and struggling to keep their heads above water. The middle chapters survey the urban scene, including the greatest housing bubble in the United States, a metropolis exploding in every direction, and a geography turned inside out. Lastly, it hits the environmental impact of the boom, the fantastical ideology of Tech World, and the political implications of the tech-led transformation of the bay region.

"With Pictures of a Gone City, California's greatest geographer tells us how the Bay Area has become the global center of hi-tech capitalism. Drawing on a lifetime of research, Richard Walker dismantles the mythology of the New Economy, placing its creativity in a long history of power, work, and struggles for justice."
—Jason W. Moore, author of Capitalism in the Web of Life

"San Francisco has battened from its birth on instant wealth, high-tech weaponry, and global commerce, and the present age is little different. Gold, silver, and sleek iPhones—they all glitter in the California sun and are at least as magnetic as the city's spectacular setting, benign climate, and laissez-faire lifestyles. The cast of characters changes, but the hustlers and thought-shapers eternally reign over the city and its hinterland, while in their wake they leave a ruined landscape of exorbitant housing, suburban sprawl, traffic paralysis, and delusional ideas about a market free enough to rob the majority of their freedom. Read all about it here, and weep."
—Gray Brechin, author of Imperial San Francisco: Urban Power, Earthly Ruin

Counterpoints: A San Francisco Bay Area Atlas of Displacement & Resistance

Anti-Eviction Mapping Project with a Foreword by Ananya Roy & Chris Carlsson

ISBN: 978-1-62963-828-7
$34.95   320 pages

Counterpoints: A San Francisco Bay Area Atlas of Displacement and Resistance brings together cartography, essays, illustrations, poetry, and more in order to depict gentrification and resistance struggles from across the San Francisco Bay Area and act as a roadmap to counter-hegemonic knowledge making and activism. Compiled by the Anti-Eviction Mapping Project, each chapter reflects different frameworks for understanding the Bay Area's ongoing urban upheaval, including: evictions and root shock, indigenous geographies, health and environmental racism, state violence, transportation and infrastructure, migration and relocation, and speculative futures. By weaving these themes together, *Counterpoints* expands normative urban-studies framings of gentrification to consider more complex, regional, historically grounded, and entangled horizons for understanding the present. Understanding the tech boom and its effects means looking beyond San Francisco's borders to consider the region as a socially, economically, and politically interconnected whole and reckoning with the area's deep history of displacement, going back to its first moments of settler colonialism. *Counterpoints* combines work from within the project with contributions from community partners, from longtime community members who have been fighting multiple waves of racial dispossession to elementary school youth envisioning decolonial futures. In this way, *Counterpoints* is a collaborative, co-created atlas aimed at expanding knowledge on displacement and resistance in the Bay Area with, rather than for or about, those most impacted.

"This collection literally makes visible intersecting lines of structural violence that produce displacement and dispossession, while also tracing creative resistances that are always challenging these processes and building more just futures. As an atlas, Counterpoints: A San Francisco Bay Area Atlas of Displacement and Resistance *is transformative and inspiring—it refuses the knowledge making and representational practices that bind cartography to settler colonialism and racial capitalism, instead developing ethical cartographies and collective praxes for mapping otherwise."*
—Sarah Elwood, professor of geography, University of Washington, author of *Relational Poverty Politics: Forms, Struggles, Possibilities*

Anarchist Education and the Modern School: A Francisco Ferrer Reader

Francisco Ferrer
Edited by Mark Bray and
Robert H. Haworth

ISBN: 978-1-62963-509-5
$24.95   352 pages

On October 13, 1909, Francisco Ferrer, the notorious Catalan anarchist educator and founder of the Modern School, was executed by firing squad. The Spanish government accused him of masterminding the Tragic Week rebellion, while the transnational movement that emerged in his defense argued that he was simply the founder of the groundbreaking Modern School of Barcelona. Was Ferrer a ferocious revolutionary, an ardently nonviolent pedagogue, or something else entirely?

Anarchist Education and the Modern School is the first historical reader to gather together Ferrer's writings on rationalist education, revolutionary violence, and the general strike (most translated into English for the first time) and put them into conversation with the letters, speeches, and articles of his comrades, collaborators, and critics to show that the truth about the founder of the Modern School was far more complex than most of his friends or enemies realized. Francisco Ferrer navigated a tempestuous world of anarchist assassins, radical republican conspirators, anticlerical rioters, and freethinking educators to establish the legendary Escuela Moderna and the Modern School movement that his martyrdom propelled around the globe.

"A thorough and balanced collection of the writings of the doyen of myriad horizontal educational projects in Spain and more still across the world. Equally welcome are the well-researched introduction and the afterword that underline both the multiplicity of anarchist perspectives on education and social transformation and the complexity of Ferrer's thinking."
—Chris Ealham, author of *Living Anarchism: Jose Peirats and the Spanish Anarcho-Syndicalist Movement*

"This volume brings together for the first time a comprehensive collection of Ferrer's own writings, documenting the daily life and aims of the Escuela Moderna, alongside reflections, often critical, by contemporary anarchists and other radical thinkers. Together with the editors' thoughtful Introduction, the result is a fascinating collection— essential reading for anyone keen to go beyond the image of Ferrer the martyr of libertarian education and to understand the perennial moral and political questions at the heart of any project of education for freedom."
—Judith Suissa, author of *Anarchism and Education: A Philosophical Perspective*

Raising Free People: Unschooling as Liberation and Healing Work

Akilah S. Richards
with a Foreword by Bayo Akomolafe

ISBN: 978-1-62963-833-1
$17.00   192 pages

No one is immune to the byproducts of compulsory schooling and standardized testing. And while reform may be a worthy cause for some, it is not enough for countless others still trying to navigate the tyranny of what schooling has always been. *Raising Free People* argues that we need to build and work within systems truly designed for any human to learn, grow, socialize, and thrive, regardless of age, ability, background, or access to money.

Families and conscious organizations across the world are healing generations of school wounds by pivoting into self-directed, intentional community-building, and *Raising Free People* shows you exactly how unschooling can help facilitate this process.

Individual experiences influence our approach to parenting and education, so we need more than the rules, tools, and "bad adult" guilt trips found in so many parenting and education books. We need to reach behind our behaviors to seek and find our triggers; to examine and interrupt the ways that social issues such as colonization still wreak havoc on our ability to trust ourselves, let alone children. *Raising Free People* explores examples of the transition from school or homeschooling to unschooling, how single parents and people facing financial challenges unschool successfully, and the ways unschooling allows us to address generational trauma and unlearn the habits we mindlessly pass on to children.

In these detailed and unabashed stories and insights, Richards examines the ways that her relationships to blackness, decolonization, and healing work all combine to form relationships and enable community-healing strategies rooted in an unschooling practice. This is how millions of families center human connection, practice clear and honest communication, and raise children who do not grow up to feel that they narrowly survived their childhoods.

"This is an insightful, brilliant book by one of today's most inspiring leaders in the realm of Self-Directed Education. We see here how respecting children, listening to them, and learning from them can revolutionize our manner of parenting and remove the blinders imposed by the forced schooling that we nearly all experienced. I recommend it to everyone who cares about children, freedom, and the future of humanity."
—Peter Gray, research professor of psychology at Boston College, author of *Free to Learn*